D1029314

EVERYDAY
INJUSTICE

EVERYDAY INJUSTICE

Latino Professionals and Racism

Maria Chávez

ROWMAN & LITTLEFIELD PUBLISHERS, INC.
Lanham • Boulder • New York • Toronto • Plymouth, UK

Published by Rowman & Littlefield Publishers, Inc.
A wholly owned subsidiary of The Rowman & Littlefield Publishing Group, Inc.
4501 Forbes Boulevard, Suite 200, Lanham, Maryland 20706
http://www.rowmanlittlefield.com

Estover Road, Plymouth PL6 7PY, United Kingdom

British Library Cataloguing in Publication Information Available

Library of Congress Cataloging-in-Publication Data

Chávez, Maria, 1968–
    Everyday injustice : Latino professionals and racism / Maria Chávez.
        p. cm.
    Includes index.
    ISBN 978-1-4422-0919-0 (cloth : alk. paper) — ISBN 978-1-4422-0921-3
(electronic)
    1. Hispanic Americans—Employment—United States. 2. Minorities in
the professions—United States. 3. Hispanic American lawyers. 4. Hispanic
Americans—Social conditions. 5. Racism—United States. I. Title.
    HD8081.H7C43 2011
    331.6'280973—dc22   2011009797

∞™ The paper used in this publication meets the minimum requirements of
American National Standard for Information Sciences—Permanence of Paper for
Printed Library Materials, ANSI/NISO Z39.48-1992.

Printed in the United States of America

To my beautiful children—Mariela, Thomas, Michele, and Donny. May the professional world in America become more accepting of the next generation of Latinos.

To David Pringle, for a life shared.

CONTENTS

ACKNOWLEDGMENTS

My deepest gratitude to the many people who helped make this book possible, especially Supreme Court Justice Charles Z. Smith, Carmen Gonzalez, Dr. Sandra Madrid, Sonia Rodriguez, Lourdes Fuentes, Alejandro Torres, Norma Urena, and Myrna Contreras. Thanks too to all the Latino attorneys who participated in this study and to the comparison group of non-Latino attorneys in Washington who graciously filled out a parallel survey.

I am appreciative of the invaluable feedback on drafts I received from friends and colleagues, especially Joanne Conrad, Ross E. Burkhart, and Sid Olufs, who read and commented extensively on the entire manuscript. It is a much stronger book because of them. I also received helpful suggestions from Eduardo Bonilla-Silva, Kevin R. Johnson, Rodney Hero, Luis R. Fraga, Gary Segura, Ron Schmidt, Kaitlyn Sill, and Lisa García Bedolla. A special thanks is due to the three anonymous reviewers; I owe a huge debt to them for their invaluable suggestions. Thanks to the Rowman & Littlefield staff, particularly to Sarah Stanton, acquisitions editor, and Jin Yu, editorial assistant, for being so kind, encouraging, and helpful throughout the publication process. Thanks likewise go to Tali Johnson for her amazing help with the citations and bibliography.

I have been extraordinarily privileged to come into contact with wonderful people in academia, principal among them, Joe Feagin. I am grateful to Joe for writing the insightful foreword to this book, for including it in his

Perspectives on a Multiracial America Series, for his support and encouragement throughout the process, and especially for his personal and professional commitment to exposing and ending racism in America. In addition, this project could not have been completed without generous support from a very special person—my dear friend and mentor, Nicholas P. Lovrich. Dr. Lovrich arranged the funding for the surveys and focus groups, assisted me in conducting my first focus group, and helped me in too many ways to list to complete my field research. I will always be grateful to him for his love and guidance over the years. Likewise, I am also very grateful for the support and friendship I received from Luis R. Fraga, another supportive mentor and friend who has taught me much of lasting value.

I am fortunate to have excellent colleagues at Pacific Lutheran University, who make academic life here very rewarding. I would especially like to thank my colleagues Peter Grosvenor, Solveig Robinson, Paula Leitz, Laura Klein, Lynn Hunnicutt, Tamara Williams, Anna Leon-Guerrero, Ann Kelleher, Claudia Berguson, Gina Hames, Joanna Gregson, Teresa Ciabattari, Karen Travis, Kaitlyn Sill, Sid Olufs, Chris Hansvick, Brenda Murray, Carolyn Reed, Norris Peterson, and Steven Starkovich. My heartfelt thanks to my 2010-2011 Wild Hope Seminar for a year of rich conversations and new friendships: Samuel Torvend, Kirsten M. Christensen, Lynn Hunnicutt, Heather Mathews, Eric Nelson, Carmina Palerm, Erin McKenna, and Neal Yakelis. Finally, I feel very privileged to have been hired at PLU by President Loren Anderson—thank you for welcoming into the PLU community, for sending me a personal congratulations card when my twins were born, for supporting me through the tenure and promotion process, and most of all, thank you for being such an inspiring and gifted leader at PLU. I wish you and MaryAnn the best.

My love and thanks also go out to Lisa García Bedolla, Melissa Michelson, Jessica Lavariega Monforti, Maggie Chon, Russ Lidman, Bitsy O'Connor, Gina Hames, Michele Shover, Byron Jackson, Wanda Costen, Ellen Lin, Brian Wampler, Ross Burkhart, Joanne Conrad, and Bridget O'Meara. Their support on so many aspects of academic life over the years has been a great source of comfort and inspiration for me. Thanks too to my in-laws, Marolyn and Don, for encouraging me to maintain balance in my life. To my dear sister, Celia Canalia, thanks for being excited over and supportive of all my accomplishments, and for doing the striking cover picture. To my wonderful daughter, Mariela Barriga, thanks for being the beautiful Latina professional on the cover and for all the years of love and frustration that only a mother and daughter can have.

Above all, I owe special thanks to my husband, David Pringle, for his patience and willingness to discuss the book over and over again, for his good nature and constant encouragement, for his pitching in during those precious family times when I would work on weekends and evenings. Thanks, David, for your love and especially for our Booboos—Thomas, Michele, and Donny.

FOREWORD

In this pathbreaking book, Professor Maria Chávez begins Chapter 7 with an extraordinary account, one cutting quickly to a set of major questions about U.S. society: A Latina graduate student asks a political science professor in a seminar about the absence of people of color in a book on American civic behavior. The white professor replies, "When are you going to get over your 'race' thing?" His tone makes clear obvious irritation and demonstrates his own racial framing of people of color, in this case of a young person trying to make her way through a historically white university. His sharply worded "your race thing" makes it clear that she and her fellow citizens of color are racially "othered" and are *the* societal problem when it comes to "race"—and not, of course, the persisting, white-generated racist realities of this society.

Indeed, Chávez's interviews with Latino professionals in one of the most distinguished U.S. professions reveal that they still are not accepted by many in the dominant group, that is, by white Americans. They are commonly framed in terms of the stereotypes, images, and emotions of an old white racist framing of Latinos.

Throughout this book, we see the many and varied ways Latino professionals must deal with such racist intrusions and barriers in their everyday lives, from early youth to advanced professional success. Chapters deal in depth with their struggles and successes in education, in the workplace,

and in their civic lives. We see them constantly struggling against marginalization, against being seen as unimportant, against being disrespected. The
in-depth interviews with Latino lawyers that make up the core of this book
constantly point us to the racialized pain of our present and past history.

This book is much needed, and for several reasons. For one thing, there
is not much literature on the everyday lives and experiences of Latinos
generally, or for any of the subgroups that make up that umbrella category.
There are very few studies that have recently involved, as here, in-depth
interviews with Latinos about their lives in this still systemically racist
country. Now this valuable book provides one that can not only be read
by general readers but also used in many social science and humanities
classes, as well as in workshops and classes for business leaders and policy
makers at all levels.

The book also provides much material to counter the toxic presentations
of Latino immigrants in the mass media. Consider the extensive attacks today in much of the mainstream media that target Latino immigrants, their
children, and their communities. One can rarely pick up a major newspaper or listen to a day's worth of television news that does not recount some
type of hostility or attacks directed against Latino Americans. There are
laws trying to get the police to crack down on darker-skinned Americans,
who might be undocumented immigrants. There are new school regula-
tions and policies trying to get rid of Hispanic studies classes and programs.
There are new city ordinances making it difficult for Latino workers to find
housing in numerous upscale white communities where they are recruited
to do the everyday "dirty work." And there are constant political commen-
taries by aggressive right-wing politicians and conservative scholars insisting that Latino immigrants will somehow destroy the English language and
the white Anglo-Saxon Protestant culture and civilization.

While those interviewed here are professionals, their experiences with
racism and the costs of racism for them are felt by Latinos in all occupations across the country. For example, not long ago, Southern Poverty
Law Center researchers interviewed hundreds of Latinos, mostly modest-
income immigrants, in several southern states. Those they interviewed
reported encountering much racial discrimination by whites. To take just
a small sample, here is part of their report:

> In Tennessee, a young mother is arrested and jailed when she asks to be
> paid for her work in a cheese factory. In Alabama, a migrant bean picker

sees his life savings confiscated by police during a traffic stop. In Georgia, a rapist goes unpunished because his 13-year-old victim is undocumented. . . . [Latinos] are routinely cheated out of their earnings and denied basic health and safety protections. They are regularly subjected to racial profiling and harassment by law enforcement. . . . And they are frequently forced to prove themselves innocent of immigration violations, regardless of their legal status. This treatment—which many Latinos liken to the oppressive climate of racial subordination that blacks endured during the Jim Crow era—is encouraged by politicians and media figures who scapegoat immigrants and spread false propaganda.[1]

One notes here racial profiling or harassment that is similar to that faced by the Latino professionals in this book, and by their parents and other relatives. One also sees similarities here to the old Jim Crow segregation that black Americans once faced in many areas of the country.

In spite of all the current attacks on Latino immigrants—and often by implication on all Latinos—no group has believed more strongly in the old American dream and sought it more aggressively than have U.S. Latinos. As we observe in this book, most work very hard, seek an education for themselves and/or their children, and take very seriously the U.S. promise of success from such efforts.

There are a great many ironies in the data presented so well in this pioneering book. The essential contradictions between the common white racial framing of Latinos and the actual reality of their lives—and their centrality to the growth, prosperity, and workings of U.S. society—are dramatic. Without Latino immigrants and their descendants, such as the professionals surveyed and interviewed for this book, U.S. economy and society would probably be on the same downward demographic, and eventually economic, slide of most European countries. Most Latino immigrants come as young workers, and for decades now they have provided those willing to work in the many of hardest and dirtiest jobs of this society, and often for modest wages and few fringe benefits. They rarely complain but fill jobs often abandoned by Americans with longer ancestral lines in U.S. society.

I have never quite understood how easily brainwashed these latter Americans have become on numerous immigration issues. The Latino immigrant communities, including those in the West that are discussed in this book, should be celebrated and welcomed for providing the workers at various class levels, including professionals, that have kept the United

States more vigorous and growing socioeconomically as compared to almost all other advanced industrial societies. They and their children and larger families also enrich this country in many other ways well beyond the economy. Moreover, except for indigenous Americans, who were already here, has not this reality of relatively recent immigrants building up the United States always been true? Is this not the loudly proclaimed "land of immigrants"? Or have we let reactionary white-framed movements encourage us as a country to give up on the fabled words of immigrant poet Emma Lazarus, as she put them in her famous poem now on the base of the Statue of Liberty in New York harbor:

> Not like the brazen giant of Greek fame,
> With conquering limbs astride from land to land;
> Here at our sea-washed, sunset gates shall stand
> A mighty woman with a torch, whose flame
> Is the imprisoned lightning, and her name
> Mother of Exiles. From her beacon-hand
> Glows world-wide welcome; her mild eyes command
> The air-bridged harbor that twin cities frame.
> "Keep ancient lands, your storied pomp!" cries she
> With silent lips. "Give me your tired, your poor,
> Your huddled masses yearning to breathe free,
> The wretched refuse of your teeming shore.
> Send these, the homeless, tempest-tost to me,
> I lift my lamp beside the golden door!"

How can a society whose dominant leaders and others forget our long history of the immigration of the masses seeking to be free and better off, and our deep history of oppression of many poor and middle-class immigrants of color, and their descendants, be truly successful in building a real democracy? That is just one of the many profound questions about which this savvy book provides much insight.

We as a nation have collectively forgotten the history of U.S. Latinos. Take the example of the largest Latino group today, Mexican Americans. Mexican-American history actually began with whites' ruthless conquest of northern Mexico between the 1830s and the 1850s. In this imperialistic conquest, white elites created a distinctive colonial situation for early Mexicans, whose land and labor were brought into the United States by force. Today, few Americans realize that the much-maligned Mexican immigrants who entered the United States later on—often parents or other ancestors of some of the professional respondents, or the respondents themselves, in this book—did not come into a totally new environment, for their ancestors have long lived in what is now the southwestern United States. The border has essentially crossed them as a group, rather than the reverse, and socially and culturally Mexican immigrants have to some extent moved within one geographic area, all of which was once Mexico. Thinking about more recent decades, we have also collectively forgotten how Mexican-American and other Latino efforts to resist racial oppression have moved this country toward more democracy. We might recall that after a Texas cemetery refused to bury a Mexican-American veteran after World War II, the now influential American GI Forum was created to organize Mexican-American veterans and work for expanded civil rights for all. Moreover, there is the now forgotten *Méndez v. Westminster* (1946) federal court case, which ruled segregation of children in California's "Mexican schools" violated the U.S. Constitution. Few know now that the legal theory expressed in this pathbreaking case anticipated the Supreme Court's more famous ruling in *Brown v. Board of Education* a few years later, which brought down the structure of legal racial segregation in public education. It is indeed time to remember how central Mexican Americans and other Latinos have been to the economic, legal, and political improvement of our still unfinished democracy.

Some years ago, the black civil rights leader and social scientist, W. E. B. Du Bois, spoke out for the major societal benefits of ending large-scale racism in U.S. society. Exclusion and marginalizing of people of color had, in his savvy view, excluded *vast stores* of human creativity, knowledge, and wisdom. In his view, and in the view of many others since he wrote this, no society can long ignore such a great store of knowledge and ability and expect to endure. In effect, all Americans should benefit from the renewed inclusion of the knowledge, abilities, and creativity of Latino Americans, as well as other Americans of color, in the public and private spheres. Indeed, the democratic ideals held so strongly at a rhetorical level by most people of all backgrounds in the United States can thereby have a better chance of actually becoming reality.

Joe R. Feagin
Ella C. McFadden Professor of Liberal Arts
Texas A&M University

$$(I)$$

INTRODUCTION:
LATINOS AND RACE IN AMERICA

Tony is a Latino man in his late fifties who wears a long black ponytail down his back. His face has the look of someone who has, as he put it, "been baptized by fire." He'd had a tough upbringing in Los Angeles. Decades later as a successful attorney in Seattle, Tony clearly holds onto some of the bitterness from his youth. His frustration is palpable. His high school teachers thought he should be an auto mechanic. Perhaps they thought that by guiding him into a trade, they were actually doing this young Latino a favor. And in a way they did. Their advice provided Tony with the motivation he needed to become a professional. "Going back to my experience as a young man and the idea that I should have been an auto mechanic made me so angry, it was the last thing I was going to be," he shared with the group of Latino attorneys in Seattle on a cold night in November. Because of the discouragement and tracking he was given by his teachers when he was young, he feels a special obligation to give back to the Latino community. He stated, "I think we owe something. You know, besides shoving it in people's faces that I'm around, I think that I owe something." One could hear the irritation in his voice. His sense of giving back is forever tied to showing people a Latino can be anything, including a successful attorney.

His experiences with racism have seeped into every area of his life, not just in his profession, and not just when he was young. When asked about the effects on his life of being a minority he said, "I'm always aware of it.

And it's subtle. It's subtle . . . for example, when I bought my home on Bainbridge [Island] and it overlooks the water. I was outside and I don't know what I was doing. My neighbor says: 'Oh, are you the gardener?' And my actual gardener, who is about 6'3" and a white guy with blonde hair, says, 'No, that's the owner.' And the face on the person was like, totally changed. And that's what I have experienced for fifty-five years. That's the kind of thing that you see. As a Latino or Native American or any kind of minority, you're just another wetback, or you're just another migrant farm worker, or whatever, until you are a professional, and that suddenly changes your stature, and you have to be aware of it whether it's been brought out to you or whether you've faced it or you've experienced it, it's there. . . . [The] whole idea of being a minority and working as a professional, you almost have to be outstanding in order to be accepted."

Being "outstanding in order to be accepted" is something Tony has accomplished. However, when pressed about what this means for him, he said, "You have to work harder, it seems, than if you were not a minority. It's like women have always said about being minorities, you know you have to work twice as hard as a man in order to do the same job. It's that kind of attitude that is out there. And especially, I think here in Washington, although it seems to be a bed of liberalism, though the discrimination is very subtle. You know, they talk about the glass ceiling. It does exist here. It does exist." To survive as a Latino professional in a white world, he stated, "You have to be able to be, I don't want to say switch hit, but you've got to be flexible, or you're going to be left out." This flexibility is not all negative. As he talked about how it unfolds, he laughed and said, "If you don't speak Spanish in L.A., you're toast."

Tony's constant navigation of issues around race produced a complicated mix of values and beliefs for him. Despite having had greater expectations placed on him as a professional of color because of perceived incompetence, or maybe because of the need to work twice as hard as his white colleagues to prove he was credible, his views are very conservative, particularly when he talked about individual initiative, drive, and ambition. He is very much against "handouts," which he believes are a waste of money. "It's like a little kid, you know, if you give them a toy, you know it doesn't mean anything as much as if they worked, saved their money, and go to the store and buy it with their own money that they feel this is something special and they take care of it. That's how I feel about my education, because I had to work for it. I missed out on all the affirmative action, you know, I was too old, and by that time I'd already been through law school—at a cost of only $10,000, I might add. All those things I think are important but I think that . . . you point them in the right direction, but not hold their hand all the way through. I think that's what's important. I think just indiscriminately throwing money out there, I think is a waste of money."

As a registered Republican, Tony sees affirmative action as just another obstacle for people of color. "One of the things that I've faced especially strong is the effect of affirmative action. And I have heard people say: 'Oh, did you get into school through affirmative action?' Which means that you weren't good enough to get through the normal ways. You got in because you were a minority. And that comes up periodically." However, Tony's conservative views are mixed with the reality of his experiences with racism, stigma, and exclusion as a Latino growing up in America. The life of a Latino professional is "a very big balancing act," he explained. As a member of the Washington State Bar Association's Committee for Diversity, he found some professional acceptance "for some degree of minorities in law firms." But this acceptance did not translate into increased diversity at the level of partner in law firms. When asked by his colleagues to name one Latina partner in a major law firm in Seattle, he replied, "Can't. You can't."

The experiences that Tony described of his life as a person of color are not unique to his chosen profession of law. *They are unique to his being a person of color in America where a Latino is treated like just "another wetback,"* as he put it. Tony's story could be the experience of any Latino professional, whether a banker, a real estate agent, a doctor, or a professor at a university. School tracking into a vocational trade such as mechanic is an all too familiar experience for Latino males, as is secretarial tracking for Latina females. Negative experiences growing up in America are shared by many Latinos. Tony's neighbor's assuming he was the gardener in a fancy neighborhood would be a simple mistake were it not repeated a thousand times in one lifetime. This repetition adds up to an assertion by others that over time makes him feel he is not wanted or accepted in America, or that if he is, it is only in the status of a poor, unauthorized, and unwanted labor-force participant. That is why Tony, and most of the people described in this book, report regular experiences of being labeled.

Tony's experience is similar to that of blacks and Asians, who also encounter obstacles in the predominately white world of professionals. For

example, African-American professionals who are pillars of their communities have discovered that they are still treated as outsiders.[1] They have
experienced disillusionment because they have played by the rules but
have not achieved equality in our government and professional institutions. Their experience is not widely understood. Hochschild found strong
evidence that white Americans overwhelming believe that discrimination
is a thing of the past. She noted that black middle-class professionals are
highly skeptical of the system and are increasingly questioning the fairness
of American society.[2] The same sentiments are found in Asian communities as well. Tuan's study of Asian-American professionals in California
demonstrated that despite the numerous generations of people of Asian
descent who have lived in this country, and despite their law or medical degrees and otherwise growing representation among the professional class,
they are still commonly seen as foreigners or considered to be "honorary
whites" as opposed to real Americans.[3]

This research attempts to give a direct voice to the experiences of Latino
professionals. Using in-depth interviews of key informants, focus groups,
and survey responses, I investigate one group of professionals—lawyers.
The experiences of Latino lawyers can provide a case study on the experiences of all Latino professionals in America. The research reveals widely
shared perceptions and experiences of negative stereotypes encountered
by Latino lawyers, whose main attribute, in the eyes of the wider society, is
that they are not white. As a group, Latinos have been racialized similarly
for decades in America, so Latino professionals, who have in fact overcome
the socioeconomic barriers placed before them, must also contend with
similar obstacles due to the systemic negative stereotyping of them. The
excerpts from interviews throughout this book describe the experience of
Latinos in search of legitimacy, respect, and acceptance by whites in mainstream post-civil rights American society.

THE RACIAL FRAMING OF LATINOS

It is a paradox that a Latino can be a successful attorney and still be in a
disadvantaged position. As Luis Fraga and colleagues stated, "Paradox appears to be a prominent feature of the contemporary lives of Latinos."[4] The
disadvantage lies in being viewed as an "outsider" within the United States,
a status that does not go away even after Latinos earn law degrees. This is

because the Latino experience in America is, as Fraga et al. argued, full of contradictions. For example, Fraga et al. detailed some of these contradictions in their analysis of contemporary Latino experiences in American society. They described what "Latino-ness" encompasses in America:

> Latino-ness cannot be understood without grappling with the nature of an ethnic community deeply rooted in U.S. and North American history and yet vaguely alien to the mainstream of American culture; a community, like preceding generations of new Americans, composed primarily of immigrants and their offspring yet understood as the perpetual "other"; a group of peoples striving for full cultural inclusion in the United States *and* insistent on the retention of the richness of their heritage; a race *and* an ethnicity; a "linguistic minority," most of whom speak English fluently; and as a "community" whose boundaries and self-definition are still evolving.[5]

Recent scholars have called this complex "othering" of Latinos the "racial framing" of Latinos—a concept that captures both symbolic and material outcomes of widespread racial stereotypes. José Cobas, Jorge Duany, and Joe Feagin[6] described it as follows:

> The racialization of Latinos refers to their definition as a "racial" group and the denigration of their alleged physical and cultural characteristics, such as phenotype, language, or number of children. Their racialization also entails their incorporation into a white-created and white-imposed racial hierarchy and continuum, now centuries old, with white Americans at the very top and black Americans at the very bottom.[7]

Tracing the pattern of racialization throughout the centuries, Cobas and colleagues provided ample evidence to demonstrate that Latinos have been constructed as "unwanted and disreputable aliens."[8] This can be seen in today's immigration debate, which links Latinos, regardless of their citizenship status, to being "foreign and dangerous."[9] Tony can never truly escape from this reality, no matter how successful he becomes.

Racialization of Latinos became codified in law in Arizona's 2010 SB 1070, which *"requires officials and agencies to reasonably attempt to determine the immigration status of a person involved in a lawful contact where **reasonable suspicion** exists regarding the immigration status of the person."*[10] Arizona is not alone in targeting public policies toward Latinos. Other states are considering similar legislation.[11] The current immigration debate highlights how Latinos are construed as foreigners, regardless of how many generations of their families have lived in the United States. Latino citizens will regularly be subjected to harassment by officials and agencies due to this anti-immigrant legislation passed in Arizona. Latino appearance now constitutes reasonable suspicion for an armed official to stop, detain, and demand proof of legal status. Claims that Latino citizens will not encounter civil liberties violations or threats to personal security are sheer fantasy.

However, over 11 million Latinos *are* foreigners, lacking the protection of legal residency or citizenship, which puts them in constant fear of deportation and makes them extremely vulnerable. For just one example, on October 5, 2006, National Public Radio's Jennifer Ludden described immigration raids in Stillmore, Georgia, in which over 126 Mexicans had been deported. One woman who escaped the dragnet was so afraid that she left her two-year-old U.S.-born toddler, a U.S. citizen, with his daycare provider and fled to another state until the danger was over. One can only imagine the fear, desperation, and confusion that would lead a parent to make such a decision.[12] The lesson here is that racial framing of Latinos produces public policies that harass citizens and spread terror among those who are unauthorized residents—many Latino families include a mix of both citizens and noncitizens. One of the perverse outcomes of Congress's failure to undertake comprehensive immigration policy reform points to a central feature of racial framing. Regardless of Latinos' immigration status, they are caught in an immigration debate that dehumanizes them. This means they are not considered as deserving the same regard as others. Part of this regard is social, as when people choose to act one way or another, as did Tony's neighbor. Another part is about rights, as when agents of the government stop, detain, and check the status of people based on how they look. Racial framing justifies exclusion and treatment that would not be considered acceptable for most people. Sadly, the United States is filled with a history of examples of the dehumanizing of groups of people according to race, ethnicity, and religion: the removal and genocide of Native Americans, the enslavement of blacks, the fear of the "yellow peril" leading to the Chinese Exclusion Act of 1882, the mistreatment of Irish and Italian Catholics, the exclusion of Jews, the Mexican Repatriation of the 1930s, and the Japanese internment during World War II, just to name a few. This dehumanizing has not only been about individuals doing awful things to other individuals. This history includes government-sponsored, as well as popularly supported, racist policies directed against racial, ethnic, and/or religious groups.[13]

One disturbing example of today's racial framing of Latinos is found in the vigilantes who arm themselves and undertake private border patrols. The "Minutemen," as they describe themselves, have spread beyond the Southwest and the physical border to places as far away as Virginia.[14] Another disturbing example was a Republican candidate for Congress in New Mexico who suggested putting landmines across the U.S./Mexico border to prevent Mexican immigrants from crossing the border.[15] Unfortunately, there are many other examples of rejection and dehumanization of Latinos and Latino culture that underscore the need to seek out community.[16] For example, in Daneen Peterson's December 2, 2005 article, "Pro-Illegal Alien Shills True To Their Hispanic 'Roots,'" she argued that both liberal-leaning Latinos such as Geraldo Rivera and conservative-leaning Latinas such as Linda Chavez have one thing in common: racial loyalty. Peterson argued that a "Hispanic 'human tsunami' . . . is invading America. A deluge of illegal aliens that has defied our laws and sovereignty, balkanized our cities and towns, corrupted our unifying English language, culture and society, degraded our hospitals, schools and jails and caused reductions in our American quality of life, job opportunities and wages."[17] Peterson's racist arguments are known as symbolic racism and are nothing new. Mingying Fu stated, "[S]ince symbolic racism is theorized to explain Whites' current attitudes better than older forms of racism, it can predict Whites' policy preferences much better than other forms of racism."[18] Eduardo Bonilla-Silva called this "racism without racists."[19] Bonilla-Silva argued in *Race without Racism* that this new color-blind racism allows whites to be against public policies promoting racial equity by rationalizing current racial inequalities as part of individual dysfunctional behavior such as blacks lack of success due to cultural pathologies or residential segregation due to individual personal preferences. And all the while, the policies and actions they support maintain their white privilege. Bonilla-Silva stated that this new racism is "subtle, institutional, and apparently nonracial."[20] It is, as he calls it, discrimination with a smile. He stated, "Whites enunciate positions that safeguard their racial interests without sounding 'racist.' Shielded by color blindness, whites can express resentment toward minorities; criticize their morality, values, and work ethic; and even claim to be the victims of 'reverse racism.'"[21] Ongoing dehumanization of Latinos may bring American society to the brink of committing another historical tragic error.

Racial framing of Latinos can also be seen in academic language. For example, Samuel Huntington[22] claimed that Latinos—immigrants or citizens—threaten to culturally divide the United States and that they reject core American values. This is an example of the racialization of Latinos in "polite" academic debates. According to Huntington, "(T)he persistent inflow of Hispanic immigrants threatens to divide the United States into two peoples, two cultures, and two languages."[23] He maintained that Latinos are different from immigrants of the past because they refuse to assimilate and charged Latinos with "threatening or diluting" American culture and society. However, Huntington's claim that Latinos "refuse to assimilate" is nowhere substantiated empirically. For example, Jack Citrin and colleagues tested Huntington's assertions and found that Hispanic immigration and assimilation follow patterns established by earlier immigrant groups. They concluded that "The balance of evidence available at present suggests that Mexican immigration is not the threat to American national identity that Huntington and others assert."[24] Huntington's assertion is purely an academic racialization lacking in substance, empirical evidence, and analytical rigor. The racialization of Latinos is that they are not accepted or welcomed in America, whether as citizens or immigrants, working class or professional. Apparently, to some, it is the culture and the people who are a threat to the white American way of life.

Other social scientists have weighed in on the Huntington argument. For example, Kevin Johnson and Bill Ong also provided strong empirical evidence to demonstrate that immigrants of Mexican descent have a strong commitment to learning English, based on waiting lists at English as a second language centers and showing that they usually read and speak English within ten to fifteen years after arriving in the United States.[25] Political scientist Lisa García Bedolla demonstrated that scholars such as Arthur Schlesinger (or Huntington), who claim that multiple languages are "disuniting" America, are really insisting that "immigrants must not simply speak English, they must speak *only* English."[26] Political scientists Luis Fraga and Gary Segura asserted that if concerns about language acquisition were really at the forefront of efforts to strengthen American national identity, they would not only include English-only laws but also resources to teach immigrants the English language.[27] Unfortunately, this information goes unheard by large segments of American society who are calling for immigration reform and English-only laws. Instead, self-styled minutemen, politicians playing the race card, and racial profiling laws are all given a stamp of legitimacy when professors from elite universities publish their support in opinion-leading journals and books.

RACIAL FRAMING AND BARRIERS TO ASSIMILATION

No Latino in America, whether a citizen or a professional, can truly escape the consequences of racialization that brand him or her as foreign, unwelcomed, and unwanted. Because of racialization, Latinos are not allowed to assimilate. Kevin R. Johnson, the dean of the School of Law at UC Davis, used his personal experience to argue that assimilation is not an option for people of color, particularly Latinos and Asian Americans, and he argued this is not for lack of trying. He demonstrated that even as a physically white male (his father was white and his mother was Mexican American), whose last name is Johnson, and who graduated from Harvard Law School, assimilation is not an option for him, nor was it an option for his Mexican-American mother and grandmother. Why? Because the reality is that "many whites refuse to accept minorities, whether they try to assimilate or not."[28] Johnson added, "Even as the new [Latino] immigrants acculturate, Anglo society continues to view Latinos, with their Spanish language and surnames, their non Anglo-Saxon culture, and their different physical appearance, as foreign, different, 'other.'"[29] Johnson tried to assimilate by at times even denying the Mexican side of his identity. However, he soon discovered that trying to pass as white was a double-edged sword for him. He eventually concluded: "Whatever I wanted to be, I could not fully assimilate. The way I looked, the way I was raised, and my memories were impediments to the assimilation process—if assimilation meant forgetting your family history, accepting racial hatred as the norm, and disregarding what you knew was right and true."[30] According to George Lipsitz, racial barriers evolve and adapt to new societal circumstances as America changes because of what he refers to as a "possessive investment in whiteness," or the commitment to the maintenance of social, political, and economic structural and material advantage by whites over people of color. So, barriers to assimilation will remain for racialized groups.[31] Based on an extensive analysis of immigration policy, law professor Bill Ong argued that Latinos, specifically those of Mexican origin, have been defined as non-American regardless of citizenship status.[32] No amount of assimilation efforts on the part of Latinos can compete with the structural barriers and cultural constructions of what it means to be an American—Latinos are not seen as real Americans.

What is the impact of this lack of acceptance on Latino's life experiences? Scholars have found that individuals living in a society that provides them limited social, professional, or political acceptance are more likely to become isolated from and disenchanted with the broader society. In other words, Lisa García Bedolla suggested the answer lies in a "context of stigma" and how this impacts Latinos' political and civic behavior. As she explained, "This less tangible aspect of racial hierarchy is very powerful, and it affects the life experiences and social interactions of all people of color in the United States. Numbers of stigmatized groups internalize societal stereotypes early in life, which negatively affects their future socioeconomic status and psychological health."[33] García Bedolla argued that stigma leads to internal and external consequences for Latinos. She stated, "Internally, feelings of stigma make it difficult for Latinos to feel positive about themselves and their larger group. Externally, their opportunities and choices are limited by a structural context that is often also the source of information regarding negative group attributions. Analyses of marginal groups must consider how feelings of stigma affect attachment to their social group(s), as well as to the political system as a whole."[34]

García Bedolla's extensive study of two Latino communities in Southern California, one middle-class community whose residents have been in the country for generations and one more recent immigrant community, suggested that members of marginalized groups respond to stigma in a variety of ways: "How a group member responds to feelings of stigma, along with the political resources and opportunities available in his or her political context, affects the group member's political engagement."[35] Another way this lack of acceptance impacts the life experiences of Latinos is by examining levels of trust among Latino immigrants as their levels of adaptation to American society increase. In addition, Melissa Michelson found that immigrants who identified with Hispanic ethnic groups and their sense of discrimination and racism "are acculturating into the society of the racialized Latino community."[36] In other words, the life experience of Latinos is one of continually adapting and adjusting to being treated as outsiders.

LATINO PROFESSIONALS

Where do Latino professionals fit into all this? Latinos are greatly underrepresented in professional occupations, comprising only 3 to 4 percent of engineers, doctors, lawyers, pharmacists, and elementary and high school teachers.[37] According to Richard Zweigenhaft and G. William Domhoff, as of August 2010, there have been only fifteen Latino CEOs in Fortune 500 companies, and most of these fifteen came from elite immigrant families.[38] These low numbers are all the more reason why we need to examine the experiences of Latinos who have successfully entered into the professions. These are the success stories. Do they perceive the stigma and marginalization too? What is the experience of Latino professionals, and what does it say about the larger story of racial progress in America today?

Research demonstrated that there are similar experiences among all Latino professionals. For example in "The University Setting Reinforces Inequality," Christine Marie Sierra stated, "Academia and its institutions foster inequality. . . . The power of academia rests upon the control or monitoring of ideas . . . its hierarchical, elitist ('selective') structures which promote rich over poor and working-class, whites over people of color, and men over women."[39] María de la Luz Reyes and John J. Halcón argued that racism is as pervasive in higher education as is tracking in the elementary and secondary school system. They use the metaphor of a wolf in sheep's clothing to show how subtle, yet potent, racism can be found in institutions of higher education. They described examples of new Latino faculty attempting to break into academia, and documented and described the obstacles that were placed before them. They stated, "We believed that our Ph.D.s paved the way to an egalitarian status with mutual respect among professional colleagues, where the new rules of competition would be truly based on merit. We were wrong."[40]

Reyes and Halcón distinguished between two different kinds of racism in higher education—overt and covert—with covert being the more difficult to handle. The examples of overt racism are not as frequent; however, they still occur far too often for new Chicano faculty. Though overt racism is out in the open, it is usually done in isolation, and most people outside the university rarely find out about it. One of the examples that they provided occurred during a faculty search at a university located in the Southwest. The local community was 40 percent Chicana/o. When five Chicanas/os from various parts of the country applied, not only did formal objections in the way of signed petitions surface, but racial slurs such as "What do they think this is, Taco University?"[41] were expressed. This comment came from a school dean. In the end, though, it was covert racism that kept all five candidates from being hired. Institutions such as universities have far too much power to need to use open and confrontational fighting to beat someone down. Reasons such as inexperience, not a good match in the department, and not "being qualified" enough resulted in none of them being hired and four of the available positions left vacant, while the fifth was temporarily filled by a white male. Major confrontations occurred, and eventually, one of the Latinos was hired. Reyes and Halcón concluded: "Covert racism is the most pervasive form of racism in higher education. Because of its elusive nature, however, covert racism is ignored by those who have never experienced it, and denied by those who contribute to it."[42] Some of the examples of covert racism that they discussed include: (1) tokenism, or the idea that Chicanas/os are only hired as tokens and that they lack the qualifications for the position; (2) typecasting syndrome, which is the clustering of people of color in departments that are "minority-related"; (3) the one-minority-per-pot syndrome, which is the view that if there is one person of color in a department that is enough or standards will be watered down; and (4) the "brown on brown research taboo," which is the devaluing or the dismissal of research by people of color about issues related to people of color (even though when white professors' chosen research is related to them, their work is not discredited or seen as lacking in objectivity). According to Reyes and Halcón, only 2.1 percent of all PhDs are held by Latinos.

The evidence suggested that Latino professionals are often trying to balance their life in American culture by doing what is expected of them to succeed, while at the same time, trying not to let the process of entry into professional life change them in ways that are antithetical to traditional Latino values. The experiences of these Latino academics demonstrated that in addition to the demands of performing in a career, they must continuously contend with the frequent insensitivity—and at times, blatant racism—on the part of their colleagues.

Latino Lawyers

There are three main reasons for looking at Latino lawyers as a case study of the experiences of all Latino professionals. By looking at how one successful group of professional Latinos has achieved success, this study adds to our understanding of race and ethnicity in America today. It also provides a measure of American democracy and citizenship. Finally, it informs us of the political and civic activities of some of the most privileged members of the largest ethnic and racial group in America.

The experience of Latino lawyers has much to teach us about the political and social incorporation of the largest ethnic and racial group in American society. Latinos comprise 16.3 percent of the U.S. population, and demographic forecasts put Latinos at 29 percent of the U.S. population by 2050. What would success look like for members of ethnic and racial communities? How significant is the role of systemic racism in America today? How does the United States continue to racialize Latinos, and how does this racialization impact professional groups such as lawyers? What additional efforts and resources are needed from Latino lawyers in normal day-to-day interactions at work or in the community? The experiences of Latino lawyers highlight many aspects of American society.

The experiences of Latino lawyers inform us of how well the United States is living up to its democratic ideals of justice and equality. America is an increasingly multicultural society. A group of political scientists concerned about the status and health of American democracy argued that inequitable institutions, low levels of trust, and lack of community connectedness undermine democracy. One of the points raised by the authors is the *"challenge of diversity or heterogeneity."*[43] How well we incorporate people who are from distinct racial, ethnic, religious, and cultural backgrounds will in large part determine just how democratic America remains. If Americans fail to accept the largest ethnic and racial group in the country, then not only is it critical to ask how well America is living up to its ideals, but more importantly, the issue becomes, as García Bedolla stated, "whether our democracy is creating a more just society."[44] This is an important point, because democracy does not necessarily equal justice, so we may have a democratic society that is far from just for many, particularly for minorities.

Finally, Latino lawyers open a window on the experiences of broader Latino professional groups. Their legal training puts them into the thick of the fight against the discrimination and injustices that Latinos experience in America. Latino attorneys have this capacity precisely because their training in the law allows them a recourse that Latinos nationally simply do not have. Because Latino lawyers are in an advantaged position compared to other Latinos, they have the capacity to remedy the civil rights violations that Latinos endure. As lawyers, they have the skills to be politically active in their communities. They have what it takes to demand to be full and equal members of American society in ways most Latinos, even other Latino professionals, do not have.

THEORETICAL FRAMEWORKS: THE WHITE RACIAL FRAME AND SOCIAL CAPITAL

In this book, two major theories useful for examining Latino lawyers' experiences are utilized: the white racial frame and the notion of social capital. These approaches are used to help frame this study and help us understand the reality of Latino professionals' experiences. Because of the racialization of Latinos in the United States, Latinos' everyday reality cannot be separated from the societal construction. It is how society has defined them, and this has affected every aspect of their lives. The latter theory is useful in analyzing the new ways in which Latino professionals can become part of the political and social communities in which they live and work. It can help us to understand how their newfound professional status impacts their overall civic engagement. The combination of both makes for a stronger guide for asking, interpreting, and analyzing the data.[45] Racial framing and social capital help us understand the patterns in the responses of the Latino attorneys.

The White Racial Frame

Joe R. Feagin's white racial frame concept provides a way of understanding race relations in American society. Feagin argued that traditional social science models and traditional social scientists have used a limited way of thinking to understand racism as an exception to societal norms rather than as a systemic problem in America. Instead, much discussion of racism in America is focused on the view that it is just a "cancer" in our system. According to Feagin, racism is not a disease but is rather a central aspect of American society that has been this way from the founding of this country. He stated:

> I argue that a much better societal metaphor is that of racism as an important part of the structural "foundation" of the U.S. "house." Racial oppression was not added later on in the development of this society, but was the foundation of the original colonial and U.S. social systems, and it remains as a foundation to the present day.[46]

This American foundational history is unique, and Feagin argued it is key to explaining the current systemic racial realities. "*Systemic* here means that the oppressive racist realities have from the early decades been institutionalized and thus manifested in all of this society's major parts. . . . Major parts of this society, such as the economy, politics, education, religion, the family, reflect in numerous ways the fundamental reality of systemic racism."[47]

Feagin seeks to understand American society and demonstrates that the white racial frame explains much about American notions of leadership, intelligence, power, wealth, crime, poverty, and dysfunction. Feagin notes in The White Racial Frame, "The dominant frame has persisted now over centuries only because it is constantly validating, and thus validated by, the inegalitarian accumulation of social, economic, and political resources. This theory explains why there are still vast differences today among whites and people of color along all these dimensions including levels of wealth and well-being and political representation. Feagin's theory is about perspective, collective memory, and ideology. It is a way Americans understand, think, and feel about their world. His theory helps make sense of the experience of Latinos in America. He stated:

In this broad racial framing of society, white Americans have combined at least these important features:

1. racial stereotypes (a beliefs aspect);
2. racial narratives and interpretations (integrating cognitive aspects);
3. racial images (a visual aspect) and language accents (an auditory aspect);
4. racialized emotions (a "feelings" aspect); and
5. inclinations to discriminatory action.[48]

However, a significant contribution of Feagin's theory is the way people of color resist racist stereotypes and negative images, actions and emotions directed at them. Rather than accepting or buying into the white racial frame, many Americans of color have created what Feagin calls counter-frames. According to Feagin counter-frames by people of color are counter narratives of traditional American versions of history and politics. Feagin's theory of counter-frames puts people of color in active positions of resistance rather than as passive recipients of injustice. This becomes important to fight against the negative effects of the white racial frame and provides people of color some dignity and sense of humanity in the face of our racialized society.[49] While there are important "counterframes," such as home culture by people of color to combat the racist oppression, the white racial frame is a powerful way to describe our racialized society today. Feagin stated:

> [T]his omnipresent white frame encompasses much more than verbal-cognitive elements, such as racial stereotyping and ideology. . . . It includes many other important elements, such as deep emotions and visceral images, even language accents and sounds, that have long been essential to the creation and maintenance of a system of racial oppression. . . . [It] is taught in thousands of different ways—at home, in schools, on public playgrounds, in the mass media, in workplace settings, in courts, and in politician's speeches and corporate decisions. . . . [It] rationalizes and structures the racial interactions, inequalities, and other racial patterns in most societal settings.[50]

Feagin reminded us that we are only forty years removed from legal racism; therefore, we are still living with the residual impact of these past institutional racist policies and practices, including segregated living conditions and "willful" ignorance among whites about the current realities of people of color in America. Feagin's use of the white racial frame calls for a new paradigm in understanding our highly racialized society—one that asserts systemic racism in America is really the norm.

According to Feagin, the anti-Latino frame has a long history in America, going back to at least the 1800s. Expanding on the previous discussion of the racialization of Latinos, Feagin applied the white racial frame to the way Latinos are viewed in America by politicians, academics, and the news media—all use images of Latinos as "lower class" "criminal," "dangerous," "burdensome," and "immigrant," to name a few.[51]

LATINO-ORIGIN GROUPS IN AMERICA

This section will provide a brief overview of the historical circumstances of the three main Latino-origin groups in America in order to understand the historical context for contemporary Latinos in America.

Mexican-Origin Latinos

Most Latinos in the United States are of Mexican background, making up 66.9 percent of the Latino population, according to the U.S. Census Bureau. They also comprise the youngest population, with 37 percent below age eighteen. Mexican-origin Latinos also have the lowest educational attainment, with the fewest college degrees of all the Latino groups, with only 8.5 percent of Mexican-origin Latinos earning bachelor's degrees.

The foundation of Mexican-origin American citizens in the United States officially began with the Treaty of Guadalupe Hidalgo of 1848, which officially ended the Mexican-American War and resulted in the United States acquiring what is now known as the American Southwest.[52] While the treaty granted Mexicans equal rights as citizens and full protection of their property under the U.S. Constitution, in reality they lost their property, and their political and legal rights were severely eroded. The ideology of Anglo cultural superiority was used to justify acts of official and unofficial discrimination and racist attacks against Mexicans, including lynchings.[53] Discriminatory laws and practices toward Mexicans have their roots in this period of conquest, which included restrictive covenants written into real estate transfers, segregation in schools, curfews (they could not be seen in town after sunset), and denying access to eating at local restaurants or shopping at local drug stores.[54] These laws "served to control the visibility of Mexicans on the streets and also to limit the public practice of traditional Mexican culture."[55]

Despite accounts that illegal immigrants are "invading" America, there is a historical basis for U.S. dependence on Mexican labor, which continues today.[56] Although Mexicans were not accepted, they were and still are needed as cheap labor. Meeting these labor needs is an important factor in the historical and current economic push/pull for immigration from Mexico. Once laborers were not needed, law enforcement officials devoted major efforts to deporting Mexicans and Mexican Americans throughout history, from the Great Depression of the 1930s[57] through the 1950s, when the Immigration and Naturalization Service removed 1.3 million Mexicans in what is today referred to as "Operation Wetback."[58] The *bracero* program, which began in 1942, was established during the labor shortage of World War II and lasted until 1965. An estimated 5 million workers from Mexico were brought into the United States to provide labor in twenty-four states over the course of the program.[59] Many Mexicans settled in the United States with their families after coming here to work. Today's wave of anti-Mexican immigration has a long history in the United States. As Schmidt and colleagues argued, "The new immigrants find themselves in an old ethnoracial order."[60]

According to Schmidt et al., the post-World War II period for Mexicans and Mexican Americans was one of segregation and anti-Mexican violence by white society, which served to isolate and intimidate the Mexican community. However, this was met with resistance and protest by Mexicans and Mexican Americans. Some examples of this resistance include the development of the agricultural labor movement headed by Cesar Chávez, the development of business and professional organizations such as the League of United Latin American Citizens, and the development of the Chicano Movement started by first-generation Chicano student activists, whose efforts led to curriculum reform in higher education, which is with us to this day.[61]

Puerto Ricans

Puerto Ricans comprise 8.6 percent of Latinos in America. They are the second youngest population, with 33.6 percent below age eighteen. They are also the group most likely to be living in a household headed by a single woman (38.3 percent of Puerto Rican households). Fifteen percent of Puerto Ricans have bachelor's degrees. Puerto Rico went from being a colony of Spain, complete with Spanish customs and language, to becoming a colony of the United States, with the signing of the Treaty of Paris on December 10, 1898.[62] Nevertheless, Puerto Rican citizenship in the United States began in 1917, with the passage of the Jones Act. However, under U.S. rule, the status of people in Puerto Rico includes "exclusion from the right to vote for President, full or meaningful representation in Congress, and equal participation in federal aid programs."[63] Roberto Suro pointed out that the status of U.S. citizenship enjoyed by Puerto Ricans still has not allowed them "into the American mainstream. . . . Puerto Ricans remain outsiders."[64]

Significant migration to the United States began in the 1950s, when an estimated 40,000 Puerto Ricans began to migrate annually. Most of them settled in New York.[65] By the early 1960s, more than 1 million Puerto Ricans were living in the United States. During the 1960s, Puerto Ricans earned close to 60 percent of the urban average income, yet by the 1990s, Puerto Ricans were earning only 50 percent of the city average. Rather than improving their circumstances in each new generation, as occurred with other ethnic groups, the situation has demonstrably worsened for Puerto Ricans.[66] Suro argued that Latinos in New York were affected negatively by changes in the U.S. economy and public policies, and the declining quality of the public education system. Thousands of industrial and light manufacturing jobs disappeared (because of automation or the export of production) in the 1970s and 1980s; Puerto Ricans were heavily concentrated in those types of jobs. Furthermore, the barrio (Spanish Harlem) was largely destroyed by municipal redevelopment. Suro highlighted the fact that "chunks of El Barrio were leveled to build public housing."[67] From colonial foundations, Puerto Ricans have engaged in a long and difficult struggle for equality, justice, and freedom within Puerto Rico and within the United States. Though they may technically be U.S. citizens, they are largely regarded as "de facto foreigners."[68]

Cuban Americans

Cuban-origin Americans comprise 3.7 percent of Latinos in the United States. They also make up the oldest Latino population at 18.1 percent over age sixty-five and 23.3 percent under age eighteen. They have the highest educational attainment among the Latino groups, with 24.4 percent of Cuban Americans having earned a bachelor's degree. This is due in part because compared to the other Latino groups discussed so far, Cuban-origin Americans received more purposeful accommodations by the U.S. government, and consequently, the first two generations of Cuban exiles have been able to adapt more easily to life in the United States.[69] Cuba, as with Puerto Rico, came under U.S. control upon the conclusion of the Spanish-American War. However, the colonial status period was not nearly as long for Cuba. This period was then followed by multiple waves of immigration of Cubans to the United States during the latter half of the twentieth century, particularly after the revolution led by Fidel Castro, who overthrew Juan Batista in January 1959, when many Cubans emigrated to Miami.[70] Since the revolution, each successive wave of Cuban immigration has been different from the previous one.

The first wave of immigration was composed of persons considered to be political exiles, and it included primarily upper- and middle-class persons, including government officials from the Batista regime.[71] Between 1959 and 1961, approximately 135,000 Cubans migrated to Miami. This was the community who received substantial federal aid with the enactment of the 1966 Cuban Adjustment Act.[72] This assistance included, for example, $1.5 billion to the Cuban Refugee Program, federal scholarship programs for Cuban-origin college students, the University of Miami's special courses to assist Cuban doctors in getting their medical licenses in the United States, credentialing programs for Cuban teachers, bilingual education programs for exiled Cuban children, and "off the books" intelligence-gathering projects financed by the Central Intelligence Agency.[73] All these forms of assistance served to create the foundation for a Cuban professional class. It can be argued that these supportive public policies were aimed more at hurting Castro than helping Cubans, because the Cubans have encountered many obstacles for full acceptance in America.

The next waves of immigrants came increasingly from the lower middle class and were more representative of the Cuban population as a whole. Portes and Stepick pointed out that in 1970, 15 percent of the exiles were professionals, but by 1973, only 5 percent of the Cuban exiles represented the professional classes.[74] During the 1980s, the Cubans on the Mariel boatlift (or *Los Marielitos*) migrated to Miami. According to Suro, they consisted mainly of wageworkers, and most have remained poor even after years of residence in Miami. The 1980s also included a visible anti-Latino backlash by both white and black Americans against the Miami Cuban community. For example, an anti-bilingual education referendum intensifying tensions between European Americans and Cuban Americans was placed on the Florida ballot. In 1990, five Cuban majors in the army uninvited Nelson Mandela from a visit to Florida because Mandela was sympathetic to Castro; blacks in Miami protested. Suro argued that after four decades of considerable economic achievement by Miami's Cuban community, they have yet to successfully integrate into American society. Portes and Stepick similarly noted the failure of Miami Cubans to integrate into American society: "The sense of having the truth but few allies with whom to share it strengthened considerably the moral bonds and self-reliance of this community: Cubans were in America, but not really of it, even after becoming U.S. citizens."[75]

The history of these three major Latino groups suggests a wide range of experiences, yet there are some important cultural and systemic similarities. Culturally, there is the legacy of Spanish conquest, including language and religion. Structurally, there is racialization, discrimination, and segregation in the United States, all of which are reinforced by public policies, particularly at the state level.[76] The impact of these systemic barriers for Latinos is profound. "The very act of racial segregation can help to create the racial stigma that is essential to racialization. Perhaps more important, however, is that tremendous disadvantage often accompanies racial segregation."[77] This disadvantage includes barriers in educational attainment and economic advancement that are experienced for generations. This continuity of experiences has contributed to a common ethnic identity among Latinos, despite their vast differences.

The white racial frame helps to understand the current socioeconomic circumstances in which the majority of Latinos live. For example, according to U.S. Census Bureau data, 29.7 percent of Hispanics under the age of eighteen live below national poverty levels compared to almost 10 percent of non-Hispanic whites.[78] An examination of median net worth revealed that Latino households are worth only around $8,000 compared to non-Hispanic white households whose net worth is close to $90,000. More than a quarter of Latinos have either a zero or negative net worth.[79] Regarding educational levels, current U.S. Census data indicated that only 57 percent of Latinos aged twenty-five or older have graduated from high school compared to 88.7 percent of the non-Hispanic white population,[80] only 12.1 percent of Latinos have a bachelor's degree or more compared to 30.6 percent of non-Hispanic whites,[81] only 5 percent of Latinos nationally have achieved master's and professional degrees, and only 3 percent have achieved doctoral degrees.[82] Lack of formal education among Latinos, in combination with living in poverty, demonstrates how far Latinos as a group have to go to combat the effects of systemic racism and discrimination. As the largest and fastest-growing ethnic and racial group in the United States, these income disparities underscore the importance of studies devoted to the problems Latinos face in America.

CIVIC ENGAGEMENT AMONG LATINOS

The second approach in examining Latino professional experiences is through civic engagement activities, known as social capital theory. As lawyers, the Latino respondents in this study are participating in their communities in many new and varied ways due to their new professional roles. This includes volunteering in local schools, playing in basketball leagues, and being involved in the Washington State Bar Association. According to Harvard political scientist Robert Putnam, this type of civic engagement makes society better on many levels, from safer neighborhoods and better schools, to greater individual health and even more effective government.[83] Civic engagement is defined as *"any activity, individual or collective, devoted to influencing the collective life of the polity."*[84] This could be anything from collecting litter on the street, to joining neighbors in a community meeting, to writing a letter to the editor in the local newspaper, to reading the local newspaper. According to Macedo and colleagues, civic engagement is important for three main reasons. First, high levels of civic engagement improve democracy. They stated: "While there surely is a role for expertise in politics and public administration, citizen input has the potential to improve the quality of public decisions by marshaling the knowledge and registering the preferences of the entire community."[85] Second, citizen participation gives government legitimacy.[86] Finally, the authors contended political and civic involvement improves the quality of one's life.[87]

This examination of Latino civic engagement adds a fourth reason—namely, that the experiences of professional and civic engagement among disadvantaged racial and ethnic groups in America are particularly important to highlight. If one is interested in having a healthy democracy with just institutions, communities of engaged citizens, and responsive and legitimate government, it is also important to understand how to include as many people as possible, especially groups who have been excluded from mainstream institutions and associations in the past. Because civic engagement improves democracy, it is important to understand how the leaders of the largest ethnic and racial group in the nation connect to and engage with their community and profession.

Related to civic engagement is the concept of social capital. Robert Putnam made the argument that the higher the levels of social capital—defined as individuals coming together through membership in a variety of community associations such as the Parent Teacher Association or the Rotary Club—the greater the benefits will be for the entire community through increased trust among community members.[88] Putnam argued that strong social capital strengthens not only our society but also our government. Although not all scholars agree with Putnam's conclusions that social capital has been on the decline since the 1960s, they do agree on one basic proposition—that broad-scale civic engagement is essential for a healthy democracy.[89]

Putnam distinguished between two types of social capital—bonding within groups and bridging across groups—arguing that it is important to have both "outward looking" (which results in bridging) and "inward looking" (which results in bonding networks of people). Bridging social capital is key in a democracy.[90] However, Putnam mentioned that bridging is the more challenging, yet more important, type of social capital to create and sustain because "birds of a feather flock together. So the kind of social capital that is most essential for healthy public life in an increasingly diverse society like ours is precisely the kind that is hardest to build."[91] This makes the civic engagement of Latino lawyers so important to understand. They are on the cutting edge of engaging in bridging social capital activities in their communities and in their profession. We need to understand groups who are civically engaged in ways that increase *bridging social capital*.

Discussions of social capital too often ignore important differences within societal groups, particularly marginalized communities. Recently, scholars are increasingly examining social capital in diverse communities. Whether examining Latino immigrant communities, levels of trust among Chinese Americans, or patterns of African-American civic life, these studies all have one thing in common—that race and ethnicity cannot be excluded from analyses of social capital if we are to have an accurate assessment of America's civic health.[92] This study is the first to systematically examine the levels of social capital and civic engagement specifically among a group of Latino professionals. By looking at Latino lawyers, this book builds on the studies of social capital and civic engagement among ethnic and racial groups. It informs us of how race, ethnicity, and gender affect Latino lawyers' type and degree of civic and professional engagement activities.

The Legal Profession and Civic Engagement

Civic activities have a longstanding tradition in the legal field. Public service, ethics, and professional responsibility in the legal profession are given serious attention and commitment. For example, almost all law schools require law students to take a class focused on the professional responsibility of lawyers in society.[93] While some researchers have concluded that the trend of ever-growing corporate law firms (which resemble business organizations) has turned the profession away from its classic duties to the public sector to the exclusive pursuit of corporate self-interests,[94] other scholars have found that measures of civic engagement and levels of pro bono work among attorneys remain high. One study found over 70 percent of Chicago attorneys were involved in community organizations or civic associations.[95]

Other studies demonstrated that there is a strong commitment by the legal profession to civic duties. For example, Brint and Levy examined the American Bar Association's (ABA) civic trends and behaviors over the period from 1875 to 1995 and compared it with various professions and associations. They found that the two organizations with the highest levels of civic engagement were the ABA and the University of California at

Berkeley. They contended that the main reasons for the success of these "highly engaged organizations" were the amount of resources available and the degree to which the organizations were connected to the public sector or state.[96] According to Ryan Blaine Bennett, lawyers have a special responsibility "to serve as community educators."[97] This view of the lawyer as "statesman" or "social trustee" is not new. It is a conscious aspect of the profession, which can be seen in the Washington Rules of Professional Conduct for lawyers: "Lawyers, as guardians of the law, play a vital role in the preservation of society."[98] Bennett added that "cultivating virtue in the community as legal educators"[99] is one of the greatest responsibilities with which lawyers are entrusted. Many law schools are committed to public service in their legal education and incorporate it into their curriculum. Bennett argued that the legal profession presents an opportunity for enhanced civic renewal in America and maintained that lawyers represent a good hope for saving and preserving American democracy.

Lawyers are an especially important profession to study with regard to civic engagement for a number of reasons. First, their training in the law is a powerful and important skill in society, which makes them uniquely situated in the political system. Aware of this powerful role in society, the preamble to the Washington Rules of Professional Conduct for lawyers states: "The continued existence of a free and democratic society depends upon recognition of the concept that justice is based upon the rule of law grounded in respect for the dignity of the individual and the capacity through reason for enlightened self-government. Law so grounded makes justice possible, for only through such law does the dignity of the individual attain respect and protection. Without it, individual rights become subject to unrestrained power, respect for law is destroyed, and rational self-government is impossible."[100] Their knowledge includes an understanding of the commercial system, of legal concepts, and of theories of justice in American law and society. This understanding of the workings of the U.S. political system, both at the state and national level, puts lawyers in a highly favorable position to exercise influence in the public policy process, the law, and in turn, civil society. As Macedo and colleagues stated, "Scholars and commentators often overlook the extent to which law and policy shape associational activity."[101] Reviewing Alexis de Tocqueville's understanding of the importance of associational life to American democracy, the authors stated, "Scant attention is paid to the ways in which, as Tocqueville emphasized, a healthy civic life depends on sound policy choices and well-designed institutions."[102] Lawyers are uniquely situated in the political system to influence policy choices because of their understanding of the law and public policy.

Second, lawyers have attained a high level of formal education, which is important for civic engagement for a number of reasons. A legal education is highly uniform across the country, as a consequence of the decades-long effort of the American Bar Association to standardize legal education. This level of formal education and the standardized curriculum found in law schools across the country allow for general comparison between Washington Latino lawyers and lawyers in other states. In addition to the standardized legal education lawyers receive is the role that formal education has on increasing civic and political participation, as noted in the literature on political participation in the United States.[103] As Macedo et al. stated, "The characteristics of individuals—their level of education, socioeconomic status, and age, among others—influence the decision to get involved, with whom, and on which causes."[104] Finally, educational institutions have historically promoted and taught citizens about civic duties.[105] According to Brian O'Connell, it is important to incorporate issues of citizenship throughout formal education, establish civic literacy as a priority for all Americans, and develop methods to emphasize and pass on the importance of civic participation to future generations of Americans.[106]

Finally, the legal profession has been the fastest-growing profession since the 1970s, growing twice as fast as the medical profession and closing the gap between lawyers and engineers as well. The ratio of lawyers to engineers was 1 to 4.5 in the 1970s and is currently 1 to 2.1.[107] Putnam argued that the unparalleled growth in the legal profession is one form of evidence of America's declining social capital, in that our "get it in writing" society demonstrates how disconnected and distrustful we are.[108] Whether Putnam's view that the great expansion in the number of lawyers is symbolic of America's fading social capital is correct or not, the fact that the legal profession has grown so steadily, in combination with the previously mentioned reasons, makes studying Latino lawyers important.

LATINO LAWYER SAMPLE

The Latino professionals surveyed in this study are an extremely diverse group. For readers interested in looking for more in-depth data at various places in the book, tables with further data are collected in Appendix A.

These Latinos grew up all across the United States—in California, Texas, Idaho, Miami, Illinois, and Michigan, to name a few of the states—and from all over Latin America, including Cuba, El Salvador, Puerto Rico, and Mexico.

The data collected for this book are derived through an examination of both quantitative and qualitative data sources. Quantitative data are derived from two survey questionnaires mailed to lawyers—one specifically mailed to all Latino-sounding surnames in the Washington State Bar Lawyer Directory and in the Hispanic Bar Association's mailing list, and another mailed to a random sample of all lawyers in Washington State. Overall, the bar in Washington is over 90 percent white, so it is safe to assume that the comparison group of lawyers in this study are predominantly white.

Qualitative data were obtained by conducting seven initial interviews, two focus groups of Latino lawyers—one in Western Washington and one in Eastern Washington—and five additional in-depth interviews of female Latina lawyers only (see Appendix B). Using snowball sampling, a total of thirty-one interviews were conducted between the focus groups and one-on-one in-depth interviews. In addition, 102 survey questionnaires from the Latino attorneys were utilized, which represent the majority of Latino lawyers in Washington State, who comprise just under 2 percent of the state's attorneys as of December 1, 2010.[109]

Finally, over 700 survey instruments from the comparison group of predominately white lawyers were analyzed. While these data were robust in their own right, for the purposes of this study, they were used only as they provided useful comparison for the analysis of the Latino respondents' experiences. Out of the 102 Latino attorneys who responded to the survey questionnaire, 41 percent were women. Most respondents had at least one parent who was a recent immigrant. Specifically, just over 40 percent of respondents' mothers immigrated to the United States, while slightly more than 50 percent of their fathers were immigrants. Therefore, most of the Latino attorneys were raised in immigrant households.

Mexican-origin Latinos are the largest group of immigrants among the Latino attorneys' parents, but there were a variety of cultural backgrounds represented (from over ten Latin-American countries), underscoring the diversity of backgrounds in this group of Latinos studied. Of the fathers who were born in another country, 24.5 percent are from Mexico, 7.8 percent from Cuba, and 6.9 percent from Puerto Rico. Other countries of origin for Latino lawyers' fathers included Bolivia, Colombia, Costa Rica, Ecuador, El Salvador, Peru, the Philippines, and Spain.

Of the 40.3 percent of Latino lawyers' mothers who immigrated, 18.6 percent came from Mexico. Almost 5 percent (4.9 percent) came from Cuba and 3.9 percent from Puerto Rico. Other countries of origin for Latino lawyers' mothers included Colombia, Costa Rica, El Salvador, the Philippines, and Spain, and one mother was even born in Japan and one in Africa.

The Latino attorneys interviewed varied greatly in their generational backgrounds, ranging from first-generation Mexican Americans and Cuban Americans to Cuban and Mexican nationals and other Latin-American nationals. Geographic diversity was also evident, ranging from growing up as a local Washingtonian, to growing up on the East Coast of the United States, to spending one's early formative years in Cuba or Mexico.

In terms of ethnic identity labels, I asked the following survey question: "When asked to describe your ethnic identity, which term would you be most likely to use?" Respondents were then given a list of categories that included "American," "Mexican American/Chicano," "Puerto Rican," "Cuban," "South American," "Central American," "Dominican," and "Other." Responses to this question were broken down as follows: 12.7 percent, "American"; 42.2 percent, "Mexican American/Chicano"; 6.9 percent, "Puerto Rican"; 6.9 percent, "Cuban"; 2.0 percent, "South American"; and 2.0 percent, "Central American." In addition, 27.5 percent indicated "Other" and wrote in one of two responses—the panethnic labels of "Latino" or "Hispanic." This finding is remarkable because a panethnic label was not included as an option, yet respondents added it in themselves, demonstrating that their identity is tied to a larger Latino community.[110] The majority of the data for this study were collected over the span of four years (between 2001 and 2004).

CONCLUSION AND OVERVIEW

Examining the experiences of this highly successful group highlights the continuing importance of race, culture, and class in America today. The following chapters reveal their stories and what those stories tell us about the larger story of race relations in America today.

Most of the Latino attorneys in this study are first-generation college students who came from working-class backgrounds. Today they are successful professionals living their lives much like other professionals. Yet, despite the fact that these Latino lawyers have achieved great success in their new professional positions, they continue to experience prejudice and discrimination. The experiences of some of the most successful members of the largest ethnic and racial group in America today reveal a lot about the strength of the white racial frame. Tony's story in the introduction reveals a lifelong experience with racism and discrimination that didn't end with the six-figure income, the professional position, or the big house overlooking the water.

Here are some of the underlying questions this book explores: To what extent are Latino professionals accepted in their professions and in the greater communities in which they live? How much do they identify with Latino culture and with American culture? Did they grow up speaking Spanish at home? Are they the first in their families to go to college? What challenges based on race, gender, and ethnicity do they face? How do Latinas' experiences differ from their male counterparts? Finally, do Latino lawyers provide a model for how other Latinos can achieve entry into the professions? What lessons of resistance and resilience do these respondents have to teach other Latino professionals?

Chapter 2 describes Latino attorneys' cultural and family backgrounds within a context of the white racial frame. It describes the socioeconomic and cultural background community that most Latinos in this study came from before they became attorneys. The cultural background includes how many Latino attorneys were raised speaking Spanish or celebrating traditional Latino holidays, as well as how many still speak Spanish and maintain cultural ties with their communities of origin.

Chapter 3 compares Latino attorneys to white attorneys in Washington State, along a number of dimensions. These include their parents' educational and occupational backgrounds while growing up, their current demographic circumstances, and even their ideological similarities and differences. It examines their experiences in law school and in their new professional lives as practicing attorneys. It includes a comparison of both groups of attorneys' challenges and obstacles in law school, their overall satisfaction with their decision to become lawyers, their current types of legal practices, job satisfaction, and pro bono efforts. It then focuses on the unique obstacles that Latino attorneys face, including a discussion on the role of gatekeepers that Latino attorneys encounter in their professional lives. This includes gatekeepers in the firm, as well as clients and those in the community.

Chapter 4 explores the impact of both race and gender in the legal profession, specifically looking at the Latina respondents' experiences. This chapter examines the findings from a combination of the forty-one Latinas who responded to the survey questionnaire, the Latina contributions in the two focus groups conducted, and finally, five additional in-depth interviews conducted solely with Latina attorneys in December 2004. This combination of data sources reveal that the experiences of Latina professionals are often unique from those of the other Latino respondents. Their experiences add to the studies on the intersections of race, class, and gender by highlighting their cultural and professional identity and challenges, the unique challenges they face in the community, and their civic contributions.

Chapter 5 reviews civic engagement among the Latino respondents and also highlights their political leanings, activities, and values. The data demonstrate that once Latinos received the benefits of higher education—in this case, a legal education—the differences between Latino lawyers and the comparison group of white lawyers all but disappear with regard to community and political involvement, especially when compared to Latinos nationally, with their much lower levels of formal education, formal political participation, and levels of community involvement. This chapter also demonstrates that despite the high level of involvement among the Latino respondents, they often sell themselves short on their actual levels of participation and activities.

Chapter 6 looks at the role of education with an examination of affirmative action as a way to keep making educational improvements among Latinos. Education is a way for Latinos to improve not only their personal circumstances but also their level of involvement in the community. Following a path similar to that of the Jews in the nineteenth century, who used education as a way out of their circumstances as outsiders in America, it argues that Latino lawyers can be a model for other Latinos in gaining access, even if not acceptance.

Finally, Chapter 7 concludes with a discussion of the major implications and findings of this study. First, the data from this study reveal what happens to Latinos in the trenches of their professions. This is similar to what other middle-class Latinos have experienced around the country. National anti-Latino framing contributes to discriminatory treatment of Latino professionals. Therefore, social capital theory, while helpful in examining this highly successful groups' hard work, is limited in explaining the continuing importance of the white racial frame with regard to understanding race, culture, and class in America.

(2)

LATINO CULTURE:
THE FOUNDATION TO PERSEVERE

Anna grew up the youngest daughter of Mexican immigrants, who earned a meager living as farmworkers in Burley, Idaho. She never would have imagined she would become a successful attorney in Seattle given where she started in life—particularly when the National Center for Education Statistics show that students whose parents had a high school diploma or less were five to six times *less likely* to enter a postgraduate professional degree program, such as law school, than those from households in which at least one parent had earned an undergraduate or graduate degree.[1] Nor would she have imagined she would win the 2009 King County Bar Association's Pro Bono Award—an award usually reserved for attorneys from big firms, not for lawyers in solo practice who devote themselves to helping undocumented workers collect wages they are owed. Anna's life is an outstanding example of overcoming countless obstacles. Reflecting on her unpredictable achievements, Anna especially would never have imagined she would also unexpectedly become the legal guardian and new mom to her niece's three-year-old son, after her niece had been shot and killed by the father, now in jail.

As Anna recalls the experiences that motivated her to go to law school, she notes they weren't all pleasant. Her reasons stemmed mostly from witnessing the way her parents were treated. She hated it that they weren't treated fairly when they worked in the fields, whether they were sugar beet, bean, or potato fields. Remembering the conditions in the fields made her cry, particularly when she described her parents having to take their own toilet paper because they didn't have bathrooms or when the ranchers would impose unfair and illegal rules such as allowing them only fifteen-minute lunch breaks. What was worse, she stressed, was that her parents would be even stricter with themselves, imposing only a ten-minute lunch on her and her family so that the rancher wouldn't get mad at them for taking lunch at all. Her dad was always especially cautious when it came to the ranchers or bosses because he didn't have any power or rights. The lack of power for her dad and the abuse endured by her family are what made her decide to go to law school.

As an undergraduate, she told her advising professor that she was interested in going to law school. He told her flat out that she didn't have what it takes to be a lawyer. She had heard this kind of "advice" from her teachers before as a Latina from her socioeconomic and racialized background. While it made her angry, like it did Tony in the previous chapter, she didn't internalize it. She had stopped doing that a long time ago. Instead, she told herself that this political science professor didn't know what he was talking about. After all, he wasn't a lawyer. When she was offered an opportunity to attend Gonzaga University's summer pre-law program, a program that her minority affairs counselor told her about while pursuing her undergraduate degree, her life really took off. It was at Gonzaga that she met other Latinas from various regions of the country, all from farmworker backgrounds. They immediately understood each other. They knew the same Mexican musicians, understood the same jokes, could speak Spanish, and shared the same negative experiences in America, so they had many of the same reasons for wanting to go to law school. Moreover, they were all Latinas who were driven and ambitious. For the first time in her life, Anna felt comfortable and at peace with others from her culture who were also striving for success.

However, it wasn't easy. Her first year in law school was difficult. She was going through a divorce from a very controlling husband and having several health problems caused from all the stress. In addition, there were family obligations and pressures to contend with during that crucial first year of law school: her oldest brother got into trouble with the law, her other brother became seriously ill with diabetes, her youngest brother's family life was falling apart, and her mother had to return to Mexico because her aunt died. It became too much. So, she went to the dean of the law school to see what would happen if she would just drop out that year. When the dean told her that if she quit she would not be guaranteed a spot the following year, she had to make a decision—she either had to finish the year or quit law school altogether. At the time, the doctors weren't sure of her medical diagnosis, so they couldn't postpone her final exams on medical grounds, and she knew she would just get further and further behind. She decided to make it through her first-year final exams. She recalls that during one final exam, she actually put her head down and started to cry. She wrote the whole exam with her head on her desk, all the while crying. She had been experiencing vertigo (later she was diagnosed with perilymph fistula, which causes vertigo), so when she put her head down to take the exam, she became so dizzy she couldn't see straight. Somehow she passed. She passed all her exams that year and made it through her first year of law school, when at times, just getting to class was a struggle.

After earning her law degree, she returned to Idaho to try to help farmworkers, but in many ways, she felt she was in a straightjacket. Due to the systemic institutional racism that farmworkers lived under, she felt as if all she could do was say "I can't help you" in Spanish. She described the story of a woman telling her that her brother was in Mexico because the rancher had called immigration to avoid paying him, but since the brother was no longer in the country, she couldn't collect his wages for him. She recalled another example in which she had been powerless to help a farmworker who had been injured on the job obtain workers' compensation, because farmwork was exempt from workers' compensation in Idaho at that time. Frustrated and ready to leave Idaho behind, she was offered a position at the Northwest Justice Project in Seattle and took it. Years later, she began her own practice with absolutely no support and only $1,000 to her name. Now in a successful practice, with the recognition of her peers in the King County Bar as the most deserving attorney of the Pro Bono Award, Anna reflects on how her life has been a tale of unpredictable success but also one of struggle as well.

Anna's story is similar to that of other Latino professionals. Set against a background of hardship she and her family experienced as farmworkers, able to succeed in her education in the face of obstacles framed by reactions to race, she has now achieved the American dream. Yet it still isn't easy. Anna now seeks to balance her life in the United States by doing what is necessary to succeed, while at the same time, trying not to let the process of success change her in ways that are antithetical to traditional Latino culture and values. Her story highlights that for first-generation Latino professionals, the Latino culture is critical for survival and success and is the foundation and motivation for all that they do. However, it also shows that because Latinos as a group are in a disadvantaged position in society, Latino professionals are never too far from the pain and dysfunction found in their communities of origin. The respondents in this study report that it seems there is always a crisis to contend with when you come from a poor immigrant or racialized community without many rights in society. This can create challenges and obstacles for Latinos trying to achieve success in America.[2] Janet Bauer stated, "The ability to adapt and the choices immigrants make are at least partially affected by whether they are accepted or rejected by their United States communities."[3]

Similar to other racialized immigrant groups of the past, such as the Chinese, the Koreans, the Italians, the Polish, and others, family expectations and economic pressures can be overwhelming and hinder even the most ambitious educational and professional goals. It is not that Latino families are against educational attainment for their children. In fact, as Luis Fraga and colleagues pointed out, "Conventional wisdom has long held that Latinos do not place the same emphasis or value on education as do others. . . . Such claims are nonsense and are unrecognizable in the comments of our focus group informants."[4] However, when one comes from a disenfranchised community, there are always many needs. The expectation also exists that with further understanding of the legal system and American society, one will help address some of those needs for the family and even the community at large. This expectation becomes both an honor and a burden for Latino professionals, who are also trying to fulfill the requirements for success expected of them.

Anna's life—from growing up in a farmworker immigrant household in Idaho to becoming a successful attorney, to raising her niece's three-year-old son as her own—demonstrates that if you don't give up, if you are there for the family, if you fight the good fight, you can become a great success. However celebratory her success story is, it also demonstrates how rare it is. Latinos must be strong enough to resist the stereotyping, the questioning, and the racialization encountered in their new professional role in society. At the same time, they have to be available to drop everything they are doing and help their family, even with something as life changing as adopting a murdered niece's son. This is a lot to balance. As Anna looks back on her life now, she realizes that part of her is and will always be drawn back to her roots, to her family, and to her culture. She hopes she can instill this cultural strength in her adopted three-year-old son as her parents did for her, because in the end, she is convinced her culture is what has helped her persevere.

LANGUAGE AND CULTURE

The stories of the Latino attorneys interviewed typically contain strategies for resistance, and those include the importance of language and culture. Similar to Anna's story, the Latino respondents' chosen career of law was often motivated by a need to help the Latino community and to fight against discrimination. Anna's experiences demonstrate not only the obstacles she and her family repeatedly encountered but are also reflective of the strategies of resistance Latinos use to confront the racial, class, and gender oppression they experience.

One reason Latinos have developed a variety of strategies is because they lack a strong counterframe, or widely shared common story such as black Americans have that accounts for their racialized experiences. Chou and Feagin stated that "among all groups of color, only African Americans have managed to create a strong counterframe and to teach it to successive generations."[5] A counterframe is simply a way of being, a way of doing or seeing things that fights against the dominant white racial frame. The counterframing process is complex and includes oppositional storytelling to counteract the dominant white group's version of historical events. For example, the popular slogan "We didn't cross the border, the border crossed us" is a counterexplanation of the U.S. war against Mexico. This statement makes the point that the war was unjust and imperialist, and serves as a reminder to Latinos that half of Mexico's land was seized as a result. Counterframes also include positive images and emotions about one's own group, for example, celebrating and teaching one's culture to future generations of Latinos. As Bauer stated: "A community's culture introduces its children to their world. It influences their impressions of themselves, of other countries, and of where they belong."[6] The Latino culture includes the Spanish language, frequent extended family interactions, and Catholic religious customs and traditions such as baptisms, first communions, and *quinceneras*. It also includes community connections with other Latinos, particularly to share in positive experiences that help fend off all the negative experiences and remind them of their human-ity. Often this includes participation in soccer leagues, Mexican dances, and Spanish-language interactions. Chou and Feagin discovered in their study of Asian Americans that communities of color are in fact displaying acts of resistance even if they are not directly visible or as well developed. Similarly, the Latino respondents in this study are also actively resisting the negative framing of who they are. Often the strategies of resistance to the openly anti-Latino climate in America begin at home. Like Anna's parents, most of the Latinos in this study came from families who wanted them to "lay low" and not make waves. Members of immigrant families are taught to never draw attention to themselves. However, one thing many of the parents insisted upon was that the respondents continue to speak Spanish at home. Speaking Spanish became a way for them to maintain some semblance of dignity when everything around them told them that they were inferior.

This reliance on language makes the politics of English-only doubly sa-lient. Schmidt suggested that "language policy conflicts can be understood best in terms of the politics of identity."[7] Schmidt argued that language is core to one's identity; to attack it is to attack a person. He stated, "[I]f language, for example, becomes an important marker of ethnic identity, then language policy represents one avenue through which to gain greater public recognition and respect for a particular ethnic community."[8] Unfor-tunately, public policies making English the official language do the exact opposite. Schmidt quoted a Los Angeles civil rights lawyer to demonstrate the effects of attacking one's language:

> I grew up in an English-only household. I was told "You're not a Japanese. You're an American." When I finally realized that it doesn't matter that I went to a top law school, that I continue to be judged by the color my skin, the slant of my eyes, and the color of my hair . . . , without that culture I'm left with a shell.[9]

Culture, language, and race are intimately intertwined. García Bedolla argued that language and culture are even *more important* than race for political and social mobilization of identity-based Latino movements.[10] Nearly half of the Latino respondents in this study spoke Spanish as a first language. Over 30 percent indicated that they currently speak both English and Spanish within their family settings and on social occasions.

Language and cultural maintenance become heroic acts of resistance on the part of immigrants and their children, who often have so few rights. For Latinos living in a larger society that rejects who they are, the maintenance of Latino culture and Spanish language does more than just "introduce its children to their world," as Bauer stated with regard to culture. For Latinos, it helps them survive that world, especially during the current anti-immigration climate.

One of the few studies to examine the experiences of Latino lawyers and doctors was conducted in Los Angeles on those who attended university during the 1960s and 1970s. It found that a strong "Chicano movement culture" permeated all aspects of their professional lives, including the type of medical and law practices chosen, the volunteer work they did, the type of networks and associations they belonged to, the shared stories of racism, and even the food served at gatherings.[11] Their professional lives were permeated by a common experience of struggle and a commitment to using their new professional status to give back to their communities. Cultural identity became the foundation for their professional lives and provided the much-needed support in their professional environments.

Both the survey data on and interviews with the Latino respondents reveal how knowing and speaking Spanish are important aspects of their cultural identity, as is being raised in an immigrant household. As previously mentioned, nearly half of the respondents spoke Spanish as a first language, and over 30 percent still speak Spanish socially; however, these bilingual skills are also utilized by the respondents in their professional circles, with 35.6 percent of the Latino respondents indicating that they currently speak both English and Spanish in the course of their work. When asked how they would describe (in cultural terms) the people with whom they associate regularly, over half (51 percent) responded with "a diverse set of persons," fewer than one in ten (7.8 percent) indicated that they associate with "mostly Latinos," and four in ten (41.2 percent) indicated that they associate with "mostly Anglos." These findings are particularly interesting given the fact that as Bonilla-Silva demonstrated, we live in a highly segregated society. For example, Bonilla-Silva documented that racial considerations are key to where whites live and with whom they form friendships, with less than 10 percent of whites who can claim to having a close friend who is black.[12] In contrast, slightly more than half of the Latino respondents interact with diverse groups, while slightly under half interact with only whites. This means these Latino respondents occupy some sort of middle-of-the-racial-road space. Their rates of intermarriage are also indicative of this new racial space they occupy, with interracial marriage rates among the Latino respondents in this study at over 56 percent (see Appendix A, Table 3.5). Nationally, interracial marriage is currently at around 5.5 percent.[13]

The survey revealed that most of the Latino respondents are also intimately connected to their immigrant roots. Just over 40 percent of their mothers immigrated to the United States, while slightly more than 50 percent of their fathers are immigrants. Therefore, most of the Latino attorneys in this study were raised in immigrant households. Over half of the Latino attorneys (54.9 percent) indicated that they participated in Latino-specific holidays and celebrations, such as *Cinco de Mayo, quinceneras,* or *Diesiseis de Septiembre,* while growing up.

Mexican-origin Latinos are the largest group of immigrants among the Latino respondents' parents, but there were also a variety of cultural backgrounds represented (from over ten Latin-American countries), underscoring the diversity of backgrounds in this group of Latinos studied.[14] Similarly, the Latino attorneys interviewed varied greatly in the diversity of generational backgrounds, ranging from first-generation Mexican Americans and Cuban American to Cuban and Mexican nationals and other Latin-American nationals. Geographic diversity was also evident, with some growing up locally, some on the East Coast, and some in Mexico or Cuba.

IDENTITY AND RESISTANCE: REJECTING THE WHITE RACIAL FRAME

I came from a community where everybody was very working class: the whites were working class, the Latinos were working class. . . . The critical thing for my survival [in law school] became getting to know other Latinos. . . . There was a group of Latinas called Latina Perspectives, and I joined that and that was a way of connecting. . . . Because otherwise you were in this world that was so alien and just inexplicable and bewildering. So, that became for me an important resource, an important way of reaffirming my

own worldview. . . . Finding community, finding a place were I could speak
to people who shared, to some extent, my life experience, culture, language,
values. It became critical to survival.

This Latina respondent grew up working class, made it to college and
then law school. However, she felt the need to seek out other Latinos
of similar cultural, linguistic, and economic backgrounds for support
throughout her undergraduate and law school days. The white professional world and the path to it were extremely wounding for her. Despite having been raised in America and growing up watching the *Brady
Bunch*, all of a sudden going to an elite university and then later law
school was an alienating experience for her, not because of the academic
challenges, but because of the vast differences in culture and class and
the negative treatment that came with this environment. This was the
case for the Latino respondents. The quotation illustrates the significance of cultural identity, particularly how identity becomes *"critical to
survival"* for groups such as Latinos.

Many scholars have written about the importance of identity as a
method to unite racial and ethnic communities. For example, Cornel
West argued that ethnic identity can and must serve as a catalyst for
improving the degrading conditions in which many African Americans
live. West stated, "The quest for black identity involves self-respect
and self-regard, realms inseparable from, yet not identical to, political
power and economic status."[15] However, self-respect and self-regard—
requirements of a healthy, productive identity—often become difficult
to achieve when the world around you disrespects you and what you
represent. According to West, too often a black middle-class professional's racial identity includes the opposite. West described it as a sense
of "flagrant self-loathing,"[16] which often disadvantages the entire black
community. The energy of a black middle-class person of means is often
spent either trying to gain white peer approval or in engaging in black
separatist nationalism, reflecting excessive obsession with white racism.
In the meantime, distressed and impoverished communities, which
could benefit from the help of more prosperous and influential African
Americans, persist in their disadvantaged state. This same phenomenon
described by West happens with Latino professionals. The frequency
with which Latino respondents sought out Latino support groups while

in school suggests that young professionals in training recognize the importance of cultural identity for self-respect.

ETHNIC IDENTITY LABELS AMONG THE LATINO RESPONDENTS

In terms of ethnic identity labels, the Latino respondents were asked the following survey question: "When asked to describe your ethnic identity, which term would you be most likely to use?" The respondents were then given a list of categories that included "American," "Mexican American/Chicano," "Puerto Rican," "Cuban," "South American," "Central American," "Dominican," and "Other." The responses to this question were broken down as follows: 12.7 percent, "American"; 42.2 percent, "Mexican American/Chicano"; 6.9 percent, "Puerto Rican"; 6.9 percent, "Cuban"; 2.0 percent, "South American"; and 2.0 percent, "Central American." In addition, 27.5 percent indicated "Other" and wrote in one of two responses—the panethnic labels of "Latino" or "Hispanic." This finding was remarkable because a "panethnic label" was not available as an option on the survey, yet respondents added it in themselves, demonstrating that their identity is tied to a larger panethnic Latino community. This may mean that a Cuban American might feel a connection with or support for a Mexican American who has just been picked up in an immigration raid. It provides hope for developing coalitions across the diversity of Latino communities.[17] García Bedolla's research applied Michael Dawson's "linked fate" to Latinos and identity politics in examining Latino political participation in Los Angeles.[18] Harvard Law School professor Lani Guinier and University of Texas law professor Gerald Torres argued that tapping into one's racial identity can be a source of political action. They asked: "In what ways can racial group consciousness function as a political asset, rather than a liability, in an ongoing struggle for social justice? And how does being raced black or brown in the United States affect one's motivation to engage in this kind of transformative political activity?"[19] They argued that "racialized identities may be put to service to achieve social change through democratic renewal."[20] Guinier and Torres used this as a foundation to go beyond identity politics to action. They stated:

Unlike identity politics, political race is not about being but instead is about doing. Political race configures race and politics as an action or set of actions rather than a thing. . . . Race becomes political when those who have been raced black in this society not only experience their identity in the form of what Michael Dawson calls "linked fate" but then act accordingly. They see that their fate is linked to others who are like them.[21]

Do Latino attorneys feel they share a linked fate of being "raced" brown or black in the United States? To answer this question, we will examine their perceptions of prejudice toward themselves and toward other Latinos.

EXPERIENCES OF PREJUDICE AMONG THE LATINO RESPONDENTS

The Latino respondents were then asked to rate their sense of Latino identity from "very weak" to "very strong." Almost 60 percent indicated that their Latino ethnic identity is "Somewhat Strong" or "Very Strong," while under 20 percent indicated that their ethnic identity is "Very Weak" or "Somewhat Weak" (see Appendix A, Figure 2.1). So, there is a sense of "linked fate" among most of the respondents. In addition, over a third of Latino lawyers in this study indicate that they currently speak both English and Spanish on social occasions and that language is very important to their identity.

While some may caution that identity politics is divisive to American politics and society, Princeton professor Amy Gutmann asserted that identity groups are actually good for democracy.[22] Specifically, Gutmann argued that "when they struggle for greater civic equality for a subordinated group, identity groups use their political power in defense of democratic justice."[23] That is, participation in the political struggles shaped by groups not only improves the circumstances of the members of the group but also contributes to the formation of a democratic civil society in important and fundamental ways. Gutmann listed four main reasons in which identity groups are important to democracy: the ability to influence individual identities, the importance of numbers in a democracy to help individuals achieve greater influence, the ability to combat injustices, and the benefit of providing mutually supportive relationships. This list precisely describes the motivations of the Latina respondent previously quoted when she joined the group, Latina Perspectives.

According to Gutmann, these reasons go beyond self-interest, because shared identity, whether based on culture, gender, race, class, or sexual orientation, is an important value in and of itself. Shared identity creates mutually supportive relationships.[24] However, Gutmann cautioned against "saddl[ing] the most advantaged members of the least advantaged groups with the greatest obligations,"[25] with which Latino professionals are often faced. Gutmann acknowledged the reality is that "ascriptive groups need to act for themselves because otherwise no one will act for them, at least not now."[26]

The Latino respondents were also asked to describe their own personal experiences with prejudice on a scale from "None" to "Extreme." Over half of them responded that they have experienced "moderate" (36.6 percent) or "substantial" (16.8 percent) prejudice. When this same question was generalized to ask how Latino attorneys would characterize their personal lifetime experience compared to prejudice of the *average Latino in Washington*, those figures went up even more, with 91.4 percent indicating either "Moderate" (49.5 percent), "Substantial" (38.7 percent), or "Extreme" levels of prejudice (3.2 percent). Figure 2.2 details their responses of the perception of prejudice among the average Latinos in Washington State (see Appendix A, Figure 2.2). These responses demonstrate that Latinos feel a sense of shared identity and sense of shared experiences along the lines of prejudice, even if they, as professionals, experience it to a lesser degree. Furthermore, while they believe other Latinos have experiences with prejudice at much higher rates than they do, over 50 percent of Latino respondents believe that they, too, have encountered this treatment. While they believed their experiences with prejudice are not as severe as Latinos statewide, they undoubtedly understand that they live in very different circumstances than do the majority of Latinos, simply because of their high levels of formal education relative to the rest of Latinos. The quotation from this Latino attorney makes this point:

> I really feel like I don't have their same struggle kind of thing and I didn't have to go through what they've been going through. But I think it was very important for me to be aware of what they were going through and what some of them have gone through and things like that . . . , you know, and a need to get more professionals in the community.

This quotation acknowledges the understanding Latino lawyers believe they should have about "what [Latinos] were going through" and the need to have "more professionals in the [Latino] community." The implication is that having more Latino professionals can become an important counterframe in and of itself for the Latino community.

PROFESSIONAL ACTS OF RESISTANCE

I think that I've given it my best good effort trying to deal with all these white groups, and I gave up! I have tried to go here and do that and do this. It's just uncomfortable and I don't like it. . . . The whole thing is just sickening to me. I mean I get tired of it. I play it because it's business. I have business things I gotta do, and I can eat cheese and crackers like anybody else, a little wine. But I miss that Budweiser with carnitas. And I just want to go in, do my thing, and get the hell out of there. . . . I'm tired of that bullshit game where I have to be a white guy. Why don't they become Mexicans? Why don't they become like me instead of me like them? There's nothing wrong with me!

After twenty years of trying to play the game, this respondent decided he'd had enough. His statement demonstrated that the Latino respondents in this study resisted the racism they experienced in the way they engaged and participated in their profession. This includes the choices they make in the professional functions they attend, the type of law they practice, where they work, and even the very decision to go into law—a profession seen as a power profession. This section looks at the motivation for going to law school and the types of law the respondents practice. Often, their decisions come from a sense of rejecting the white frame, from a sense of wanting the tools with which to fight back against the oppression they had experienced all their lives.

I was involved in a lot of things politically [while in university]. I had decided that lawyers play a significant role in this culture. And that it's really important to understand the legal system if you're going to have any effect.

This sentiment was shared by the overwhelming majority of study respondents. They went to law school to effect change. They included a sitting judge, attorneys in private practice, partners in sizable law firms, and attorneys working with government agencies. They also varied by generation, ranging from recent law school graduates to those who had practiced for decades. Across the profession, they had felt a legal career would help them make change. The majority of respondents believed a law degree would give them the tools to change the status quo or, one could argue, the white racial frame with which they lived.[27] They may not have understood the theory of the white racial frame, but they definitely understood the experience of it, as indicated by their many stories and comments, just as Anna's and Tony's experiences demonstrated. Nearly all have experienced racism, believe almost all Latinos do, and that their identities are centered on these experiences.

FAMILY SOCIOECONOMIC BACKGROUND AS A MOTIVATOR

Another important factor that ties culture and identity together is the role of family as a motivating force for these respondents. Most of them indicated it was the importance of family and identity within the Latino culture that made the biggest difference for their career choice. When participants were asked how they got to where they are today as Latino professionals, most of them credited their families. One key informant interviewee, whose parents were migrant farmworkers with few English skills, stated:

> Oh, my parents were a big influence. They were the influence in my going to school. I mean, since I could remember, they always encouraged us going to college even though we didn't have any money. It was a question of "Well, I don't know how we're going to do it, but you're going to go."

Another interviewee talked about the sacrifices his mother, who was a housecleaner, had made to get him where he is today and how that extraordinary effort on her part has impacted his desire to help other Latinos pursue their own education goals. This respondent grew up in the city and arrived in the United States in the fifth grade without English skills; however, he used his strong knowledge of math to demonstrate that he was intelligent. Soon he was able to work his way through private high school through his mother's direction and personal sacrifices made for his advancement. He stated:

> [M]y mom worked very hard for [us], and I started at a public school here. My mom worked very hard, you know, cleaning jobs. Anybody that has had the most influence on who I am, it's my mom, my mother, because she's the

one that had to make the sacrifices of working constantly, not being there for us as a mom, you know, but providing just sufficient enough to live [on] and also worked with the school administrators at private schools, parochial schools, you know, to get us in there at a discount or something. So, from fifth grade through the end of high school, we went to private schools, parochial schools through the eighth grade, and then a private Catholic school for my four years in high school. The only thing my mom could promise us is help in our first year through high school. After that, we would have to finance it. So, from the third year, I guess, tenth, eleventh, and twelfth grade, anybody who wanted to stay at the private school had to finance it him- or herself. And all my siblings did.

This story of how his mother earned a meager income as a housecleaner but still managed to find a way to send this Latino respondent and his siblings to private schools for one year and how he and his siblings worked to finance their way through the final three years of private high school demonstrates this family's dedication and sacrifices made in exchange for access to education and a better life. This Latino attorney stated that he hopes to give back to his community of origin by helping Latinos from similar economic circumstances complete their education. This trajectory was common among respondents and central to their identities as professionals. Stories of family sacrifice are a significant piece of the Latino lawyers' narratives.

When examining the Latino respondents' parents' educational and occupational history, the circumstances in which the Latino respondents in this study grew up are quite similar to those of Latinos nationwide. For example, according to U.S. Census Bureau data, 29.7 percent of Hispanics under the age of 18 live below national poverty levels compared to almost 10 percent of non-Hispanic whites.[28] An examination of median net worth reveals that Latino households are worth only around $8,000 compared to non-Hispanic white households, which are worth close to $90,000. And more than a quarter of Latinos have either a zero or negative net worth.[29] As noted earlier, current U.S. Census data indicated that only 57 percent of Latinos aged twenty-five or older have graduated from high school compared to close to 90 percent of the non-Hispanic white population,[30] only 12.1 percent of Latinos have a bachelor's degree or more compared to 30.6 percent of non-Hispanic whites,[31] only 5.0 percent of Latinos nationally have achieved master's and professional degrees, and only 3.0 percent have achieved doctoral degrees.[32] Most of these Latinos grew up with parents who lacked high levels of formal education and who lived in poverty.

The survey data reveal that these Latinos grew up in very different socioeconomic circumstances than they currently experience as lawyers. This mirrors the experiences of African-American professionals as well. For example, in their analyses of university admissions into elite colleges and universities, Bowen and Bok observed that the "gap in pre-collegiate preparation" for black and white students was due to long-standing differences "in resources, environments, and *inherited intellectual capital (the educational attainment of parents and grandparents)*" [emphasis added].[33] The notion of "inherited intellectual capital" is an important factor for the Latino respondents in this study as well. The survey data concerning parental educational experience and work background provide dramatic evidence of their *lack of* inherited intellectual capital in their upbringing. This means that Latino attorneys most likely did not grow up surrounded by books in the house. They could not ask their parents for help with applying to university or count on financial assistance from them once they enrolled. Because the majority of Latino attorneys' parents did not attend university, let alone law school, they had less access to resources that could guide their children through college preparatory courses, SAT exams, college essays, and financial aid applications, nor could they provide much assistance with the financial resources required for higher education.

In this study, at the same time the survey was sent to Latino attorneys, a second survey questionnaire, "Civic Engagement Among Members of the Washington State Bar," was sent to a random cross-section of 1,900 attorneys, 90 percent of whom are Caucasian according to the Washington Bar Association's demographic figures.[34] A total of 757 (41.7 percent response rate) non-Latino attorneys completed and returned questionnaires (see Appendix B). The reason for sending a survey to a random sample of predominately white lawyers is to make comparisons. Comparisons between these two groups of attorneys are to assist in understanding the reality of Latino professionals' upbringing and help to highlight how far they have come. Table 2.1 presents survey findings regarding the educational backgrounds of the mothers and fathers of Washington's Latino and non-Latino lawyers (see Appendix A, Table 2.1).

The survey results displayed in Table 2.1 clearly indicate that the percentage of the respondents' mothers and fathers who did not have a high school diploma—43.4 percent and 38.4 percent, respectively—compared to the percentage of mothers and fathers who did not have a high school diploma determined from the survey sent to the random sample of Washington attorneys—5.4 percent and 7.6 percent, respectively—is the most pronounced. Similarly, only 15 percent of the parents of Latino lawyers held bachelor's degrees compared to 27.5 percent of non-Latino attorneys' mothers and 24.4 percent of non-Latino attorneys' fathers. The difference holds with respect to the completion of advanced degrees as well, with the comparison group of non-Latino lawyers' fathers holding twice the percentage of graduate degrees (at 21.9 percent compared to 10.1 percent) as those of their Latino lawyer counterparts. Furthermore, 9 percent of the comparison group of attorneys reported having fathers who were lawyers themselves, while only 2 percent of Latino lawyers' fathers were reported to have been attorneys. Not surprisingly, the stark differences in parental educational backgrounds connect directly to the differences in the reported occupational status of the parents of Latino and non-Latino attorneys in Washington.

Table 2.2 displays survey findings regarding the distribution of occupations listed for the parents of Washington's Latino attorneys and for the non-Latino attorney comparison group (see Appendix A, Table 2.2). Latino attorneys' fathers were twice as likely to have worked in manual labor (44.9 percent) than were non-Latino attorneys' fathers (20.2 percent). Furthermore, 40.6 percent of Latino attorneys' mothers were full-time homemakers compared to 51.5 percent of non-Latino attorneys' mothers. The comparison group attorneys were nearly twice as likely as the Latino attorneys to report that their mothers (22.9 percent versus 13.9 percent) were professionals (defined as lawyers, teachers, doctors, etc.) and were 1.5 times as likely to report that their fathers were professionals (45 percent versus 29.6 percent) as were their Latino counterparts. Given the obstacles regarding parental level of education and occupation, it is remarkable that any Latino attorneys went on to attain a university education and then a law degree. Thus, Latino lawyers do not come from privileged backgrounds. They had to beat the odds to get where they are.

When I asked the respondents to describe how being Latino has affected their experiences in college, law school, or their professions, one of the major themes that stood out was the lack of opportunity (including economic opportunities) that their parents had also experienced. Considering the socioeconomic background of the respondents, it is obvious that they came from families where there was little opportunity for economic advancement. In addition, as Anna's and Tony's experiences demonstrate, their parents not only faced poverty but also open discrimination and injustice. This is not surprising given the documented racialization of Latinos in America, the lack of educational and occupational opportunities, and the experiences with white discrimination and racism. Because Latinos as a racialized group often do not have many role models to look to as they pursue their educational goals, the fact that they gathered tremendous courage and support from their family and their culture to pursue their educations comes as no surprise.

The survey questionnaire asked the Latino attorneys to write in the one or two most important reasons for going to law school. Many of the reasons given overlap due to the open-ended format of the question. However, the answers still reveal important insights. The reasons fell mainly under the categories of "employment/career opportunities" (with twenty-three responses) and "income security and opportunities" (also with twenty-three responses). However, another common response is best represented by a survey participant who stated, "To help others and support myself." This desire to help others in need (listed by fourteen respondents) was often prevalent before completing law school. For example, the survey participant just quoted had founded AMISTAD, a Latino college organization; served in international clubs, including involvement in an Iranian club; and was also involved in mainstream student government organizations. The next most important reason given for going to law school was to join a "prestigious and respectable profession" (twelve responses). Related to the "help others" response, eleven respondents stated their reason for going to law school was to "Advance social and economic justice." Both the "desire to impact public policy issues/public service" and having an "intellectually challenging career" had nine responses each. Other reasons listed for going to law school were "interest in the subject of law" (eight responses) and "wanting an advanced degree" (also eight responses). Six respondents specifically indicated that "helping the Hispanic community" was their *main* motivation for going to law school. Again, this reason overlaps with others provided and could be categorized with the topic of "advancing social and economic justice" and "to help others." Finally, seven respondents listed "encouragement from family" as their main reason for attending law school. Four people listed "self-empowerment" as the main reason for choosing law school. There were other reasons listed once or twice, which included helping Native

American tribes decide their own fate; the drama of the courtroom; encouragement from a teacher, a mentor, or a friend; current political events; and the desire to be a leader.

Finally, consider how one Latina attorney replied when asked what she believed the advantages or opportunities of higher education, such as law school, were to members of minority groups such as Latinos. Her answer shows the complex role into which Latino attorneys are placed. Her response underscores how the role of the family in Latino culture is intertwined with the professional role of Latino attorneys:

> The education, first of all, the knowledge of how the world works, which is something that so many people just don't have access to, so many don't have access even to the language, much less the knowledge base. The status. The fact that you can speak authoritatively and be heard in a way that you can't if you don't have that credential. That credential means so much. It means particularly a great deal, because as Latinos we wouldn't be heard without it. The credential comes first. It's more important for people of color in general to have the prestigious credentials because it's the ticket to being taken seriously—and without it, there's nothing. And I wish that was not the case, but it is. So, it's the education, the knowledge, the status, the access to people in power that others do not have. And at the same time, most Latinos—or many Latinos—have maintained ties to their families, their communities, so that we're not operating in a vacuum without any contact with anyone else. So, there remains that—that ability, that connection, that knowledge—of what the circumstances are and for many of us because we're first-generation professionals, the personal experience of having grown up in this system and understanding what it is like to be not just at our current professional level but a bunch of other levels as well.

As suggested by her words, the act of becoming a professional for racialized groups is a way to exert self-respect, to fight back, and to say to the world that they do matter. As she stated, "As Latinos, we wouldn't be heard without it. The credential comes first. It's more important for people of color in general to have the prestigious credentials because it's the ticket to being taken seriously—and without it, there's nothing." For racialized groups like Latinos, becoming a professional is a strategy of resistance. It is an "I'll show you" attitude that helps racialized groups fight against the white racial frame. And this can become a powerful motivator.

CONCLUSION

This chapter described the ways experiences with racism affect Latino attorneys' identity. For most of them, being raised in immigrant households was a defining focus for encountering that experience. It also described the ways culture, language, and identity had become counterframing strategies of resistance among the Latino respondents. Most interestingly, the Latino respondents indicated choosing a career in law as a way to counter their experiences with white prejudice and help the Latino community.

The respondents in this study faced complex challenges, revealing much about how race, class, and cultural identity impact not only one's experiences in the United States but also one's motivations for resistance as well. Because of their situation as members of an ethnic and racial group and their experiences with discrimination, as well as their perceptions of discrimination toward other Latinos, these Latino attorneys were intimately aware of the larger context of political and social rejection that not only they have faced but that their parents have faced as well. This explains why 34 percent of Latino attorneys listed in an open-ended question on the survey that the main reasons they became lawyers were to "help the Hispanic community," for "self-empowerment," to "help others," and to "advance social and economic justice."

These Latino lawyers were also culturally connected and strongly identified with the larger Latino community. Almost half of the Latino attorneys in this study spoke English as a second language. Close to 40 percent of these Latino lawyers still speak Spanish, and language is a key link to culture and community. In addition, the fact that almost 40 percent had parents who did not graduate from high school allowed them to relate even more to the experiences and struggles Latinos in the wider community face. The familial, cultural, and linguistic background of their parents remains with them in important ways and serves as their motivation for pursuing successful careers. Many Latino attorneys also indicated their motivation to go to law school was to gain financial security, something they did not grow up with. In many ways, their career choice has become a strategy to resist the white frame on all levels: culture, class, and race. The next chapter describes some of the most significant professional obstacles they faced on their path to a better life.

③

LATINOS IN THE WORKPLACE

Luis was the child of an immigrant father from Central America who came to the United States to work on the freighters. One day, the ship docked in the Seattle harbor. He looked up the hill and saw Saint James Cathedral, and he knew this was where he wanted to make a life and to raise a family. He eventually met his wife, and they had Luis; however, the family would be separated soon after. When Luis was only five years old, his father was deported back to Central America. Luis would not see him again until he was close to ten years old. It is difficult for most people to imagine the pain and confusion that Luis must have felt growing up for years without his father. It is also hard to understand the struggles Luis's father encountered as he spent the next few years trying to reunite with his family. For many Latinos, either they or someone they know has been separated from a parent for years because of the perverse rules in the U.S. immigration system.

In the United States, almost everyone is descended from immigrants. In the previous era of globalization, which lasted from about 1850 to World War I, people moved across borders as easily as commerce. The values of that time remain engraved on a plaque on the Statue of Liberty, describing what many immigrants truly hope they will find once they arrive:

Here at our sea-washed, sunset gates shall stand
A mighty woman with a torch, whose flame

Is the imprisoned lightning, and her name
Mother of Exiles. From her beacon-hand
Glows world-wide welcome; her mild eyes command
The air-bridged harbor that twin cities frame.
"Keep ancient lands, your storied pomp!" cries she
With silent lips. "Give me your tired, your poor,
Your huddled masses yearning to breathe free,
The wretched refuse of your teeming shore.
Send these, the homeless, tempest-tost to me,
I lift my lamp beside the golden door!"

Much has changed since then. Our history of conflict over our immigration policies and practices demonstrates we've clearly lost our way with regard to our founding ideals of being a place of refuge and welcome to those needing both, as expressed in Lazarus's poem. Instead, immigration policy is a product of the polarity and gridlock that characterize so much of our politics. Immigration and workplace politics are products of the racial framing described in Chapter 1. A perfect example is the fact that Congress failed to pass the DREAM Act, which would have allowed unauthorized children who immigrated to the United States with their parents before the age of sixteen and who have lived their entire adult life in the United States a path to citizenship through either higher education attainment or military service. Instead, these American-raised, but foreign-born, children will continue to be in a vulnerable position because people argued the act was a backdoor amnesty program rewarding illegal behavior.

Missing from much of the debate on immigration are the factors that contribute to unauthorized immigration. Immigrants are doing the most difficult work for low pay, day in and day out,even when they are ill, tired, homesick, lonely, or in dangerous working conditions. They are needed by the economy and yet regarded as criminals. As Michele Wucker, a senior fellow at the World Policy Institute at the New School in New York City, stated, "The population of immigrants who are in this country without legal papers did not grow to more than 10 million people without America's full participation in the legal charade."[1]

Another element that is missing from the debate on immigration is the humanity of immigrants. What happened to Luis during the most important years of his childhood is not only increasingly common, but it is a product of the dehumanization in racial framing and a prelude to a lifetime of identity as the "other." Most people cannot imagine the destructive long-term consequences these policies are having and have had on immigrant families—for years. It should take something far more severe than trying to earn a living, even though without proper documentation, to justify the government's separating parents from their young children, as Luis and many others like him have experienced. The act of dividing families, particularly families of color, reveals a very dark side of America—one we have seen before with black slave children removed from parents and sold as property and with Indian children who were removed from their homes and placed in boarding schools to teach them how to be white people. Dividing families is part of the racialization of immigrants, particularly Latinos.

As Luis discovered very early in his life, immigrants are not widely accepted in this country. Current claims that immigrants threaten to culturally divide the United States or that they reject core American values and refuse to assimilate are nothing new. The same was said of white Eastern and Southern European immigrants in the nineteenth century, who were predominately Catholic or Jewish and who did not speak English as a first language. These white immigrants who came in the 1800s and 1900s were almost all undocumented because the United States had few exclusionary laws until the 1920s.

IMMIGRATION POLICY AND THE WHITE RACIAL FRAME

In a historical overview of immigration, Wucker demonstrated that contrary to popular belief, immigrants did not leave behind everything from the old country and not look back. In fact, many even returned home.[2] Wucker noted that during the first great waves of immigration, more than a third of all immigrants returned home, and that between 1880 and 1920, 50 percent of Italians returned to Italy. Those who did stay in America remained civically, culturally, and politically connected to their home countries. Wucker argued that although immigrants were involved in the old country, they simultaneously wanted to participate in and embrace their new society; however, this all changed after two world wars, when civic engagement in the home country became less acceptable in the United States. During this period, immigrants had to blend in as much as possible and leave their old ties behind. Wucker maintained this history is important to know because the consequences of this amnesia regarding our immigrant origins include the "age-old scapegoating of foreigners" today.[3] Wucker stated that the "false idea that white Americans had no ethnic traits was an illusion that helped lead to the culture wars of the late twentieth century."[4] According to Wucker, re-racialized arguments directed toward Latinos or Asians are examples of this ahistorical perspective on American immigration.

However, because of the white racial frame, the American model of *e pluribus unum*, or the so-called melting pot, does not work well for people of color. Eduardo Bonilla-Silva said, "That melting pot never included people of color. Blacks, Chinese, Puerto Ricans, etc., could not melt into the pot."[5] Other scholars such as Alejandro Portes and Rubén Rumbaut[6] maintained that educational attainment for Latinos is the key for overcoming some of the negative effects of racialization. However, because Latinos often have low levels of human capital and migrate into an environment of hostility directed at them by mainstream society and institutions, their chances of success are daunting. Portes and Rumbaut argued that the negative experiences Latinos encounter (e.g., educators who instill in them the belief that English is superior to Spanish) can be damaging to their educational success. Children of immigrants are often placed in a vulnerable position in which they grow up feeling shame for their parents' culture but at the same time, not fully adopting American culture. Such ambivalence creates negative or dissonant acculturation, with negative consequences for all. One consequence of dissonant acculturation is called "downward assimilation." Many of these children will grow up reacting against the system that has rejected them. The consequence of their anger often means they may end up doing worse than their parents financially and materially. Therefore, Portes and Rumbaut argued for a system that slowly acculturates immigrants into American culture and the English language, while maintaining Spanish and the value of their parents' culture. However, slowly acculturating immigrants would require addressing the white racial frame with strong counterframing that leads immigrants toward success.

Unfortunately, what Luis and his family experienced years ago is still all too common. In fact, on July 28, 2010, thousands of children marched in Washington, DC, in front of the White House, in Los Angeles in front of the Federal Building, and in Mexico City at the U.S. Embassy. They marched to deliver a letter to President Obama protesting the tragic situation of children taken from their undocumented parents following deportation.

Luis was one of the lucky ones—he had at least one parent who wasn't deported. But often this is not the case. Children separated from their parents often end up in the foster care system. Once in this system, it becomes almost impossible for parents to get them back because of language difficulties, legal status, and lack of resources and understanding regarding how to negotiate such a complex system. Immigrant parents lose the most important and precious thing in the world to them and all because they had wanted an opportunity for a life better than destitution and poverty. We've come a long way from Emma Lazarus's words written in 1883: "Give me your tired, your poor,/Your huddled masses yearning to breathe free."

Our history is filled with blatantly racist laws that have purported to simply "regulate" immigration laws but in reality were bad public policy, with racist motivations and intents. Recall the 1882 Chinese Exclusion Act and the 1907 Gentlemen's Agreement Act with Japan limiting immigration as examples of racist immigration laws in America's past. Today our immigration policy is one-sided—the only thing required of employers is that they not *knowingly* hire undocumented workers. However, instead of focusing on our unjust, one-sided immigration policies, public leaders—from church groups to civic organizations to the public at large, on all sides of the ideological spectrum—have hypocritically taken the stance that undocumented workers are "lawbreakers" who need to learn to "follow the rules" and "do it the right way." If undocumented immigrants don't "do it the right way," then apparently they must be prepared to be separated from their children.

However, Luis's experience of being separated from his dad for an important part of his childhood did not break him. As a second-generation Latino American trying to balance two worlds, education became his path to success. He dreamed of joining one of the most prestigious and powerful professions in America. What were the chances he would get to college and complete a bachelor's and then a law degree? Struggling against financial, societal, and sometimes even cultural obstacles, he eventually joined the ranks of Latino professionals. Now Luis is a successful attorney with his own law firm, not far from Saint James Cathedral. He has been practicing law for over thirty years. Luis has received numerous awards, including the University of Washington Law School's Alumni Service Recognition Award. He has been president of the Alumni Association's board of trustees and active in diversity efforts by having served as chair of the Commission on Opportunities for Minorities in the Profession, and has mentored countless law school students. There is no doubt that Luis has been extremely successful in his life and in his professional career. He is

seen as a leader in his community. He also enjoys the kind of financial freedom most Latinos in America can only imagine. By all measures, his life is
a success story. Yet, do he and other Latino professionals have experiences
that are unique because of how the United States racializes Latinos?

The racialization of Latinos is the link between immigrants and Latinos,
and affects the way both end up being viewed and treated by others in
our political, social, educational, and economic institutions. In *Newcomers, Outsiders, and Insiders: Immigrants and American Racial Politics in
the Early Twenty-first Century*, Ronald Schmidt and colleagues examined
how immigration impacts the way U.S. minority groups achieve equality
in all aspects of American life, from politics to economics. Based on their
extensive research, they found that immigration in America over the past
forty years has greatly affected minority groups in society.[7] Specifically,
the authors wanted to know how a "racial hierarchy" in public life affected
U.S. Latino, black, and Asian populations. Their findings were bleak. They
stated "that a significant number of Latinos continue to experience a substantial degree of racial hierarchy in U.S. political life . . . [and we] believe
that there will likely be large numbers of Latinos facing a continuation of
these conditions of racial hierarchy for decades into the future."[8] In other
words, the authors believed that without committed federal public policies that address ways to socially and politically incorporate immigrants,
such as the DREAM Act would have done, the racialization of Latinos in
all aspects of American public life—including the workplace, the political
sphere, and interactions in institutions that affect one's daily lived experiences—will only worsen.

This chapter will next describe experiences of Latinos in American
public life by focusing on Latinos in the workplace. This will be done by
examining the experiences of the Latino respondents, including comparing
Latino attorneys' and white attorneys' law school experiences and current
professional experiences before describing some of the more significant professional obstacles the Latino attorneys stated they face. Their experiences
help us understand the reality of what it is like to be a Latino professional
in America. How do the professional experiences of Latinos differ from
those of whites? In what specific ways are the experiences of Latinos
unique from their white colleagues'? How do race, ethnicity, and gender
affect Latinos in the workplace? No one has asked these questions in a
systematic and rigorous manner. Therefore, this chapter specifically asks
Does membership in a historically disadvantaged minority group create

unique challenges and obstacles in professional environments? The empirical evidence from this study showed that it does. Consider what this Latina respondent had to say about discrimination in the workplace:

> The primary difficulty being Latino/Hispanic has caused [me] has been in the interview process as I was seeking my first job. Later, it has been a problem working within the system due to systemic and long-held racial discrimination issues. I served on the original Minority and Justice Task Force, and that confirmed my view about widespread discriminatory practice.

This Latina respondent experienced obstacles trying to get a job and in working in the legal profession. It wasn't until she joined the Minority and Justice Task Force that she realized she wasn't the only one experiencing discrimination. Serving on the task force helped her to realize that the professional legal environment had widespread discrimination problems. Because racism has been around since the very foundation of our country, it has permeated all aspects of our society, including the professional work environment. Joe Feagin argued that understanding this aspect of American society is key to understanding our current racial realities.[9]

This makes racism and discrimination similar to environmental pollution. They aren't just in the air, the soil, or the water—they are everywhere. The workplace is no exception. Feagin contended that "the oppressive racist realities have from the early decades been institutionalized and thus manifested in all of this society's major parts . . . , such as the economy, politics, education, religion, [and] the family . . . ."[10] Therefore, it should come as no surprise that the Latino respondents' experiences in the workplace reflected the "broad, persisting, and dominant racial frame that has rationalized racial oppression and inequality and thus impacted all U.S. institutions."[11]

Feagin and Cobas offered insights into the way the dominant racial frame impacts Latinos, with their research on middle-class Latinos.[12] Through interviews with Latinos across the country, they found that Latinos supported and internalized the dominant white racial frame, especially because of the pressure by dominant white society for them to assimilate. They stated:

> Whites with socioeconomic and political resources transmit subtle and overt messages of racial stereotyping, imaging, and interpretation of Latinos/as. Such negative views of Latinos/as seriously handicap them as they try to survive and thrive within white-controlled institutions.[13]

Similarly, Zulema Valdez's research on Latino business owners in "Little Latin America," in Houston, Texas, demonstrated that even when Latino business owners tended to identify by nationality, eventually they adopted the white racial frame, placing whites at the top, blacks at the bottom, and Latinos in a middle ground.[14] Valdez stated: "The imposition of race is always required; it is not an option."[15] If the power of the white racial frame could permeate a segregated immigrant Latino community in Houston, Texas, as well as middle-class Latinos across the country, how would this racial frame impact the Latino respondents in predominantly white legal environments such as in law schools, courtrooms, and law firms? This will be answered by comparing Latino attorneys' and white attorneys' professional experiences. First, though, it is important to underscore that there are so few Latino professionals, period.[16]

Looking at the numbers specifically in the legal profession, the American Bar Association's (ABA) Commission on Racial and Ethnic Diversity in the Profession found that as of the year 2000, *all* non-white groups combined comprised only approximately 10 percent of lawyers and judges nationally.[17] More recent figures from the U.S. Equal Employment Opportunity Commission (EEOC) indicated African Americans represented 4 percent, Latinos 3 percent, and Asian Americans 6.5 percent of the legal profession nationally.[18]

Diversity in the legal profession in Washington State is even worse than it is nationally. As of 2003, there were a total of 23,632 active Washington State Bar Association (WSBA) members.[19] According to a 2010 voluntary demographic information survey of the Washington State Bar Association's active membership, 23,828 out of 34,368 active attorneys participated. Of the 23,828 attorneys who participated, 429 checked the category "Hispanic," representing only 1.8 percent of the state's active attorneys. Latinos comprise 11 percent of Washington State's total population, making them the largest ethnic and racial group in Washington. Latinos are projected to comprise 12.9 percent of the population by 2030.[20] According to the WSBA, 90 percent of the attorneys participating in the survey checked the category "Caucasian," 0.8 percent checked "American Indian/Alaska Native," 2.9 percent checked "Asian/Pacific Islander," and 2 percent checked "African American."[21]

Lack of diversity in the legal profession has a long and well-documented history. First, immigrants coming from Southern and Eastern Europe, who were culturally, ethnically, and religiously different from previous immigrants from Northern Europe, were excluded. Later, the profession excluded blacks and Latinos.[22] As late as the 1940s, a lawyer who was not of white Anglo-Saxon Protestant background would not be admitted into the American Bar Association in some states.[23] In Pennsylvania, between 1933 and 1943, not one black lawyer was allowed to enter the ABA.[24] In combination with increasingly prohibitive costs of a law school education and fees for taking the state bar, traditionally excluded groups continue to be largely excluded from the legal profession. Current low levels of diversity in the legal profession (verified by both the ABA's *Goal IX Report, 2003–2004* and the Washington State Bar Association's statistics) underscore the importance of diversifying the legal profession if it is to become a truly public profession representative of American society. Since 143 active members of the WSBA are Latinos and 102 Latinos participated in this study, one can extrapolate that the responses were highly representative of all Latino lawyers in Washington State. One would expect that by comprising such a low percentage of the legal profession, Latino attorneys would experience greater professional and social isolation, in addition to the usual demanding and stressful work environment. This study confirms this.

PROFESSIONAL EXPERIENCES

The Latino respondents in this study are a highly educated, sophisticated, intelligent, and knowledgeable group. Because of the very nature of their training and legal education, they understand the major legal and business institutions of America. These respondents can handle difficult challenges and are accustomed to heavy workloads and trained to deal with confrontations in a professional and determined manner. In short, the Latino lawyers studied here are not a group who is easily discouraged. With that in mind, let's examine their professional workplace experiences, beginning with their experiences in law school.

Law School Experiences

How do the distinctly different backgrounds of Latino attorneys, as opposed to the predominately white attorneys' from the comparison group surveyed, impact them in their law school experiences? Would they make the same career choices over again? To answer these questions, a variety of questions documents their professional experiences (see Appendix B), beginning with some of the biggest obstacles faced in law school, including family obligations, knowledge, and costs. The question-and-response format used in the survey reads as follows:

How big an obstacle to your law school education were each of the following: *Family obligations, Knowledge about how to get into law school,* and *Cost of law school?*

| None | A little | Uncertain | Somewhat | Substantial |

The survey findings reveal that the greatest difference in the obstacles faced by the two groups of lawyers resides in the areas of family obligations and knowledge of how to get into law school. Both groups indicated that the cost of a law school education presented the biggest obstacle they faced in obtaining their law degrees (for the percentage differences for each category, see Appendix A, Tables 3.2, 3.3, and 3.4). The proportion of survey respondents identifying *family obligations* as an obstacle differs significantly across comparison groups, with the Latino respondents indicating that family obligations were a much bigger obstacle. Differences in cultural expectations for Latino lawyers could explain this large difference, since Latino culture, as previously mentioned, is considerably more family oriented versus mainstream American culture, which places a higher value on individualism. In addition, as Anna's story in Chapter 2 illustrates, the reality of living in a society that is highly stratified along racial lines means that Latinos, especially first-generation Latino professionals, are never too far removed from the tragedies found in their communities.

There is also a difference in the survey responses with regard to *knowledge* of how to get into law school, with Latino respondents indicating that knowledge was a much bigger obstacle than it was for the comparison group. Given what we know about the differences in inherited intellectual capital previously discussed in Chapter 2, this finding should not surprise anyone. As first-generation college students, and then law school students, these Latinos were entering a different world from the one in which they began. Most of them did not grow up with people they could turn to for help on how to navigate the higher education bureaucracy and law school. This includes knowledge of how and when to apply to college, which schools to apply to, preparatory courses to improve law school entrance exam scores, and even the costs associated with applying to law schools.

The overall *cost* of a law school education was seen as a formidable obstacle for *both* groups of attorneys. While the majority in the comparison group may have considered cost an obstacle as well, based on the information about parents' occupation, they (at least theoretically) had resources available to them to assist in law school expenses, whereas the Latino attorneys, who grew up with much more modest means, would not have had access to the same levels of family resources.

Despite these substantial differences in difficulty of obstacles experienced during law school, overall satisfaction with law school education was comparable for both groups. When asked about their overall satisfaction with the professional law school education they received, both Latino attorneys and the comparison group of white attorneys held similar opinions. On the high end of the "satisfaction" scale, 47.5 percent of the Latino attorneys indicated that they were "Very Satisfied" with their law school education compared to 49.9 percent of the comparison group of white attorneys. On the low end of the scale, the percentage expressing dissatisfaction ranged from 12.9 percent of Latino attorneys who indicated that they were either "A Little Dissatisfied" or "Very Dissatisfied" to 8.7 percent of the comparison group of white attorneys expressing dissatisfaction. So, once both groups were in law school, their perceptions about the experience are very similar, which could be, in part, because of the generalized law school curriculum that everyone must go through.

In contrast, there was a bigger gap between Latinos and white attorneys when asked how likely it would be that they would attend law school all over again if given the choice: 52.5 percent of Latino attorneys indicated "Very Likely" compared to only 39.5 percent of white attorneys. There is also a smaller gap in those who replied "A Little Unlikely" or "Very Unlikely," with 18.2 percent of Latino attorneys compared to 22 percent of white attorneys. Perhaps this 13 percent difference between Latino and white attorneys attending law school all over again can be attributed to the fact that by the measures listed above, Latino attorneys made greater sacrifices to get there or attended for different reasons. Because they are also most likely the first in their families to become professionals, it means a lot to their extended family as well. Coming from the backgrounds that the Latino attorneys do, one can easily see that there would be pride and a sense of accomplishment among the larger family.

Latino attorneys did experience some additional challenges while in law school, which they believed were based on their cultural and ethnic background. These challenges included complaints about the professors or teaching methods in law school. Specific comments by Latino attorneys included descriptions of their professors as "unfair," "arrogant," "prejudiced," and even "disinterested." "Alienation" or "cultural isolation" was another common challenge noted by the Latino attorneys. Several Latino attorneys listed such challenges as experiencing difficulty being the "only Latino" or having "White upper-middle-class environment/no peers to relate to," and suffering the stings of "institutional sexism, racism, and classism (not knowing how to think like a white upper-class male)." Similarly, the following statement represents a perspective mentioned several times by the Latino respondents: *other students questioning my right to be there*" or "peer comments/opinions on affirmative action." Another common challenge listed by almost a dozen Latino attorneys was the lack of academic preparation in K-12 for success in law school. These comments in combination highlighted some of the unique obstacles that membership in a historically disadvantaged racial and ethnic group can create in an already challenging environment like law school. Such things as feelings of isolation, nonminority students believing Latinos were not qualified to be there, and inadequate elementary and secondary academic preparation to meet the demands of college and then law school presented significant obstacles for Latino attorneys while in law school. We now turn to see if these challenges continued once they received their law degrees and became active members of their new profession.

Professional Work Experiences

How do the two groups of attorneys compare with respect to their current professional experiences? To compare both groups along professional dimensions, respondents were asked how long (in years) they had been practicing law in Washington, whether they were presently practicing law, how satisfied they were with their work, how many law-related professional organizations they belonged to, what type of law they practiced, and if they provided any pro bono legal services in the course of their work.

Nearly all the attorneys surveyed were currently practicing law. The survey data revealed that 80.4 percent of the Latino attorneys currently practice law, while 89.3 percent of the comparison group of white attorneys are currently practicing. However, the comparison group of attorneys' average years of practice in Washington is fourteen, with a median figure of twelve years, while the Latino attorneys have an average period of practicing law of only nine years, with a median of seven years. Latino lawyers are a relatively newer group of attorneys in Washington, in contrast to attorneys generally.

The level of overall job satisfaction is high for both groups, with 84.2 percent of the Latino attorneys and 82.9 percent of the comparison group indicating that they were either "Very Satisfied" or "Moderately Satisfied." On the low end of the "satisfaction scale," 11.9 percent of Latino attorneys indicated that they were either "A Little Dissatisfied" or "Very Dissatisfied" with their work, while 12.9 percent of the comparison group indicated the same. It is clear that both groups of attorneys are quite satisfied with their jobs.

In terms of professional organization membership, over half of the attorneys from both groups belong to at least three professional organizations, with 54 percent of the Latino attorneys listing at least three professional organizations and 53.5 of the comparison group listing membership in at least three organizations. Thus, both groups are very active in their professional organizations.

When asked the question "Do you personally provide any pro bono legal services?" well over half of all the attorneys surveyed indicated that they do in fact provide pro bono legal services: 66.3 percent of the Latino attorneys compared to 65.2 percent of the white attorneys. So far, both groups of attorneys provide comparable levels of pro bono legal services, are involved in the same number of professional organizations, and experience similar levels of job satisfaction. However, do they hold similar types of legal jobs?

With regard to type of law practice, Latino attorneys and the comparison group of white attorneys are also quite similar, with both groups being quite diverse in the types of legal practices in which they are engaged (see Appendix A, Table 3.1). Twenty-two percent of both groups are in solo practice. A higher proportion of the comparison attorneys work in smaller firms compared to the Latino attorneys. For example, 16.5 percent of Latino attorneys work in small firms compared to 21.7 percent of the comparison group. Similarly, 9.3 percent of Latino attorneys work in large firms, while 13.5 percent of white attorneys do. Latino attorneys have slightly greater representation working for government, with 10.3 percent of Latino attorneys working for city or county government, while 8.7 percent of the comparison group is employed by a city or county government. However, at the state level, the comparison group of white attorneys has a bit higher representation (5.2 percent of the white attorneys work for the state, while only 2.1 percent of Latino attorneys do). Latino attorneys are much more likely to hold federal government jobs at 8.2 percent than white attorneys at 3.8 percent. Only 1 percent of Latino attorneys are working as in-house counsel in comparison to 3.8 percent of white attorneys. Finally, in the judge or magistrate category, we find 3.1 percent of Latino attorneys compared to 2.4 percent of the white attorneys. The greatest difference can be found in the "Other" category (write-in responses). A full 16.5 percent of Latino attorneys do not engage in any of the legal practices listed, while 7.9 percent of the white attorneys do not engage in the listed legal practices. This could be because many Latino attorneys are employed in "legal services" types of practices. These are nonprofit organizations that provide legal services to people who do not have the resources to get legal representation. Two examples of these organizations in Washington State are the Northwest Justice Project and Columbia Legal Services. It would be fair to infer that at least some, if not most, of the 16.5 percent of Latino attorneys who checked "Other" are engaged in these types of organizations, especially because many of the Latino attorneys who participated in the interviews for this study indicated that they worked in one of these two specific nonprofit legal organizations.[25]

Now that the Latino respondents have made it into the professional world of law—they made it through law school and are practicing law—what is their current demographic information? Not surprisingly, both the Latino and the comparison respondents are quite similar with regard to their current background characteristics, despite the fact that these two groups of attorneys are from completely different worlds (see Appendix A, Table 3.5). Both groups of lawyers are more male in composition than female; 58.8 percent of the Latino respondents are male compared to 63.9 percent of the comparison group. Overall, marriage rates are high for both groups, at 68 percent for Latinos and 73.2 percent for the comparison group, with Caucasian/White spouses being the majority ethnic/racial group for all attorneys—close to 50 percent of Latino attorneys intermarried with Caucasians. While intermarriage rates were higher among the Latino respondents, intermarriage rates with blacks were low for both groups, with only 2.1 percent of Latinos in black/Latino marriages and none among the comparison group of white respondents. Over 60 percent of both groups have children, with 64.7 percent of Latino attorneys indicating that they have children compared to 67.4 percent for non-Latino attorneys. Interestingly, median annual income for both groups fell in the range of $70,000 to $99,000, a huge difference for the Latino attorneys compared to what Latinos earn nationally, with over 73 percent of Hispanics nationally earning less than $35,000 per year, according to the 2001 U.S. Census information. These demographic figures show that Latino lawyers have successfully overcome their economic and educational disadvantages. In summary, professional work background, income earned, overall satisfaction with their law school education, and job satisfaction are quite similar between both groups of respondents.

LATINO ATTORNEYS AND THE ROLE OF GATEKEEPERS

So far, we have seen that both groups of attorneys sampled in this study engage in similar types of legal professional activities, express similar levels of job satisfaction, do similar levels of pro bono work, and earn similar amounts of money. Why, then, do so few minority attorneys make it to the ranks of partner? Both lawyers of color (who combined represent around 10 percent of the profession) and white lawyers (over 90 percent of attorneys in Washington State checked the category "Caucasian") are behaving the same way professionally, but lawyers of color are not achieving the final prize of becoming a partner in a firm. Why is this the case?

Diversity in the legal profession has long been a problem. In fact, in 2009 to 2010, a group of eleven minority bar associations in Washington State began compiling data on the top fifty law firms in the state and based on the survey information they received, began grading those law firms with regard to diversity.[26] Prominent law professors contend diversity is at a "crisis stage."[27] An article titled, "Law Firms Short on Diversity," in the 2005 issue of *The News Journal*, stated that "lawyers of color nationwide account for 4.32 percent of partners at big firms."[28] In 1998, the American Bar Association published a report, *Miles to Go: Progress of Minorities in the Legal Profession*.[29] It was found that representation by racial and ethnic minorities among partners in large law firms was 2.97 percent as of 1997. The *Miles to Go* report also noted that minority attorneys face additional obstacles to "full and equal" participation in the profession, which include isolation from important social networks, lack of mentors, lack of a friendly environment for people of color, and lack of access to important clients and referrals. This should not be too surprising, considering the historical exclusion of racial and ethnic groups from the legal profession.

Based on these studies and the professional experiences of Latino law-yers, the reasons why racial and ethnic group members are not entering the upper-level positions in their profession can be linked to the white racial frame. If white lawyers comprise most of the legal community, this means that once Latino attorneys make it through law school and begin legal practices, much of their professional interactions in the legal com-munity will be with white colleagues. There must be some troublesome interactions that lead to so few attorneys of color becoming partner. One of the conclusions is actions and decisions of white lawyers are impeding the successful entry into the upper ranks of the legal profession among the racial and ethnic minority members. The unwritten rules of the game result in minority professionals having to do more to prove themselves in order to succeed. What else could explain this ceiling for minority lawyers and specifically for the Latino respondents in this study?

These claims are the product of the experiences of Latino profession-als, based not only on the survey results but also on focus-group and individual interviews (see Appendix B for the focus-group protocol and interview questions). This established that a sizable percentage of the Latino respondents experience significant levels of marginalization in their new roles as professionals. Based on the evidence from these ad-ditional interviews, it appears that although Latino attorneys are active and productive members of their profession, they encounter additional obstacles in their path because of the role of "gatekeepers." Gatekeepers are those who have the power to place barriers on the social, economic, and professional inclusion and/or advancement of racial and ethnic communities, who have only recently begun to make some inroads into professional circles, as demonstrated by the low numbers of attorneys found in the ABA's *Goal IX Report, 2003–2004*, the Washington State Bar Association's statistics, and the Washington Minority Bar Associa-tion's Joint Committee on Law Firm Diversity. The role of gatekeepers can be defined as follows:

> These gatekeepers are comprised of individual and organizational pow-erholders within institutions who, in the exercise of their responsibilities, are in influential positions to affect the experiences (whether negatively or positively) with social trust and civic engagement of broad cross sections of a community's residents. Given that communities of color are often at the lower end of an asymmetrical distribution of social, economic, and political

power, groups such as Latinos and African Americans may be especially vulnerable to the decisions made by these gatekeepers.[30]

Similar to the ABA's *Miles to Go* report, study data on these Latino professionals reveals there are gatekeepers who negatively impact Latino attorneys from a variety of sources. There are three specific types of "gatekeeper activity" in various areas in the legal profession, which result in experiences of discrimination and marginalization for Latino attorneys. These include (1) organizational, as found in the Washington State Bar Association or other mainstream organizations, (2) law firms, and (3) client interaction.

Organizational Gatekeepers in the Bar Association

Organizational gatekeepers can be found in the professional associations in which Latino lawyers are now involved as part of their role as attorneys. White members have largely dominated these organizations. Culture and environment naturally reflect that membership composition. For new members from distinct cultural backgrounds such as Latinos, this can be very alienating, even with one's professional credentials in hand. The interviews and focus-group data revealed that at times, there is even limited acceptance of the Latino respondents' participation, efforts, and contributions. Participating in mainstream professional organizations was not as comfortable as participating in Latino organizations, as this focus-group participant described:

> [I]nitially, when you first graduate from law school and you . . . look around the table and you see these are people who have been involved in Hispanic organizations, and I think that when you first graduate that's really important and there's a certain amount of comfort and support that comes from the people that you know and you have similar background and so . . . it's easier to become involved in these organizations. You immediately feel welcomed. Though, once you get that sense of, I guess, confidence in your professional life, then it becomes easier to join or participate in other organizations. *Not necessarily that you're more welcomed*, but that you're more mature in your own career that you can easily deal with the *unwelcome* that comes.

Another issue besides sensing that one is "unwelcome" in the mainstream organizations is whether or not the Latinos' presence was symbolic or substantive. Regarding participation in professional organizations, Latino attorneys often feel as though they are not given any "real voice." Whether or not there were any substantive contributions by Latinos in the mainstream organizations became the subject of internal debate among the Latino focus-group participants. For example, this interchange took place during the Yakima focus group (the "Y" stands for the Yakima focus group, and the number represents the number assigned to each participant):

> Y11: It's easier to get into these other [mainstream] groups and kind of become a minority and do nothing because you're just there—a minority. I mean, they want a minority person on these boards, *but you really have very little voice there*, at least from my point of view.
> Y1: I think that depends on the board.
> Y3: I disagree on the "voice." At least in the boards that I've been involved in, I have as much voice as I want to have and be as involved as I want to be, and that may just happen to be the luck that I'm involved in boards that give me that opportunity.

Whether having a Latino professional on mainstream boards and organizations made a difference or not, some of the Latino respondents clearly expressed being tired of "not being welcomed." After years of encountering hostility, one Latino respondent (quoted in Chapter 2) has decided to give up on dealing with mainstream civic and professional organizations altogether. The following exchange expands on his ideas and on why he has declared that he is "giving up" on the WSBA. However, this position did not go unchallenged, as the following exchange demonstrates, when a young female attorney insisted that it is the Latino lawyers' responsibility to remain active in the bar:

> Y8: It's a dual responsibility, but when I walk into that all-white, you know, forum, that means that they're going to see me and I'm the only brown face there. They have to understand that I may be the brown face that they have all the stereotypes that I'm coming in with. They're like, "Oh, she's going to be this, this, and this." But the moment that they get to know who I am, they're going to know that I am just as *Mexicana* as the next person, but I can also relate to them, and at the same time, it is my responsibility to educate them on who, on this *Mexicana* that I am.
> Y11: But it gets old. I've done that.
> Y8: I understand that.
> Y11: I've done all that, and I am tired of that little game, so I don't want to educate nobody!

Y8: I may be assimilated, or whatever you want to call it, and I can relate to them, but at the same time, they have to know that . . . maybe the next time they see another brown face, they're not going to have those presumptions and, you know, we might be having . . . carnitas and Budweiser, or whatever. I mean, I think it's a balance, and I mean we're taking from them, and they're taking from us, and I really feel it's a responsibility.

Y11: I see, but the problem is that they're absorbing—it's like you're over-whelmed by this.

Y8: Well, that's, your back is on me then to . . .

Y11: I know, but it's like a resistance, and you're always fighting, fighting, fighting, and pretty soon, like you're part of this thing, and I say wait a minute! So, I've reached the point in my life where I don't want to deal with it.

Y3: I think you're talking about being tired, not that you're not . . .

Y11: That whole game, my God! I don't want to do the Bar Association. I don't want to all the, I just don't want to do it.

This passionate debate during the Yakima focus group among Latino attorneys illustrates the level of alienation and discomfort experienced by the Latino respondents as they try to participate in mainstream professional organizations.

Gatekeepers in the Firm Environment

Another example of the gatekeeper role can be found in the firm environment as revealed in the following comment:

It's been a tough go. It's been a real tough go. . . . I have seen a lot of transition for the Latinos and Latinas in Seattle. . . . Most of my friends started off in law firms and have transitioned completely out. And what I'm saying, I mean, they've transitioned into government kinds of jobs as opposed to being, you know, part of the firms. And there is a real significance to that, which I don't want to have lost here, which is that firm jobs tend to have more money associated with them. So, the earning capacity is higher. . . . I can probably name to you a half a dozen attorneys that I know from the last five years—we're not talking about ancient history here—who have now transitioned out of law firms into government work.

This participant went on to detail specifically how little diversity there is at one particular law firm that has been in existence for over one hundred years:

My last law firm had been in existence for over 100 years. It has forty-five attorneys. I mean a large firm, not huge, but large. In the top twenty-five size-wise. It had forty white men, and the other five were either women or people of color. Some of us counted twice. Of those five, *two* of those were people of color, myself and one Asian-American man. . . . Towards the end, while I was there—and I was there for just under two years, twenty-three months—they had hired seven new white men in the time that I was there. . . . It turns out that there had been three of us [and] added up to less than ten years [of work] total. Total! For a firm that had been in existence for over a hundred years!

She went on to state how little support Latino lawyers encounter in large law firms: "I mean most of these firms have no ability in-house to like deal with [diversity], there's nobody there that really is your ally." Because there is little support, and in some cases outright hostility, in many law firms toward people of color, this Latina attorney goes on to describe how one other Latina in the legal community actually hid her Latina identity to cope and survive in her legal career:

There was a judge in this town, a Latina, who during her entire judgehood changed her name to a Caucasian name and only switched it back like months before retiring. . . . I understand why people do it. Don't get me wrong. I mean, I also remember in Shakespearean days women dressing as men so they could be actors. I understand why they do it. [But] it's not acceptable. Our numbers are too low for us to be able to just hide. We can't hide anymore. Because we're perpetuating the problem by hiding.

Unfortunately, since this interview, this Latina attorney has quit her firm as well because her firm became much too hostile for her to endure any longer.

Not everyone had negative experiences in the law firm environment. For example, a very successful Latino attorney in Seattle shared his experience. Although his experience may be the exception, it is important to highlight it as well:

I started as an associate and . . . it's just going to be hard work and just doing the job right, you know, be willing to pitch in to work with others, have the right communication skills, be able to do the legal analysis. In this law firm, also the ability to work with others and people liking working with you and who you are, your personality, is also very important. So, I must have done several things right for that to happen, and it's true, *without a lot of support*, I guess.

Again, since this interview, this Latino respondent has also left the firm. The lack of ethnic and racial diversity in major law firms and the propensity of Latino attorneys to transition out of these firms are examples of constrained social mobility for Latino attorneys by gatekeepers. As one of the focus groups came to a close, the Latino participants began discussing lack of diversity in major law firms in Seattle. The participants in the Seattle focus group were hard-pressed to find a single Latina as partner in any of the major firms:

S3: I think that the studies that the Supreme Court just finished on the glass ceiling is indicative of it. I think it's really tough for women and women of color in particular to make it into partnership in this state.

S1: It's a very big balancing act.

S3: A very big balancing act. And I don't think [it] can be [done], at least in most firms. I'm just speaking from that perspective 'cause I really don't have any other experience in any other field within the law but firms, it is a balancing act. Everything that you do is a balancing act.

S1: One of the things we saw in the State Bar Committee for Diversity is that there is an acceptance for some degree of minorities. For a number of years they would never make partnership. And that is something that is just real tough.

S3: The numbers never go up if you stop and look.

S1: It's amazing.

S3: I mean, and the joke for Latinas is to name me one Latina partner in a major law firm in Seattle. I dare you.

S1: Can't. You can't.[31]

Clients as Gatekeepers

A final example includes the role of clients as gatekeepers. It seems regardless of Latinos' professional status and credentials, they often have to deal with demeaning stereotypes and discrimination. They have a sense that they have to work much harder to prove their credentials to clients. This is highlighted in the following comments from one of the Latino respondents:

I do see it with certain clients. . . . When I get first introduced to clients, especially over the phone, I think my accent comes out a little bit stronger, and so they do a review of checks, well, "Where did you go to school?" and they always get great comfort to find out where I went to school, and then, you know, "How long have you been practicing?" But it's kind of like they're checking. Now I know they don't ask this or they may ask [it] of everybody, but certainly they have to check to see what my qualifications are as an attorney. *"Did you get in" for example, "through affirmative action?" or "Did you actually get the degree?"* Now that's just the sense I get, but I do get those questions *often*. And definitely where you're from and "How long have you been here?" kind of things. So, it's interesting. It does exist.

Sometimes discrimination is not as subtle as "Where are you from?" or "Where did you go to school?" as another prominent Seattle attorney shared:

> When I graduated from law school . . . one of my very first clients complained to the managing attorney and said that he didn't want a Mexican attorney. So, he actually ended up writing a letter to the managing attorney and to the director of legal services asking for a replacement attorney. The managing attorney wrote back to him and told him this is your attorney, and if you don't want the attorney that we assigned to your case, then you can go look for a different attorney elsewhere.

This Latina respondents' manager was supportive, but what about the managers who would have simply preferred not to deal with this challenge and would think twice before hiring a Latino? Another Latina respondent noted her experience with community stereotypes when she mentioned the following negative experience:

> It's like putting yourself on the fire front to be a target. And when I worked for the *Yakima Herald* . . . , we did this [Latino] series just to be educational and informational about our culture. We got tons of letters to the editor telling us, calling us beaners and telling us to go back to Mexico, and if the reporters loved them so much why don't they go back to Mexico. You know, you have that kind of mentality out there. Who wants to be out there saying, oh, I'm behind this action, you know. And so it goes hand-in-hand with, I mean unless you are ten times better than everyone else, I don't feel like I can take it on, so I don't. It's easier not to.

These experiences of discrimination and marginalization and lack of acceptance in law firms, the WSBA, and even with clients in the community who don't want a "Mexican attorney" hinder the efforts of Latinos as professionals. Academics of color experience the same kind of questioning and marginalization as previously discussed. It seems regardless of the profession chosen by Latinos, regardless of their advanced degrees or work experience, they will encounter "gatekeepers" in their colleagues. At least, this is what the thoughtful and insightful reflections shared by the Latino respondents during the interviews revealed.

To conclude this discussion of the professional workplace experiences of Latino attorneys, a question was included on the survey that asked them whether they felt that being Latino/a has caused them difficulties in their profession as a lawyer. This was a two-part question. It had a "Yes" or "No" box available to check and then just two lines to add a comment. Forty-six percent of the Latino survey respondents answered "Yes," that being Latino has caused them difficulties in their profession. Also, fifty of the 100 Latino lawyers who completed this particular survey question included a comment. Here are some representative statements they listed, reflecting the negative experiences with stereotypes and discrimination. Many of the comments written in the survey support the comments raised in all the focus groups and in-depth interviews:

- "Societal stereotypes are very common in the legal profession. Most people believe you are a clerk/bailiff or interpreter."
- "Having to overcome other people's prejudice; feeling different due to different values."
- "Only to the extent that persons of color must be better than others to succeed. I truly believe this."
- "Difficult to do jury trials because majority of jurors are retired white people."
- "Not treated the same as my counterparts by courts, colleagues."
- "Do not fit in with the big firm culture."
- "Only initially with other attorneys. Anglo clients rarely contact me, but Latino clients constantly do."
- "Latinos are not well regarded in this country, and other professionals do not know how to interact (threatening?)."
- "I was not considered a good 'mix' for certain firms; looked upon as unqualified or undesirable."
- "People don't take you seriously."
- "Presumption of incompetence."
- "Negative stereotypes: lazy, affirmative action."

There were also a small number of comments such as:

- "I appear 'white.' Most people don't realize I'm Hispanic."

One person stated, "But being female has caused more problems."

I can only speculate that some people in my profession continue to stereotype Latina professionals. So far, however, the challenges have not been a major obstacle to doing what I want to do with my degree.

And finally, a few attorneys felt being Latino was an asset in their professions, and they wrote positive comments:

- "Being bilingual is an advantage in my area of practice."
- "My answer might be different if I had chosen a different area of practice. In immigration law, it is an asset—gives me credibility."
- "It has also been a great advantage."
- "If anything, it makes my perspective unique, and that's what the legal community needs."

CONCLUSION

This chapter has described a pervasive experience of Latino professionals in the workplace. The experience is framed by a racialized immigration policy, which is echoed in workplace practices that produce markedly different outcomes between white and Latino attorneys. It should be no surprise that these Latino respondents have overcome significant obstacles, often from a very early age, as Luis's story at the beginning of the chapter demonstrates. Yet, they continue to face unique challenges based on their race and ethnicity that transcend their educational and economic success. Their stories reveal insights into how Latino attorneys are often pulled in many directions as they try to meet their professional obligations and demands, while at the same time trying to remain active and positive members of the Latino communities from which they come.

Despite their personal successes, their stories demonstrate that they still have a long way to go in achieving full acceptance and inclusion in America. Latino attorneys still face obstacles in their professional lives. These include gatekeepers in all aspects of their professional lives, from the Washington State Bar Association, to law firms, to client interactions. Sadly, the stories reveal that some of the Latino attorneys in this study have given up believing that they will ever be treated as equals in their chosen profession. They spend too many days searching for justice. Some of them have given up hope that they will ever find it in their careers.

The Latino attorneys well may be aware that their feelings of exhaustion and doubt, associated with having to continually prove themselves, have more to do with a historically unsupportive and openly hostile environment in the legal profession than with anything lacking in them. Nonetheless, it is still a difficult and exhausting phenomenon with which they must continually deal. Unfortunately, this is simply the reality of being a Latino professional. Many of their colleagues, and even their closest friends and most of their clients, may find this difficult to understand. The reality for Latinos and other people of color, especially those from working-class backgrounds who are lacking in inherited intellectual capital, is that they apparently do indeed have to work twice as hard as traditional middle-class and upper-middle-class white people to get ahead and to prove themselves. This notion of having to overcome stereotypes in the legal profession, in which *"persons of color must be better than others to succeed,"* is the one topic that was mentioned in all three types of data collected. The significance of this finding cannot be overemphasized.

4

LATINA STRUGGLES: CHALLENGES FOR WOMEN

Josefa had the most difficult time trying to describe her story for this study. She is among the few successful Latina attorneys in Washington State. An immigrant from a working-class background to an accomplished attorney, she finds that very few people understand what she's been through. Cuban born, Josefa emigrated to the United States with her family when she was six and a half years old and was raised in the Midwest. Even though she was a young child when she left Cuba, she still remembers the warmth of its sun. Though her parents did not have the opportunity to return, one day she plans to visit the place of her birth and early childhood.

Josefa decided to go to law school after moving to Washington when her teaching certificate was not honored in the state. She chose law because it was a helping profession but one that would garner respect. And helping is what she does best. With a huge smile on her face, she talks about how much she loves the clients she represents now that she is in solo practice. Josefa shares a story of one young Latina client who was brought to the United States by her parents, without papers, when she was six months old. This young woman was caught by authorities at an underaged drinking party. Although she had not been drinking, she is currently facing deportation back to Mexico—a country she does not know, where she has absolutely no resources and cannot even speak or read the language. To make matters worse, she has a three-year-old child who is an American citizen and who will also be sent to Mexico if the deportation is not stopped. Her life would be hell. And Josefa is eagerly taking on her case. Cases like this are what motivated Josefa to go to law school in the first place.

Josefa's legal journey started as a law school student and after graduation, as a clerk at the Washington State Supreme Court. She then became an associate and then partner at a prestigious law firm. She encountered years of dismissive treatment at the firm. The years of condescending behavior toward her took a toll, and one day, she just quit her firm. After a couple of different career moves, including teaching at the University of Washington Law School and working as a recruiter, she eventually opened her own private practice. As a Latina professional, it has not been an easy journey.

She has always had a strong level of involvement and commitment to the Latino community. She understands that with her privileged education and respected voice, there is a huge responsibility and opportunity to give back to the community. She stated, "We have a voice where a lot of our community doesn't. It is a responsibility, and we need to take it on. It is who we are. And it is easy to do. I could have easily ended up where many of our community end up."

She has been heavily involved in two Washington State Supreme Court appointed positions with the Minority and Justice Commission and the Gender and Justice Commission. She has also served on numerous boards, including the Latina/o Bar Association of Washington, the local chapter of the American Immigration Lawyers Association, and Mujeres of the Northwest. When asked about who is doing the heavy lifting in community involvement, she was quick to say, "I see women more involved. Men often get the limelight, but women do the work. It's like men don't have the same sense of needing to give back to the community. What's ironic is that women are not reaping the benefits and success that men generally experience as a result of community involvement. All you have to do is look at the rate of women making partnership in firms. The percentage is absolutely dismal."

Reflecting on her time in law firms, Josefa commented, "There is such isolation. Even after you 'make it,' you are probably the only Latina or the only woman of color. You are always viewed as the outsider, with little support to help you succeed. No one tells you of the land mines because, frankly, you make them uncomfortable and they really want you to go away." Even receiving awards and accolades, and repeatedly being one of the top income producers, did not afford her the respect that her underperforming male counterparts experienced. Males were given deference because of their "potential," while the firm merely referred to Josefa as the "cash cow." With a laugh, Josefa said, "This never stops." She reveals her father was a lawyer in Cuba, but when the family emigrated to the United States, he had to pump gas. According to Josefa, he was a firm believer in the philosophy that what doesn't kill you makes you stronger. Josefa notes that he was a person who was filled with gratitude and appreciation for his life.

Josefa believes that she has helped chip away at some of the problems that women of color have in law firms. Many firms have "revolving doors," with people of color lasting a year or two before being forced out or opting out because the environment is too toxic for them. It's hard to see this problem when merely looking at numbers from year to year, but recently, questionnaires are starting to focus on this fact. When asked if there were additional barriers for Latina professionals, Josefa quickly stated, "As Latinas, we don't boast about ourselves or seek recognition. We feel more comfortable letting somebody else get the limelight. We think that 'good work' should speak for itself, but ironically, this generally leads to doing more behind-the-scenes work without getting any recognition. Unfortunately, this has long-term impact on the promotion to partnership."

Josefa recently opened her own firm. She cited the benefits of running her own business: "You can take the clients that pull at your heartstrings without having to explain and justify it to others. I see my parents' struggles in my clients' faces when I first meet them. Instantly I know that I am doing the right thing. Perhaps it is our past that prevents Latinas from fitting into a profession where people frequently come from very privileged backgrounds."

Josefa's case shows that even the highly successful Latina professionals encounter experiences such as these. The legal profession is not the only place where Latinas experience what Josefa describes. It is the reality of being a Latina professional in America.

There is a growing collection of scholarship looking into the negative experiences of Latina professionals. For example, Professor Jody Vallejo documented the experiences of a group of Latina middle-class women in Southern California. She found that Latina professionals encounter negative stereotypes based on their race and gender by the whites around them. This group of Latina business owners also lack many of the resources that middle-class whites have at their disposal. Consequently, this group of Latinas face unique financial and societal obstacles, and therefore, they create "Latina spaces" to navigate their situation.[1]

Another example from Jessica Lavariega Monforti documented the experiences of Latina political scientists in graduate school and as faculty members in the anthology, *Presumed Incompetent: The Intersections of Race and Class for Women in Academia*. Lavariega Monforti convincingly documented the experiences of seventy-three Latina respondents in political science. She found that as women of color in academia (particularly in a male-dominated discipline like political science), Latinas were marginalized based on race and ethnicity, and also based on gender.[2]

This marginalization is true in Josefa's experiences as well. As one of the founding members of *Mujeres of the Northwest*, Josefa is an active member of an organization of professional Latinas—medical doctors, PhDs, artists, musicians—women looking for a community of support and a safe space to discharge the emotions associated with the day-to-day sexism and racism encountered by them in their professional roles. Josefa laughs as she shares some of the worst stories she has experienced as a Latina professional over the years. She sighed and said, "They never stop. After all these years. They never stop."

LATINAS AND INTERSECTIONS

Josefa's case shows that for Latinas and other women of color, the combination of race, gender, and class inequality leads to unique experiences of marginalization and discrimination that theories of race alone cannot explain. Scholars such as Kimberlé Crenshaw[3] and others have provided the foundation for analyses that examined how multiple identities resulted in increased oppression. bell hooks's *Feminist Theory: From Margin to Center* demonstrated how the experiences of injustices for black women are distinct from those of white women.[4] Scholars working within the concept of *intersections* insist that attention to these multiple categories is essential in order to not only understand oppression but in working toward ending it.[5] The ways in which multiple categories work simultaneously to impact one's life chances often get left out of the conversation because race, gender, and/or class get treated as separate categories, serving to mislead and decrease their combined importance.[6] Studies focused on race and gender often include an oversimplification of categories, particularly in the legal field and in academic fields like political science. Lisa García Bedolla contended that "popularly held understandings of group membership . . . are overly simplistic and do not accurately reflect the diversity of our lived experience."[7] For example, the following remarks from a Latina respondent in this study clearly show some of the issues around intersections:

> The intersection of race, gender, and CLASS is rarely discussed . . . .Almost without exception, white colleagues and colleagues of color come from middle-class or elite families—and they cannot begin to understand the ways in which our lives were radically different. Sadly, this often leads to condescension toward us rather than respect for the extraordinary things we've overcome to get where we are. Moreover, many colleagues deeply resent our achievements.[8]

This statement reflects years of experiencing marginalization based on race, ethnicity, gender, and class for this Latina respondent. García Bedolla developed a model for scholarship conducted in the area of intersectionality. Her model included "(1) a multi-faceted understanding of collective identity; (2) the relationship between stigma and group membership; (3) the role of social networks; and (4) the effects of the larger sociohistorical context."[9] The complexity of the stories shared by the Latina professionals in this study underscore how race, gender, and class taken together help us more fully understand their experiences.

What is the nature of Latina lawyers' personal, political, and professional experiences? The literature on Latinos and politics has not, until recently, specifically addressed the attitudes and behaviors of Latinas. While some of the research on Latinas and their political behavior viewed them as a "double minority," other research saw Latinas as having a "multidimensional nature."[10] Some research also demonstrated that Latina political activism encompasses more than narrow definitions of political behavior to include community-organizing efforts.[11] In addition, there is a general lack of information on Latinas and the law. This chapter systematically examines the data from the Latina professionals in this study and documents the struggles they encounter.[12]

GENDER AND RACE IN THE LEGAL PROFESSION

The marginalization of women of color by both men and women has been well-documented.[13] Studies have shown that women of color are not treated as equals by women in feminist circles, who downplay the role of race and ethnicity and argue that gender issues trump all else. At the same time, they are dismissed by many men of color, who believe the struggles they face are race-based or class-based.[14] The legal field is no exception.[15] For example, although the number of female attorneys is on the rise, they will very likely earn far less than male attorneys.[16] Additional biases that female attorneys face in the workplace include gender bias in the courts, sexual harassment, and lack of support systems.[17]

According to the American Bar Association's Commission on Women, Native American female attorneys faced race and gender discrimination. They also found that Native American women constantly struggle for legitimacy as attorneys with their colleagues, clients, and judges. According to the ABA's report on Native American Women:

> The difficulties encountered by Native American women in law school follow them into their law careers wherever they practice: their credibility is questioned; as a group, they are marginalized; and they face frequent discrimination, in the form of insensitive remarks, prejudicial assumptions, extraordinary scrutiny, or outright antagonism.[18]

The Latina respondents in this study faced many of these same obstacles. Not surprisingly, the American Bar Association's Commission on Racial and Ethnic Diversity found that gender is an additional obstacle (to race), finding that minority women leave the firm environment at higher rates than minority men, with 85.7 percent leaving by the seventh year compared to 76.6 percent for minority men.[19] Specifically, the Commission found that men of color do better than women of color on many measures, from outnumbering them in upper-level legal jobs, as administrative law judges, and as federal patent attorneys. *Additionally, they found that Latino lawyers in Chicago law firms outnumber Latina lawyers by five to one.*

Former president of the Washington State Bar Association, Ron Ward, said: "We've still got a long way to go"[20] when it comes to diversity in the legal profession. Citing figures from the U.S. Equal Employment Opportunity Commission (EEOC), Ward indicated that nationally, women make up 40 percent of the legal profession. According to Ward, this is up from 14 percent in the 1970s. On the positive side, the increase of females in large law firms to almost half demonstrates that progress is possible.

Ward also noted:

One glaring statistic that is not part of the EEOC study is the plight of multicultural women (women of color) in the legal profession. At the end of their initial eight years of practice, **100** percent of women of color have left their first employment, or left the practice all together. . . . While we should be proud of the progress women and people of color have made in joining the ranks of legal professionals, we must also be mindful of how far we have to go to ensure that diversity of America is reflected and sought by the legal profession.[21]

The fact that after eight years, 100 percent of women of color (documented by the American Bar Association's *Miles to Go* report) had quit practicing law or had moved into a different position points to the difficulties in negotiating multiple kinds of marginalization. As one Latina respondent in this study said, "Damned if you do; damned if you don't. If you succeed, you are 'uppity' and must be taught your proper 'place.' If things go badly, they offer tea, sympathy, and plenty of bad advice, but secretly delight in your failure—because you are 'proof' of the inherent inferiority of those of 'your kind.'"[22] This same Latina respondent made the following poignant commentary on the personal effects of gender and racial discrimination, first in college and later in law school:

I think the term is "micro-aggressions," the little digs, the snubs, the lack of respect that someone in a similar position would be accorded . . . . the difficulty of getting through undergraduate and law school surrounded by people who are extraordinarily privileged, and yet they've never used that privilege to educate themselves about other cultures within this country and outside of this country and just saying the most God-awful thoughtless things over and over—and just what that does to you that you either have to constantly be jumping—which exhausts you—or pick your battles, which means that you swallow some things and let it go by, even though you are furious. But what that does to your morale and your mental state . . .

There was a sense of melancholy and resignation in her tone as she said this. Her remarks illustrate that there is a high personal cost paid for the way Latina attorneys are treated and viewed by many people—a personal cost that includes a negative impact on one's overall mental health and spirit. This is probably similar to the experiences that women who first went to law school in larger numbers in the 1970s had to endure when they were assumed to be court reporters rather than lawyers. Latina professionals today have to endure this type of sexism as well, but they also have to endure racism.

For example, even as Jody Vallejo was conducting research to document the experiences of Latina professionals in Southern California, she personally encountered some of the common Latina stereotypes herself. She stated, "I personally experienced the stereotype that Latinas have high fertility rates when I worked at Orange County's largest business mixer. A white woman, dressed in a three-piece suit and heels, said to me, 'Good for you Mexicans. Usually people take over countries with wars, but you Mexicans are doing it by having lots of babies.'"[23]

The data analyzed for this chapter demonstrate the problem is greater than marginalization in professional environments for the Latina professional.[24] As the quotation from the Latina respondent highlights, common stereotypes of Latinas are played out in their professional environments, placing *additional obstacles* in their path of professional advancement. Another example of how Latina professionals endure "micro-aggressions" can be found in Lavariega Monforti and Michelson's and Lavariega Monforti's studies specifically focusing on Latina political scientists. Both of these studies highlight problems found in the academy for Latinas including underrepresentation (Latinos overall represent less than 2 percent of political scientists) which leads to marginalization, lack of mentoring from senior colleagues, excessive service demands placed upon, sexism, and even sexual harassment by senior colleagues.[25] Similarly, the data analyzed for this chapter demonstrate the problem is greater than marginalization . . . their paths to professional advancement. In short, there is a lot to contend with besides meeting professional standards and expectations. In short, there is a lot to contend with besides meeting professional standards and expectations.

LATINAS' LAW SCHOOL EXPERIENCE AND PROFESSIONAL SATISFACTION

To get a sense of law school experiences among Latinas, this section will examine both gender and racial breakdowns of responses to select questions from the survey questionnaire, introduced in Chapter 3. This section will focus on comparisons dealing with obstacles to law school, the decision to go to law school, and satisfaction with career choice. It is worth reiterating that the WSBA demographic survey (discussed in Chapter 2) indicated that 90 percent of the lawyers in Washington State are Caucasian.[26] The comparison survey, which was taken from this group, suggests there is a strong likelihood that it is composed of mainly white attorneys. The surveys reveal many substantial gender differences regarding obstacles to law school, the decision to go to law school, and satisfaction with career choice.

The survey question "How big an obstacle to your law school education were each of the following: *Family obligations, Knowledge about how to get into law school,* and *Cost of law school,*" has *distinctly different results by gender* in a number of ways (see Tables 3.2, 3.3, and 3.4 in Appendix A). For example, looking at the issue of knowledge of how to get into law school, 40.5 percent of Latina attorneys indicated that it posed "Somewhat" of an obstacle or a "Substantial" obstacle compared to only 17.6 percent of females in the comparison group of attorneys. For the males, 30 percent of the Latino lawyers compared to only 10.9 percent of the males in the comparison group indicated that knowledge posed "Somewhat" of an obstacle or a "Substantial" obstacle. Clearly there are gender and cultural differences regarding understanding the process for applying to law school. Breaking it down by gender is very informative. Specifically, Latinas didn't have a lot of knowledge about how to get into law school.

Family obligations are also an impediment by gender. In this case, Latino males experienced the greatest obstacles at 41.6 percent, indicating "Somewhat" of an obstacle or a "Substantial" obstacle compared to 20.1 percent of the males in the comparison group. For the females, 38.1 percent of the Latina lawyers compared to only 28.8 percent of the females in the comparison group indicated that family obligations posed "Somewhat" of an obstacle or a "Substantial" obstacle. Family obstacles were higher among Latino males *and* females, with both race and gender making the difference. One possible explanation is that the traditional gender roles found in many Latino families are an obstacle to educational requirements and expectations, particularly for first-generation college students.[27] Cultural expectations such as commitment to marrying, raising children, and caring for family members often come before individual professional goals and aspirations. For example, it might be difficult for Latino males to explain why they should work only part time in order to keep their grades up. Similarly, Latina females may have a hard time explaining that they cannot assist in the preparation of family celebrations such as a baptism or *quincenera* celebration because they are studying for their law finals. In both cases, traditional Latino culture often places the needs of the family before the needs of the individual.[28]

The cost obstacle is interesting to examine, as a majority of the respondents said cost was "Somewhat" of an obstacle or a "Substantial" obstacle: 61.9 percent of Latina attorneys indicated that it posed "Somewhat" of an obstacle or a "Substantial" obstacle compared to 59.7 percent of females in the comparison group of attorneys. For the males, 68.3 percent of the Latino lawyers compared to 49.6 percent of the males in the comparison group indicated that knowledge posed "Somewhat" of an obstacle or a "Substantial" obstacle. Cost as an obstacle was higher among Latinos and Latinas, but it was still an obstacle for the comparison group. This reflects the fact that costs are rising in general for education in the United States but that they are rising substantially for professional programs like law school.

In sum, looking at the three different obstacles to law school, never was it the case that any of these questions were *less* of an obstacle for Latinos and Latinas than for the comparison white group of attorneys. Except for family obligations—which were highest for Latinos—*the obstacles were always greatest for Latinas*. This finding goes along with the research by Marcela Raffaelli and Lenna Ontai.[29] Looking at gender socialization in Latino families, they found that the concept of *familismo*, which focuses on the priority of family and family life, and the role of traditional Latino culture, including strong distinctions in gender roles, play a significant role in gender socialization among Latinos.

Despite the greater obstacles in attending law school experienced by Latinas, some interesting findings are the responses to both the level of current work satisfaction and whether or not they would go to law school all over again. A high percentage of the Latina respondents indicated that they were either "Very Satisfied" or "Moderately Satisfied " with the type of law they currently practice (87.8 percent) and 70.7 percent indicated it was "Very Likely" or "Moderately Likely" that they would go to law school all over again. While 82.8 percent of females from the comparison group were either "Very Satisfied" or "Moderately Satisfied" with the work they currently do, 62.6 indicated it was "Very Likely" or "Moderately Likely" they would attend law school all over again. Among the men, 81.6 of Latino attorneys indicated they were either "Very Satisfied" or "Moderately Satisfied" with the work they currently do, with 68.9 percent indicating it was "Very Likely" or "Moderately Likely" that they would go to law school all over again compared to 83 percent of the males in the comparison group, who indicated the same level of satisfaction with their current law practice and 64.4 percent indicating it was "Very Likely" or "Moderately Likely" that they would go to law school all over again.

Clearly, the majority of the attorneys surveyed are satisfied with the work they do as attorneys and would attend law school all over again knowing what they know now. In addition, the fact that Latina lawyers expressed the most satisfaction with their professional lives and indicated the greatest likelihood that they would go to law school again was an important finding. Perhaps this is because the Latina professionals have not only survived the many obstacles on their paths to becoming lawyers, but they have also succeeded in accomplishing their goals and fulfilling their dreams. This creates a tremendous sense of achievement for them. Earning something against overwhelming odds is a great accomplishment, requiring a determination among Latina professionals that many people would find incomprehensible. This may explain why Latinas have the highest levels of satisfaction on the survey questions, even though they also face the greatest obstacles. After not only surviving, but succeeding in spite of all the struggles they have had, they know their self-worth and they feel it in their level of satisfaction as indicated on the survey.

Now that some comparisons of Latina lawyers have been made with Latino lawyers and with females in the white comparison group, this section will focus solely on the experiences of the Latina respondents. In addition to the forty-one Latina respondents to the survey, the two focus groups, and the key informant interviews with Latino lawyers, additional interviews were conducted solely with Latinas in 2004.[30] The findings for this section are based on the female responses from these four different datasets. They teach us a lot about the unique experiences of Latina professionals.

Of the forty Latinas who checked on the survey the type of law they practice, only three Latinas (7.5 percent) indicated they practiced law in a large firm. This is a really low number and goes along with the comments by Josefa in the opening of this chapter. Fifteen percent had solo practices. Twenty-five percent practiced in either a small or middle-sized firm. Another 22.5 percent practiced law in a city, county, state, or federal government agency. Interestingly, the largest percentage (30 percent) indicated "Other" for their type of practice. These included various legal occupations, including one policy director, one law professor, three who worked in legal services, three who worked in nonprofits or public interest law, and finally, one who indicated she worked in the software arena. Also, quite telling is that there were no Latinas in this survey group who were working as judges or magistrates at the time the interviews or survey was conducted.

LATINA PROFESSIONALS' ACTS OF RESISTANCE TO THE DOMINANT WHITE FRAME

The personal interviews of the Latina respondents illuminate how their often painful experiences are intertwined with their sense of themselves as professionals and as lawyers—including the type of law they chose to practice. Many of the Latinas interviewed engage in acts of resistance to the white frame, through their strong sense of cultural identity and in their professional identity as well. One motivates and informs the other. As Rosalind Chou and Joe Feagin stated, "Everyday resistance to racism comes in many guises."[31] The following remarks from a Latina in Seattle highlighted this point:

> I consider myself Mexican even though I was born here. I am proud of being fluent in Spanish and love to celebrate Mexican holidays. I strive to make my clients, of which the majority are Mexican, to feel respected in how my staff deals with them and in how I represent them.

For this Latina attorney, not only is her pride in her Mexican heritage one that sustains her personally, but her strong sense of cultural identity spills over into her professional identity. Most of her clients are Mexican, and she expects her staff to treat them in a positive and respectful manner, a manner in which many Mexican immigrants are not treated. She goes on to add: "I cater to the Latino community, so it impacts my work greatly. What I am doing now is not what I intended to do out of law school, but I do think that being bilingual more than being Latina has impacted my work."

Similarly, another Latina attorney noted that helping people who do not speak the English language and are in need of assistance is what drives her professionally:

> It is important to me to be able to help those who don't speak English and could easily be taken over by the system. Also, it is important to me to help those even if they cannot afford to pay me $200 per hour, depending on the case. If there are domestic violence issues, I will help them for free because I was a domestic violence victim for ten years, and that is one promise I made was to always lend a hand in that arena.

For this respondent, her negative experiences as a battered woman are now used to provide legal help to others who are also victims of abuse. As a Latina who grew up speaking Spanish, it is also important to her to help others who may have language barriers. She noted:

> Being Latina impacted my work as a lawyer because I am bilingual, so I have had opportunities to help persons that other attorneys may not have been able to due to language barrier. I chose family law because of all the personal life experiences I have. I have personal experience in almost everything that could happen to a person or their family, so I can really relate to my clients' situations, and they trust me because we can talk about things because they know I understand because I have been there.

The connection between cultural identity and professional identity has been strong for all the Latina respondents interviewed, and a strong "I'll show you" attitude prevailed among them. For example, the comments from a prominent attorney originally from Eastern Washington were commonly expressed by the other Latina attorneys as well:

> Helping individuals through the maze of so many varying laws, giving some relief to the extreme stress new immigrants undergo in a country with different cultures, social norms, and language. Practicing in this profession also allows me, as a woman of color, to demonstrate the same or better abilities that women are capable of in a job dominated by white males.

The white racial frame is as pervasive in the legal profession as it is in society. Resistance to white discrimination and stereotypes, in the form of being a competent professional woman of color who has "the same or better abilities" than the white males, highlights the powerful counterframes being constructed by some of the Latina respondents. These include being motivated to help immigrants survive a country that racializes them and showing that women of color are able to succeed in a white male-dominated profession. This respondent's comments pointed out she has rejected the white racial frame. In her mind, everything she does, from the law she practices to the way she engages her colleagues, is an act of resistance. The insistence on proving oneself in a profession and practicing law in areas that preferentially benefit or help the Latino community, such as immigration, employment, and criminal law (instead of corporate law), are ways that Latina professionals are rejecting the white racial frame.

However, for those Latinas experiencing recurring discrimination and marginalization, it is not easy. As one Latina respondent stated, "There is still an 'old boys network,' but I think that as more and more Latinos continue to pursue education and take over high professional positions, and start their own successful small businesses, I think we break down the barrier more and more with each new person and each new venture." Another Latina respondent from Yakima reflected on her years of legal experience:

> I have found that in order to be respected, I have to work twice as hard (at least!) to prove myself. The element of having to prove myself at all shows the bias that we as women, and especially women of color, undergo in this profession. I personally experienced the "glass ceiling" when I was passed over for appointment to court commissioner over a white man that had much less experience than I have.

As Feagin demonstrated, the white racial frame is systemic, pervasive, foundational, and historical.[32] As we have seen from these Latina respondents, the white racial frame also includes the notion of intersections, with gender discrimination and stereotyping by white males. The gender discrimination in the profession includes more than being passed over for positions. One young, attractive Latina attorney from Yakima mentioned that an opposing counsel frequently asked her "What do I have to do to get a date with you?" whenever they worked on opposite sides of the same case. The Latina respondent described the lack of feeling valued by the legal organization in which she used to work and the lack of having any supportive mentors available to her as she negotiated her way through her career. Even working for a public interest organization, which was supposed to be focused on justice, has been a negative experience for her. She further commented that she believed it was ironic that an organization focused on promoting justice for one's client did not achieve justice for the lawyers involved, in any concrete manner. Giving up on the whole thing, but not on practicing law, she is currently in solo practice and enjoying tremendous financial success. However, she expresses doubt that she would choose a legal career if she could do it all over. Describing her life as "chaotic," she stated, "Sometimes I feel as though I'm so far into it—I don't know if I'd get into it again. It's too hard for me. I want to come home and not worry about whether I've screwed up people's lives. Maybe I would still do it. But I want a job where I come home and enough already." The comments expressed by a couple of the Latina attorneys about not wishing to be a lawyer correspond with data from the survey, in which 17 percent of the

Latina attorneys indicated that they were either "a little unlikely" or "very unlikely" to choose to go to law school all over again. However, 50 percent were definitely likely to go to law school all over again.

In the previously discussed study, *The Burdens of Both, the Privileges of Neither: A Report of the Experiences of Native American Women Lawyers*, Native American female attorneys also encountered frequent racial and gender discrimination in their profession and faced impediments to professional growth and advancement.[33] Similarly, Latinas have countless stories about not feeling valued in their profession (ironically, even as one Latina attorney from Yakima discussed, at a public interest firm that is supposed to be focused on justice), expressing what it is like to be "the only one. I've been in tears. I've been so lonely for so long."

These Latina professionals continue to resist the white racial frame in their position as women of color and as professionals. Their commitments are motivated by a resistance to the dominant views about who they are and about what they represent in helping those with less opportunities in the Latino community. Despite these Latinas' commitments and problems with dominant white framing, they also describe having to struggle within the Latino culture as well.

CULTURAL CHALLENGES

As discussed in Chapter 2, culture is an important source of identity and support for Latino professionals. Cultural maintenance, including speaking Spanish and helping the Latino community in one's line of work, becomes a counterframing strategy of resistance among the Latino respondents. However, it is both a source of support and a source of additional obstacles for the Latinas. This is a consequence of the idea of intersections mentioned earlier. Specifically, there are obstacles Latinas face based on race and ethnicity. In addition, there are obstacles based on gender as a consequence of limiting gender roles in the culture.

Therefore, despite the importance of cultural identity for Latinas in their life's work, they also face many obstacles from their culture. Some of these obstacles are even found in their personal relationships. As one Latina respondent shared with me, "When I was in law school and I'd go to Latino dances with my friends, we would have to lie to the guys so they would ask us to dance again." She and her friends started doing this because they discovered that once they revealed they were law school students they would not get asked to dance again. So they developed the strategy of telling the Latino men whom they were interested in dancing with again that they were secretaries in order to be asked for more dances. Sharing this experience made this Latina respondent laugh. However, she quickly stopped laughing when she went on to share that one of her greatest personal challenges has been with her family. This Latina respondent from Seattle said that it was really difficult "to be taken seriously . . . being taken seriously that this was my career choice and that I would be good at it." She added, "I feel that many Latinas with whom I went to school are real good friends and do not participate in the Mexican crab attitude. I can rely on them to discuss the ups and downs of it all. The challenges of lawyering, of dealing with our families, and life in general." This "Mexican crab attitude" that she describes is the idea that Mexicans are all trapped in a bucket. When someone begins to climb out of the bucket and make a better life for him- or herself, he or she will be brought down by others who are still in the bucket. In fact, a Latina respondent from Yakima also said, "The hardest part for me is when it comes from *las misma gente, la misma raza* [from our same people, our same race]. One time, I was representing a mother in a custody case, and the day before fact finding, opposing counsel called and told me my client was looking for another attorney." It was clear from this Latina attorney's description of this experience that there was a lot of disappointment and frustration that her client, another Latina, was shopping for a "better" attorney without even contacting her first about doubts or issues she may have had about the quality of representation. The most painful part of this experience for the Latina respondent was that she believed the reason her client was looking for someone else was because she did not believe that a Latina was as good as a white male with respect to legal practice. The pain and disappointment that come from facing obstacles within one's own community are not easily explained away with theories of internalized racism—the notion that the socialization of a dominant society with racist perceptions about a group are internalized by members of that group, sometimes so much that members try to distance themselves from their own culture. Internalized racism is a common experience in many cultures that have experienced larger societal oppression by living in a society with a systemic white racial frame.

Many of the Latina respondents also expressed feeling trapped between unreasonably rigid gender roles in Latino culture and stereotypes and limitations from mainstream society. As one attorney from Seattle stated:

I think people need to understand the challenges of becoming a lawyer in spite of our culture that expects different from us, from our families that expect less from us, from our husbands that are not always supportive. The fact that in our culture humbleness is a virtue but not in American culture. That culturally we sometimes feel caught between acting as advocates for Latinos in an American system or acting as Americans representing foreigners.

This Latina attorney has an enormously successful law practice in Seattle and has been a member of the community for over twenty years, but there are days when she would not choose to be a lawyer again if she could relive her life. Thinking about her greatest success, she stated, "My greatest success is being able to have a successful practice built on helping the people that have needed legal assistance the most, without ripping anyone off . . . , whether it is me in writing a letter or it is me in helping them get legal counsel elsewhere." However, as she reflected on her life she added, "I probably wouldn't have chosen this. . . . I most likely would have become a professor or a teacher."

COMMUNITY CHALLENGES

Gender bias is pervasive in the community as well. Living in Yakima for most of her career, this Latina attorney had to endure many examples of discrimination. Not wanting to give up and leave, she worked hard to try to make things better for herself, her family, and other Latinos in the area. However, after a couple of decades of struggle, her tenacity understandably wore thin. Without a sense that the cultural and socioeconomic environment would eventually improve for Latinos in Yakima, she eventually sold her successful law practice and moved her children to the Seattle area. Looking back on the obstacles in Yakima for Latinos she stated,

The challenge in the community is trying to make changes in a community that is virtually close-minded to the progression of people of color, especially a community that refuses to see any problem to begin with. The area in which one practices makes a tremendous difference as far as whether any "success in change" happens. For example, in Yakima County, the expectation that Mexicans are farmworkers or at best warehouse workers continues to a vast degree. For whatever professional and more open-minded persons exist there, the belief seems to be that espousing assistance by way of talking and holding meetings, but not actual individual participation in cultural events or groups, is sufficient. I have also seen many times, the condescending attitude that city leaders have in regards to what is "best" for us.

CIVIC CONTRIBUTIONS OF LATINA LAWYERS

Despite these challenges, Latina attorneys are actively involved in their communities and in their professions. While a more detailed account of both Latino male and female lawyers' civic behavior will be the focus of the next chapter—including a comparison to non-Latino attorneys and to Latinos nationally—it is important to provide an overview picture of the civic contributions of Latina attorneys compared to Latino attorneys to determine whether there are any gender differences in their commitment to civic involvement. After comparing civic involvement of male and female Latino attorneys, discussion of some of the challenges Latinas revealed about their involvement follows.

What is the nature of Latina lawyers' political and civic involvement? Is it diminished or at least affected by a sense of hopelessness, because of the constant challenges and obstacles that many Latina attorneys face in their everyday lives? Based on the results found in this study, it appears that despite the obstacles faced by many Latina attorneys, they are just as actively involved in their communities as Latino attorneys. Latina attorneys use their professional skills in ways that contribute to positive changes in their communities, similar to Latino attorneys.

Involvement in the community begins with an active interest in one's community. This includes being informed about what is going on in one's local community through, for example, reading the daily newspaper, discussing current political issues, and being actively involved, such as by voting. Over 80 percent of both Latino and Latina attorneys read the daily newspaper (85.4 percent of Latinas and 84.2 percent of Latinos). When these Latino attorneys were asked to rank interest in local community politics, 66.7 percent of the Latinas indicated they were moderately or very interested, while 75.8 percent of Latinos chose those categories. Similarly, regularly engaging in political discussions illustrates an interest in local politics. Close to 40 percent (39.7 percent) of the Latinos indicated that they discussed politics every day or nearly every day, while 45 percent of the Latinas did. Another 37.9 percent of the Latino attorneys and 25 percent of the Latina attorneys talk about politics at least once or twice a week. High rates of political discussion translate, in this case, to voting: 92.9 of Latina attorneys reported that they voted in the 2000 election compared to 98.3 percent of Latino attorneys.

The interest in their community is evident in a variety of other ways, including the use of their law degrees to help others through pro bono legal services. When asked if they provide any pro bono legal services, 63.6 percent of Latina attorneys indicated that they did, and 67.9 percent of the Latino attorneys did as well. Table 4.1 summarizes a variety of other important types of civic activities occurring among Latino and Latina attorneys (see Appendix A). Both Latino and Latina attorneys contribute to a wide variety of civic activities in their communities. In some instances, Latino attorneys contribute more (for example, time to charities, church attendance, and "other" volunteer activities), while in other instances, Latina attorneys do (political campaigns, money to politics, activities that promote the Latino community, and giving money to charities).

Despite the relatively similar levels of civic involvement among male and female Latino attorneys, there is one very important finding that demonstrates a significant gender difference. Latina attorneys feel less connected to the local communities in which they work than Latino attorneys do. When asked "Do you feel part of the local geographic community where you work?" just over half (53.8 percent) of the Latina attorneys said that they did, while 72.9 percent of the Latino lawyers indicated that they felt part of the local community in which they work. This is the greatest gender difference between the male and female Latino attorneys. Both the male and female Latino attorneys are highly informed about their communities through reading the local papers and discussing politics; both participate civically in a variety of ways, with their money and their time; and both vote at extremely high levels. Despite the similar active involvement in many categories, the women felt much less connected than the men, with only half of them feeling connected to it. Some may say that just over 50 percent is a classic illustration of "the glass is half full" or "the glass is half empty" interpretation. However, it does not explain the fact that over 70 percent of the men felt connected to the communities in which they practiced law. This gender difference serves to support the testimonials Latina attorneys have been giving about their negative experiences throughout the various interviews conducted on both sides of Washington State.

Further, despite the fact that Latina attorneys feel less connected, many feel that they are doing as much (if not more) of the work in the community. As one commented, "There is a gender difference—yeah, I think there is. Latinas tend to do more than the men." In terms of civic involvement in the community, this same Latina attorney had this to say:

> As far as who's involved? I tend to see women being more involved, and I'm not sure if that's specific to Latinos and Latinas. I think that's across the board. It seems to me like men, it's almost like they don't have to work as hard as we do. You know what I mean. It's sort of like the "Oh, I don't have to do it. So why do it?" So, I don't know, I think it's true for the Latino/Latina community. I guess my point is a little bit broader, which is I think that's also, I don't think it's unique to us. And I would love to see statistics on that, because I think it's pretty prevalent everywhere that women are just doing more for the community.

Reflecting on her own experiences, this participant went on to add that even when Latinas do more of the work, they do not, however, seek out the spotlight or go out of their way to get recognition for their efforts:

> I think that Latinas don't seek the recognition or the flashiness, which is why they end up doing a lot of the work behind the scenes and not getting past the pats on the back and the "Oh, you did well. You did well. Go do it." You know what I mean. I think that we're more comfortable letting somebody else get sort of the limelight, you know. And I don't know how we break that. I mean, I think that's a really tough one. I mean, I just finished my, we just got self-evaluations. I mean, I find it really hard to sort of say: "Sigh. I'm terrific!" I mean, and when you read my self-evaluation it's like well, you know, I exceeded the goals set by my manager and met all of the billable hours, and I met the income goals. I mean, sort of the very neutral kinds of, I mean, it's like I should be going like: "I'm terrific! Look! I've exceeded every goal this firm has set for me!" It's like, I can't do it. It's like, oh, there's a real uncomfortableness about like, writing that down. It's like nooooo. I mean, come on. I was like, let me just write my little sort of, you know. And I think that that's part of why Latinas don't get promoted and elevated and advance at the same rate.

Whether Latina attorneys actually "do more" did not bear out in the statistical responses from the men and the women, as much as the fact that Latinas do not feel part of the local geographic community in which they work. Nor do Latinas feel a part of the individualistic dominant culture, which can hold them back from taking advantage of promotional and status-seeking opportunities.

With this in mind, we now turn to the Latina attorney interviews to gather additional insights about the obstacles that they experience around gender, in the hope of developing a greater understanding of why there is such a huge gender difference in sense of community connectedness among this highly active group of Latino lawyers.

ISOLATION OF LATINA ATTORNEYS

Part of the problem may be that Latina attorneys are often the *only* Latinas in their work environment. Being the only Latina in a particular work environment in and of itself would not be so isolating if it were an accepting environment. There are many different types of environments that are accepting and welcoming. However, as expressed by these Latina attorneys, many times the professional and community environments in which they function are filled with sexist and/or racist people—filled with a negative culture that contributes to an increase in a Latina's sense of isolation. For example, this Latina lawyer's comments describe what it felt like for her to be the only woman of color attorney in a rural area: "When I first started practicing law, I was the only attorney of color in three of the four counties I worked in, and the only woman of color. It's VERY difficult being in a small, rural bar. At one point, I filed a complaint with the Washington State Bar Association against the local president of the bar association due to racist/sexist/homophobic, etcetera, derogatory comments published in our local bar newsletter." This Latina attorney's experience is a theme consistently reported in the interviews. For the Latina professionals in this study, it is difficult to feel connected to the professional locations where they work, especially when the professional and community environments are such that it is acceptable to publish or state discriminatory remarks in the local bar newsletter or at professional meetings. This connectedness is understandably even more elusive for Latina attorneys to achieve.

This isolating professional environment does not just occur in rural settings. One prominent Latina attorney from Seattle describes the law firm
environment as particularly harsh for Latinas, in which even the most politically astute Latina lawyers may not survive the environment:

I mean if you look at Seattle, which I think is a hell of a lot more progres-
sive than the rest of the state—and it's hard because you can't like tell
what's going on in statistics—but every year statistics come out of how
many people of color do you have, how many women, how many men, how
many are partners. You know, part of the problem is you can't tell what's
what from just your statistics, but it's, I mean, even sort of giving everything
the benefit of the doubt and sort of saying, okay, we're just going to paint
this as rosy as we possibly can, the numbers still are horrible. They're horrible! I mean we used to have one [Latina] female partner at [major Seattle
law firm] who left. She's now in-house counsel for [a corporation]. And I
sort of look at her, and I sort of think God, if [any Latina] couldn't make
it, the rest of us are like, I mean. Because she was very corporate-minded
and very savvy, she knew how to play the game and the politics and that.
You know, she's the one who understood how to do that, which is really
tough to learn unless you've got a good mentor that can sort of say to you,
"Bombshell." Yeah, really. I mean, which is the most difficult thing is understanding where there are bombshells if there's nobody to like hold your
hand and tell you.

In addition to the isolating professional environments in which many
Latina lawyers find themselves, there are often cultural gender barriers
with which they must contend. These barriers are not only found in Latino
culture, as the first remark focuses on, but they are also found in society
overall, in that a woman is still considered the primary caretaker of the
family. While this is well understood by professional women who have
found themselves caught balancing their careers and their desire to have
a family, it is also increasingly recognized by men as well. One of the male
Latino attorneys relayed the following experience during one of his Latino
youth educational outreach efforts:

One thing during undergraduate work at the business school, once in a
while they sent out brochures and those kinds of things, and we asked high
school students from Eastern Washington, especially [which] is where we
were trying to focus. You know, get them here to the U [the University of
Washington] so they can experience it. And I remember one response from

this high school girl that she really wanted to come but her parents felt that a girl's position was in the house. So you had those cultural barriers as well.

Cultural obstacles begin very early for ambitious young Latinas who have dreams of becoming professionals when they grow up. However, the socialization girls and young women receive about which paths are appropriate to pursue and which are better left for men is part of American society as well. One only need look at the media, advertisements of all kinds, top political leaders from countries around the globe, or the messages much closer to home to see the distinct spheres for men and women regardless of race. Compounding this situation is the lack of role models for women of color, who are frequently coming from lower socioeconomic circumstances. These circumstances make becoming a professional for a woman of color all the more daunting and are the reason given by two Latina attorneys for why they continue on in a profession that does not accept them. As one Latina respondent from Yakima stated, "The one thing that makes a difference for me is being a role model and being there for others. When I go to court and it is a family law context, it is very crowded—mostly all *gabachos* among the attorneys and judge—but half of the audience is people of color, and I look out to the audience and I get a smile from one of them. So, being a role model and being out there is very important to me."

Another Latina attorney from Seattle went further by pointing out how more women leave law practice because they have additional family burdens:

> One practiced for awhile and got pregnant and left. Another one is still practicing. One was basically lost [went crazy]. I mean, it's "Oh, my God! This is not good." I mean statistically, I think it's probably the same as the rest of the population. The problem is that when you're starting with such low numbers, to lose even one person, it's like: No! No! You can't lose them. I mean you're too valuable.

She then went on to discuss the latest statistics for female attorneys in general, stating:

> The report, *Miles to Go*—that's an ABA report that was done—states that 85.7 percent of minority women leave law firms before their seventh year of practice—85.7! Almost 86 percent leave within seven years! Now, granted, that's leaving law firms, but it's still a lot of folks make the transition totally

out of the practice, and it's like, we can't afford it! I mean, we can't! Am I
emphatic enough about this? I'm very passionate about it 'cause I sort of feel
like, I mean, I understand why people leave, but at the same time, how do
we keep those [female] numbers up?!

POLITICAL AND PROFESSIONAL IMPLICATIONS

The experiences of Latina attorneys demonstrate that the concept of intersections is a useful theory in understanding their experiences. Examining
the intersections of how race, gender, and class impact Latina attorneys'
lives results in four key findings: (1) their high degree of satisfaction with
their current profession as lawyers, despite having encountered greater
obstacles and professional challenges than white female attorneys and
Latino attorneys; (2) the strong connection between cultural identity and
professional identity; (3) unique cultural challenges they encounter that
others, in some cases even Latino attorneys, do not experience; and (4)
additional community challenges they experience. One of the great differences between Latinos and Latinas is found in the level of connectedness
to the geographic community in which they live. What are the political
and professional implications of this type of marginalization that Latina
professionals experience in their chosen legal field, their culture, and in
their communities?

One can infer that opportunities for professional advancement, such as
the kind needed to make partner in a law firm, will be difficult to acquire
for these Latinas—much more so than for white female attorneys or for
Latino attorneys. As of this writing, Josefa, one of the few Latinas who
had successfully negotiated the firm world, has quit and started her own
practice. This was surprising. Josefa was one of the ones everyone thought
would be able to survive the firm environment. She was on her second
career, extremely politically savvy, and tough. Sadly, her experience is
typical for Latinas. They face difficulties in finding and building important
professional networks, mentors, and allies, leaving them isolated and marginalized in the firm environment.

Their location as women of color in the legal profession leaves them very
little professional support that they can turn to. Lack of support makes it
difficult to build and maintain solidarity within the women's bar groups,
who do not understand their racial location, or with the Latino bar groups,

who do not adequately understand their unique challenges as women. In order for professional progress for Latina attorneys and other women of color in the law to improve, there must be a consideration of how multiple identities can create special obstacles.

Latina attorneys' ability to engage in political leadership is also impacted by their experiences. Both Latinos and Latinas have recently made many strides in political leadership. Focusing on Latinas nationwide, "between 1992 and 2001, the number of Latina political officeholders grew by 146 percent—from 792 to 1,952 elected positions."[34] However, overall in the United States, Latinas represent only 0.6 percent of state legislators.[35] We have seen that Latina attorneys are very involved in the civic affairs of their communities. Because of their training in the law and their experience and civic commitments, they have the skills to take on leadership roles at the local and state level, which is often the training ground for national political representation. There is a great untapped leadership potential resulting from this group of highly educated and civically engaged women spending so much energy fighting against societal, professional, and cultural barriers rather than being able to use their talents in positive ways as community and political leaders not only in the Latino community but also in the greater community in which they live. This drain on important political and social capital is unfortunate. The civic engagement that Putnam advocated, which is so important to community life, is in no small way hampered by discrimination for these Latina professionals and results in profoundly antidemocratic effects.

CONCLUSION

This chapter described some of the experiences of Latina professionals and demonstrated how the concept of intersections provides insights into their unique experiences as women of color—even in the legal profession where everyone goes through similar educational training, the bar examination, and professional socialization. This serves to highlight just how powerful multiple identities are in creating additional obstacles for women of color. However, as we saw from the Latina respondents' comments, they resisted the white racial frame in their choice of law practice, in their commitment to help the Latino community, and in their "I'll show you" attitude.

This research documents that for these Latina professionals, they experience additional obstacles in their culture and in their communities as well. They often face distinct family obligations and rigid gender roles that do not affect Latinos in the same way; they encounter additional professional stereotypes and challenges that white women do not face; and they experience broader community obstacles in their roles as professional women of color. Because of these obstacles, it is not surprising to find that these Latina respondents—who are civically engaged and committed—do not feel connected to their communities.

The following closing comment by the Latina respondent quoted earlier, in which she discussed "micro-aggressions," summarizes many of the barriers faced by Latina professionals. Her comment points out how the intersection of one's gender, ethnic, racial, and economic positions impacts one's experiences in all areas of life:

> Your everyday experience in the world is shaped by your gender as much as it is by your culture, and so there are certain commonalities, but there are also certain great differences—how we're treated, the assumptions made about us, the equality or lack thereof in our friendships, in our girlfriend/boyfriend relationships, in marriage, how we're treated in the workplace. So it sort of cuts more broadly around gender lines, and it's played out in the Latino community just as it is in any other community. And, of course, there are unique stereotypes of Latinas versus African-American women. There are differences, but there are the commonalities in terms of how our status is lower. And so, if you look statistically at how much money people are earning, you find Latinas at the bottom of the heap. So, it's a separate issue that needs to be addressed. And just as it's a mistake to lump all women's issues together, it's a mistake to lump every group's issues together and not differentiate by gender and class and many other things.

Despite all this, law, as practiced and experienced by many of these Latina attorneys, is closely connected to their sense of cultural identity, to their experiences as women, to their civic activities, and to their ongoing acts of resistance.

(5)

CIVIC PARTICIPATION AMONG LATINO PROFESSIONALS

Juan Gabriel Ibarra, or Gabe,[1] was one of seven children raised in Eagle Pass, Texas, and also in Piedras Negras, Mexico. After graduating from the University of Texas in 1993, he did what some other Latino respondents in this study have done—he began his career as a teacher. First, he taught history at Eagle Pass High School. Shortly thereafter, he went back to college to earn a master's degree in Latin American studies from Washington State University. This enabled him to teach history at a community college in Seattle. He then began attending the University of Washington School of Law, where he received his JD in June 1999 and was admitted to the Washington State Bar Association on November 12, 1999. He died only five years later, on November 18, 2004, while driving back to Yakima from Seattle, over 2,000 miles from where he was raised. He was only thirty-three years old and had purchased his first home just one month before he died.[2]

Gabe had law practices in both Seattle and Yakima, so he traveled across Washington State frequently and was deeply committed to the Latino community on both sides of the state. According to the King County Bar Association memoriam, Gabe "was a dedicated volunteer attorney for the Bilingual Spanish Clinic and volunteered the night before he died."[3] One of the people with whom he worked, Catalina Cantu, is quoted in the memoriam as saying, "I remember that first observation shift Gabe did with me at the legal clinic. His sincerity and legal acumen demonstrated to me that he would be a positive asset to *La Clinica*. Gabe was sincerely dedicated to the Latino community in this state. He had a great sense of humor. I could always count on him and will miss him."[4]

Three years before his death, he participated in the Yakima focus group conducted for this study. When asked about his civic engagement activities he had this to say:

> I'm somebody whose civic involvement consists of being in the Yakima City Basketball League, and I'm sitting here thinking about, in terms of, you know, getting involved in Latino-focused versus more broader non-Latino [groups]. Somebody said Rotary or all these other groups versus [Latino organizations], and I'm thinking, "Why don't I get involved in either of these?" And I guess from my perspective . . . I don't know. Like in the Rotary, I grew up in Texas, and I don't really identify . . . with different groups of that nature. But then again, any other more political groups . . . when I was in college, yeah, I used to go out and protest or whatever, but in undergraduate school. But now, you know, I don't really. I don't know, I guess I'm a little more detached from that, and I haven't had an opportunity to, I mean it just doesn't . . . I don't associate . . . I understand the significance of it, but how I could help or how I could make a difference in that sense, I don't see my role there. . . . I hope it's not a cop-out.

Gabe minimized his activities in professional organizations in two locations. Despite the fact that he had two law practices in two different parts of the state, despite the fact that he did volunteer activities in both areas, he minimized his efforts. In part, he did not feel he could relate to mainstream associations such as the Rotary Club. He also felt he could not relate to identity-based Latino political groups such as the kinds he participated in during his college years. Why did he minimize his community involvement?

Why do Latino professionals such as Gabe not feel they have a role to play by actively participating in community associations even while they are participating? Why do many of the Latino professionals, who in reality participate in civic activities at high rates, elaborate during the focus groups and personal interviews that they had negative experiences, such as being stereotyped and discriminated against when they participated in mainstream civic organizations? Latino attorneys participate a lot, but it is often a negative experience. Latino professionals' high level of volunteer and community involvement is an ignored aspect of their professional lives.

Gabe's experience is illustrative of how racial framing undermines social capital. His ambivalence is typical of the lawyers in this study. Yet, their civic engagement activities include participation in community projects and community events or celebrations and on boards and commissions, and volunteering in local schools, giving time to Boys & Girls Clubs, and participating in church causes, and so on. That a Latino professional should find himself not fitting into various types of civic associations illustrates what Latinos encounter in their new role as professionals: They do not feel they fit in, and many of their experiences are negative.

Many of the Latino respondents also feel they have to balance commitments to both mainstream organizations and to the Latino community. As Gabe's remarks illustrate, they do not feel they can identify with mainstream organizations such as the Rotary, but at the same time, they view Latino civic groups as too controversial. The idea of civic engagement—and with it, increased social capital—simply does not apply neatly to professionals of color—despite their trying. Social capital is a white idea that seemingly works quite well for white people. This does not include professionals of color.

Consider Robert Putnam's definition of social capital (presented earlier in Chapter 1) as "connections among individuals—social networks and the norms of reciprocity and trustworthiness that arise from them."[5] Putnam reached his original conclusions by applying his theory without consideration of marginalized groups. "Connections among individuals" really means the connections among white individuals that matter most. For example, it is a well-known fact that connections matter regarding hiring decisions. Networking in professional arenas often leads to greater opportunities, especially for people who have large networks. But it does not matter how large your network is if you are a person of color who gets passed over for opportunities time and time again. The lie is that it is mostly whites who get these opportunities. After a few tries, white people can usually "make it." People of color, on the other hand, have to bang their heads against the wall to make it.

For example, Joe Feagin highlighted that in study after study between white and black job applicants, white job applicants were far more likely to receive callbacks from employers than black applicants.[6] Feagin noted that in a study of 350 job applicants in Milwaukee, 34 percent of whites were called back, while only 14 percent of black applicants were, despite the fact there was a subgroup of the white applicants who had served prison time for cocaine possession. In a study of Massachusetts Institute of Technology applicants in Chicago and Boston, black applicants had to have at least eight years of work experience before receiving the same consideration for jobs that white applicants who had no experience received. Finally, Feagin reviewed a study on Florida school districts that demonstrated such disparate treatment begins early, when elementary school children with black-sounding names received less assistance from teachers.[7] According to Putnam, social capital theory is believed to be an important component of trust, community cohesion, civic participation, and overall civic health.

However, looking at the experiences of people of color, social capital does not seem to work as well for them as it does for whites. The explanation for this goes far beyond individual prejudice and discrimination. In other words, it goes deeper than what individuals in Milwaukee, Chicago, Boston, or even Florida do with black job applicants or with black students. Feagin argued that the only thing that can explain this type of ongoing phenomenon is systemic racism in America. According to Feagin, "Systemic racism is far more than a matter of racial prejudice and individual bigotry. It is a material, social, and ideological reality that is well-embedded in major U.S. institutions."[8] Without contextualizing social capital within the "historical foundation and systemic character of contemporary racial oppression,"[9] we cannot understand it. Feagin went on to state:

> Very important in the perpetuation of systemic racism across the generations is the role of social networking, which is an essential type of social capital. For long periods . . . most whites have had access to critical social networks beyond those of their immediate families. These networks of white friends, acquaintances, and neighbors provide access to critical networking resources, such as information about decent-paying jobs, health care, political participation, and educational opportunities.[10]

Putnam is not completely uncritical about the role social capital plays within diverse populations. In more recent research, Putnam looked at levels of trust and argued that immigration and ethnic diversity tend to reduce social capital; however, he does not include an analysis of how systemic racism, or the segregation of networks, impacts racialized communities.[11] Putnam argued, with growing immigration to advanced countries, social capital will decline, including trust among co-ethnics. However, Putnam was optimistic about the ability of advanced societies to incorporate immigrants. Research by Maria Chávez, Brian Wampler, and Ross Burkhart also demonstrated that social capital declines with increased immigration; however, their conclusions were not as optimistic as Putnam would like to suggest.[12] Chávez et al. analyzed the levels of trust and social capital among 555 migrant seasonal farmworkers (MSFW) and found not only do they exhibit lower levels of generalized trust than do Hispanics nationally but they had low levels of trust toward whites and Mexican Americans. They concluded: "The odds are long that the MSFW community will demonstrate high levels of trust in the immediate future. Considering recent anti-immigrant initiatives such as the 2004 Proposition 200 in Arizona (the Arizona Tax-payer and Citizen Protection Act), the 1994 Proposition 187 in California (Save Our State), the recent targeting of immigrants after the September 11 terrorist attacks, and the growth of the minutemen in the United States, it is little wonder that immigrants in our study have such low levels of trust."[13] Professor Rodney Hero more convincingly documented this phenomenon.[14] Taking a broader approach, Hero argued that social capital theory does not take racial diversity into account. Once racial diversity is included in the analysis, most measures of social capital are not as good as they appear to be. Even in states with high measures of social capital, Hero found that high rates of segregation and mistreatment of people of color are the norm. Looking at a variety of policy outcomes on people of color, Hero concluded that ideas of social capital do not work when "racial diversity" is considered in the analysis.

By their very presence in associations of all types, the Latino respondents in this study are engaging in what Putnam referred to as *bridging* social capital. Putnam stated: "To build bridging social capital requires that we transcend our social and political and professional identities to connect with people unlike ourselves."[15] However, Putnam was making a normative assumption that bonding (or one could infer, identity-focused associations) is bad and bridging social capital is good. This assumption, though, did not take into consideration that, as Gutmann argued, identity groups (found in bonding social capital) provide much-needed mutual support for marginalized communities—even among professionals who find themselves negotiating a system that has historically excluded them and that presently does not welcome them. Furthermore, rather than seeing it as "hunkering down," as Putnam stated in his most recent article, bonding can help marginalized communities.

Rogers Smith demonstrated in *Civic Ideals* that the history of U.S. inclusion of racial and ethnic groups, particularly through citizenship policies—an important requirement for many types of civic engagement—has reflected racial and gender hierarchies just as much (if not more) than it has reflected liberal and republican traditions.[16] He stated that throughout U.S. history, "lawmakers pervasively and unapologetically structured U.S. citizenship in terms of illiberal and undemocratic racial, ethnic, and gender hierarchies, for reasons rooted in basic, enduring imperatives of political life."[17] More importantly, Smith argued that this aspect of our history has not been discussed widely in our literature on American political theory and history, with the consequence that the potential for the accomplishment of a truly liberal democratic society has been seriously weakened. Furthermore, according to Smith, many scholars, especially in the civic engagement and civil society literature, have espoused a Tocquevillian myth of universal extension. With regard to Tocqueville's legacy, Smith stated:

> By frequently writing in unqualified terms about America's supposedly egalitarian conditions, by relegating blacks and Native Americans to the status of tangents in a final chapter, by neglecting the rising intellectual respectability of racism, and by ignoring women entirely while discussing political institutions (and then implying that their unequal domestic status was natural), Tocqueville did much harm. He made it easy for readers to conclude that the dynamics of democracy, sparked by a setting of initial equality, simply were the story of America.[18]

As illustrated in Gabe's opening quotation, Latino professionals have ambiguous relationships with social capital. It is not something Latino professionals easily engage in, or even enjoy, because civic engagement and the related idea of social capital do not work for them as professionals from a racialized group. The data on Latino professionals support Feagin's, Hero's, and Chávez et al.'s conclusions that racial framing dilutes and complicates social capital. Mainstream social science accounts of social capital are incomplete and limited in their accounts of racism. The stories from the Latino respondents in this study reveal the social and personal costs of what they have accomplished as professionals of color in a society that constantly imposes barriers and obstacles along their path.

The civic commitments of the Latino respondents begins with an analysis of the role of education in enhancing civic engagement. This is followed by a comparison of Latino and white attorneys, on measures of social trust, types of community involvement, rates of volunteerism, political participation, and ideology. This introduces the analysis of why some of the Latino respondents do not participate in any civic organizations. Scholarly analysis of civic engagement needs to examine its relationship to education, racism, and democracy in the United States.

CIVIC ENGAGEMENT: THE ROLE OF EDUCATION

The story of American democracy and civic involvement has been very different for immigrant groups, the poor, people of color, and Latinos—who can encompass all three categories—in America. Without the access provided by the benefits of a higher education, these groups have remained marginalized in the important organizations of community life. However, examining Latino professionals' patterns of civic engagement demonstrates that once Latinos have received the benefit of higher education, their civic engagement rates go up dramatically, compared to Latinos nationally who do not have the same high level of formal education.

With this in mind, it is important to understand the crucial role that education, particularly a legal education, plays in civic engagement activities. This is important for a couple of reasons. Beyond teaching about civic responsibilities, educational attainment for marginalized communities becomes the means to acquire *access* to civil society, which has not always been available to racial and ethnic group members. American civil society has not always been too "civil" when it has come to including people of color.

The Role of Civic Engagement, Higher Education, and African Americans

Looking at black professional experiences demonstrates that increased social capital and civic engagement are the results of increased levels of higher education. In their analyses of university admissions to elite colleges and universities, William Bowen and Derek Bok measured black student success rates with data and surveys from 1951, 1976, and 1989, to test how successful affirmative action admissions policies have been at elite universities.[19] They examined the use of race as one of many possible selection criteria to admit blacks in higher education, as well as black graduation rates, rates of matriculation from graduate school or some other professional school, income, employment, levels of civic engagement, job satisfaction, college experience, and diversity both in college and in the workforce. This research, taken from the College and Beyond (C&B) database,[20] indicated that the level of civic engagement for blacks who are professionals is higher than for whites with comparable educations (included among their subjects of study were lawyers, doctors, and PhDs). Bowen and Bok stated, *"In every type of civic activity . . . , the ratio of black male leaders to white male leaders is even higher than the ratio of black male participants to white male participants."*[21]

The most important factors underlying these high levels of civic engagement surprisingly did not include standardized objective measures such as SAT scores or grades but rather (1) having children, (2) earning high levels of income (the higher the income the more involvement, especially in leadership positions), (3) attending highly selective universities (especially important for leadership positions), and (4) earning an advanced degree— most significant for the purposes of this extrapolation to Latino lawyers. The largest gap in civic participation rates was witnessed among those who held PhD degrees, with 6 percent of white PhD degree holders engaged in leadership activities in their communities compared to 33 percent of black PhD holders. Bowen and Bok demonstrated that, "whereas 15 percent of the white C&B lawyers were leaders of community or social service entities, an even higher percentage of black lawyers (21 percent) held such leadership positions."[22] The evidence from the Latino professionals in this study leads to similar findings as the research from Bowen and Bok on black professionals.

Civic Activities of Latino Attorneys

It is important to gather information on the civic behavior of Latino professionals who have benefited from higher education (specifically a legal education), not just because they are the largest ethnic and racial minority group in America. It is critical to highlight the civic behavior of Latino professionals because, as mentioned in Chapter 1, there are so few Latino professionals of any type. Therefore, what the few do matters greatly for the growing Latino community in America.

Contextual Background on Trust and Civic Engagement. How do measures of civic engagement, levels of trust, and political participation among Latinos nationally compare with Latinos who have had the benefit of a legal education? To answer this question, data was used from the Social Capital Community Benchmark Survey (SCCBS) to establish baseline measures of civic activity of Latinos nationwide. [23] These survey data produced the following variables: level of parents' education, political participation, and values associated with social capital and civic engagement—such as level of political involvement, pattern of volunteer activities, and trust in others.

This is not to suggest that the Latino professionals in this study are similar to Latinos nationally with regard to current socioeconomic factors. Rather, just the opposite. The differences between the Latino lawyers and Latinos nationally are profound in many ways. As we know from our examination of the Latino attorneys' parents' backgrounds, discussed in Chapter 2, these differences arise only after Latinos have achieved a college education and then a legal education. The point in comparing them is that research shows how far the Latino lawyers have come with regard to community commitments and involvement—once they have received higher education. When the general Latino population rates of civic engagement are compared to the Latino lawyers' rates of civic engagement, it becomes evident just how important the role of education is to increasing levels of trust and civic involvement. [24]

Although they started out in similar circumstances, particularly with regard to parental levels of education, the SCCBS findings revealed that Latinos nationally generally come from very different socioeconomic backgrounds than do the Latino lawyers featured in this study. According to the SCCBS, 45 percent of Latinos had less than a high school diploma, only 6 percent had a bachelor's degree, and only 6 percent had a graduate or professional degree. When comparing indicators of civic engagement, such as giving money to charities and measures of general trust, there is also a big gap between Latinos nationally and Washington State Latino attorneys: 79 percent of the Latino attorneys, compared with only 41 percent of Latinos nationally, indicated that they contributed money to charitable or voluntary service organizations. With regard to measures of trust, 23 percent of Latinos nationally surveyed indicated "People can be trusted," and 68 percent indicated "You can't be too careful." In comparison, while only 3 percent of the Washington Latino lawyers indicated "You can't be too careful," 18 percent responded that "It's good to be careful."

There are substantial differences between Latinos nationally and the Latino lawyers with respect to political participation and interest in politics. According to the SCCBS, 36 percent of Latinos nationally voted in the 1996 presidential elections compared to 98 percent of Latino lawyers in Washington State. With regard to interest in politics and national affairs, 47 percent of Latinos nationally indicated that they were either somewhat interested (29 percent) or very interested (18 percent) compared to 72 percent of Latino lawyers in Washington State indicating that they were "Very" or "Moderately" interested "in local community politics and local community affairs." With regard to keeping up with political and community affairs, Latinos nationally were asked how many days during the past week they had read a daily newspaper: 46 percent responded with "0," and 18 percent said they read the paper "5-7" days a week. These figures compare to 85 percent of Latino attorneys who indicated that they read the newspaper daily.

To analyze more specific measures of civic engagement, the researchers associated with the SCCBS created several indices from their database to measure levels of civic engagement.[25] Looking at levels of associational membership for Latinos nationally, 36 percent had no associational memberships at all, while only 19 percent of the Latino attorneys in Washington State fell into this category. Thirty-one percent of Latinos nationally indicated they belong to only one or two civic organizations compared to 39.2 percent of the Washington State Latino attorneys. Only 16 percent of Latinos nationally belonged to three or four civic organizations compared to 27.5 percent of the Washington State Latino attorneys. Finally, 17 percent of Latinos nationally belonged to five or more civic organizations compared to 13.7 percent of the Latino attorneys. This can easily be explained by the fact that over half of the Latino attorneys belonged to three or more professional associations.

In sum, Latino professionals, specifically Latino lawyers, are distinguished from Latinos nationally in their political and civic behavior, and with regard to social capital views such as those measured by levels of trust. They are more likely to be in organizations that promote the public good and are also more likely to participate in nonminority associations. Similar to Bowen and Bok's findings with African Americans, Latino lawyers were extremely civically active in the community. This group of Latino attorneys not only transcended educational and class boundaries to a remarkable extent, but they were civically engaged at about the same levels as non-

Latino attorneys. These findings serve to underscore Bowen and Bok's argument that the benefits of higher education (in their case, with specifically the policy of affirmative action) include increased civic engagement. Bowen and Bok contended, "It is the contributions that individuals make throughout their lives and the broader impact of higher education on the society that are finally most relevant" to explaining high rates of civic engagement. [26]

To review, Latino professionals, specifically Latino attorneys, are distinguished from Latinos nationally in their civic behavior and social capital orientation. They are more likely to be in organizations that promote the public good and are also more likely to participate in nonminority associations. Also, the Latino respondents in this study come from very similar socioeconomic backgrounds as Latinos nationally. The key difference with regard to civic engagement that separates them today is their level of education, which in turn, distinguishes them in their levels of trust and civic participation, particularly their participation in *bridging* activities.

Comparison of Latino Attorneys with White Attorneys.   When comparing Latino attorneys to white attorneys, except for childhood socioeconomic background, the distinctions in all other areas of civic engagement disappear. For example, voting rates were extraordinarily high for both groups of attorneys, with 96 percent of the Latino attorneys and 97.3 percent of the non-Latino attorneys indicating they voted in the 2000 presidential election. Moreover, when asked if they were interested "in local community politics and local community affairs," 72.1 percent of the Latino attorneys responded they were either "Very Interested" (41.2 percent) or "Moderately Interested" (30.9 percent) compared with 78.4 percent of the white attorneys (with 33.3 percent responding "Very Interested" and 45.6 percent indicating they were "Moderately Interested").

Both groups of attorneys also share a strong interest in local government. Regarding community politics and community affairs, the amount of time and money spent on political activities is comparable for both groups. Over four out of ten (41.6 percent) of the Latino attorneys indicated they had worked as volunteers for a candidate running for national, state, or local office, and 57.9 percent of the white attorneys indicated they had done so. In the last four years, 63.4 percent of the Latino attorneys had contributed money to a political candidate, political party or political action committee, or similar type of organization compared to 71.4 percent of the white attorneys who had done so. When asked how often they discuss local politics with others, 41.8 percent of Latino lawyers indicated they discuss politics every day or nearly every other day compared to 44.8 percent of white attorneys who do likewise.

Turning to analysis of specific measures of lawyers' civic involvement, the same thirteen categories used in the Bowen and Bok study were used to see to what extent they have participated as nonemployee volunteers and/or leaders in civic activities in their communities since becoming attorneys.[27] Bowen and Bok found that close to 90 percent of their survey respondents featuring black and white graduates of elite colleges and universities in the C&B database participated in one or more of the mentioned civic activities in 1995. Especially likely was involvement in the areas of professional associations, alumni activities, cultural and arts organizations, and environmental and conservation group activities (p. 157). With regard to lawyers specifically, Bowen and Bok found that 15 percent of white lawyers in their sample participated as leaders in the areas of community or social services compared to 21 percent of black lawyers.

The survey in this study (see Appendix B) reveals that 80.4 percent of the Latino attorneys were engaged in one or more civic activities compared to 86.9 percent of the comparison group of white attorneys. Latino lawyers are very close to white attorneys in terms of membership rates across the various types of civic categories. However, just as Bowen and Bok found with the black graduates from elite law schools, Latino lawyers participated as members in most of the civic associations at comparable, but slightly lower, rates than the comparison group of white attorneys. Out of the thirteen categories of participation, only three show a statistically significant difference (Mann-Whitney U test) in rates of participation by Latino and white attorneys: youth organizations, political clubs, and educational organizations. However, Latino lawyers did participate at higher rates as members in one especially important category—"Community Service." Latino lawyers participated as members in civic activities concerned with community service at the rate of 23 percent compared to 18 percent for non-Latino attorneys. However, the difference is not statistically significant.

But of importance to this discussion are their participation rates in youth, educational, and alumni activities at 20 percent, 8 percent, and 15 percent, respectively. Figure 5.1 sets forth comparisons of Latino and white attorneys with respect to their patterns of membership (affiliation) in thirteen categories of civic activities related to community affairs (see Appendix A).

The Latino and the white comparison groups show even more significant differences in the rates and types of civic leadership activities reported. With regard to patterns of the assumption of leadership roles in the same types of civic associations, these survey results demonstrate findings similar to those reported in the Bowen and Bok study. As was the case for African-American professionals from the Bowen and Bok study, Latino lawyers participate in leadership roles at higher rates than do the comparison group of white attorneys in some very important categories—namely, community service and alumni/ae activities, but at lower rates in regard to youth and educational leadership roles, at 22 percent (compared to 25 percent for non-Latinos) and 6 percent (compared to 9 percent for whites), respectively (see Figure 5.2 in Appendix A).

It would appear that when it comes to assuming leadership roles in these civic activities, in general, Latino attorneys are reporting patterns of civic engagement very much in line with Bowen and Bok's findings regarding black graduates of law schools.

Levels of Trust Among Lawyers.   Another important area in social capital theory is studying the variation in "trust in others." The distribution of responses on the two trust items was very similar for both groups. Respondents were asked to rate their "general outlook on life" on a five-point scale. Table 5.1 sets forth findings regarding the degree of trust in others between the two groups of attorneys (see Appendix A). As the results displayed in Table 5.1 demonstrate, it is evident that the two groups of attorneys are quite similar in their general outlook with regard to trust in others and believing "others are honest."[28] There are some differences, notwithstanding the overall lack of statistical significance, between the two groups within the category "It's good to be careful/Some people are always cheating," with Latino attorneys exhibiting greater caution over non-Latino attorneys (18 percent compared to 11.5 percent, respectively, for trust, and 12 percent compared to 8.3 percent, respectively, for honesty) in their general outlooks on both categories.

With respect to political beliefs and ideology, three survey items were used to ascertain the political viewpoints of both groups of lawyers in this study: political preference in terms of political labels, views on social issues, and views on economic issues. Substantially more Latino lawyers labeled themselves as "Republicans" than did white attorneys. Specifically, 38 percent of Latino lawyers identified themselves as either "Strong Republican" (4 percent) or "Republican" (34 percent) compared to 23.4 percent of non-Latino lawyers who self-identified as either "Strong Republican" (5.4 percent) or "Republican" (18 percent). A very similar proportion of Latino lawyers and the group of comparison lawyers labeled themselves "Independents"—24 percent and 24.9 percent, respectively. The difference that is the most pronounced applies to the labels of "Democrat" and "Strong Democrat," with 29.6 percent of the non-Latino comparison group of lawyers identifying themselves as "Democrats" compared to only 8 percent of Latino lawyers who did so. Almost 20 percent (19.4 percent) of the comparison group identified themselves as "Strong Democrat" compared to 24 percent of Latino lawyers.

To further measure lawyers' political ideology regarding economic and social issues, the following Likert-type scale, ranging from "Very Conservative" to "Very Liberal," was used to ask the following questions:

- "Thinking about your views concerning *economic issues* (such as taxes, government spending), where would you place yourself on the scale below?"
- "Thinking about your views concerning *social issues* (such as women's rights, gay rights), where would you place yourself on the scale below?"

Table 5.2 summarizes the responses on these two items (see Appendix A). There are notable political and ideological differences not only along political party label lines but also along economic and social attitude dimensions. In terms of economic issues, Latino lawyers as a group are very diverse in their perspectives, covering the entire ideological range. The survey findings also reveal that the greatest ideological differences are with respect to social issues among both groups of attorneys. The comparison group of white attorneys were more than twice as likely to label themselves as "Moderate" (18.1 percent) compared to Latino attorneys (7.1 percent). Furthermore, there is a substantial difference in the proportion of attorneys who label themselves as "Very Liberal" on social issues: 46.5 percent of Latino attorneys compared to 30.4 percent of the comparison group of attorneys. The survey revealed that both groups of attorneys held very comparable views with regard to measures of trust and very diverse views with regard to measures on ideology.

Other Civic Activities.   How does all this relate to their levels of interest in civic activities as varied as voting, giving money, or attending church services? To further measure lawyers' patterns of civic engagement, additional questions concerning volunteerism were asked.[29]

The survey results are summarized in Table 5.3.[30] They show the proportion of attorneys who indicated a simple "Yes" when asked from a list of typical activities in which they have participated in the past twelve months (see Appendix A). It is clear that both groups of attorneys are *highly* involved in a variety of civic activities, from politics to church attendance, indicating they are inclined to follow public affairs in their communities.

The survey data revealed that 63.6 percent of the Latino attorneys spent time on charitable or voluntary service activities, while an even higher rate—71 percent of the comparison group of non-Latino attorneys—was so engaged. Overall, money contributions to charitable or voluntary service activities are even more frequently noted than is any time commitment for both groups—78.6 percent of the Latino attorneys and 89.8 percent of the comparison group reported contributing money to charitable and/ or voluntary service organizations. However, the proportion of voluntary activities decreased substantially for both groups with regard to church-related volunteer activities in the previous twelve months—23.5 percent of the Latino attorneys compared to 30.2 percent of the white attorneys reported being active in special projects and/or serving on committees in their churches or synagogues. Although close to 80 percent of both groups of lawyers indicated they subscribe to a religious faith, these lower figures of church involvement indicate that their civic activities are focused in political activities to a much greater extent.

Both groups of lawyers were asked to check the reasons why they participate in political activities. They were asked: "Thinking about a time that you decided to participate in a political activity (campaigning, contacting politicians, making campaign contribution, protest, community board, etc.), which of these lists of reasons best describes your motivations for your activity (check **all** that apply)?" They were then provided with a list of reasons they could check off.

Looking at a few of the reasons, we find that categories that improve democracy and the community were strong motivators, whereas categories that could be characterized as more self-interested such as "The chance to further my job or career" were not listed as often. For example, only 12.9 percent of the comparison group of attorneys and only 9.8 percent of the Latino attorneys indicated that the chance to further their job or career was their motivation for involvement. At the other extreme, 55.1 percent of the comparison group of attorneys and 43.6 percent of the Latino attorneys checked "The chance to make the community or nation a better place to live" as an important motivator. Furthermore, "My duty as a citizen," while still respectable for both groups, was stronger for the comparison group of white lawyers, with 44.5 percent checking this category compared to 29.4 percent of Latino attorneys. "The chance to influence government policy" was also strong for both groups, again with the comparison group responding at higher rates than the Latino group of attorneys at 49.5 percent and 38.2 percent, respectively. This demonstrates an important aspect of legal culture that shows commitment to community as a strong part of professional and public roles. And these civic commitments are strong over time.

With regard to how these different aspects of voluntary activities have changed over the last four years, attorneys were asked if their volunteer activities were "Increasing," "Staying the Same," or "Lessening." Nearly one-third (30 percent) of the Latino attorneys responded they were "Increasing," 31 percent indicated they were "Staying the Same," and 39 percent said they were "Lessening." Similarly, 29.6 percent of white attorneys indicated that their volunteer activities were "Increasing," 40.2 percent responded they were "Staying the Same," and 30.2 percent said they were "Lessening." Both groups of attorneys share a robust pattern of voluntary activities in civic associations and community-based organizations that has remained strong for the last four years. Ron Ward, former president of the Washington State Bar Association, in arguing to improve diversity in the legal profession stated, "Lawyers are gifted with the tradition, privilege, and heritage of accomplishment. We have an obligation to be societal leaders in every area of endeavor; an obligation to do more; and [an] obligation from lawyer generation to generation, to lead and to provide to our clients, to the public, and to our profession. Lawyers are leaders."[31] These data underscore this statement.

Both groups of lawyers in this study exhibit the type of civic behavior that Ward would categorize as "societal leaders." However, what is even more astounding is that compared to Latinos nationally, it is clear that education makes a huge difference for community involvement, civic engagement, and social capital for the Latino professionals in this study. The survey data revealed that Latino lawyers are highly engaged in their communities. They report similar levels of civic engagement and associational membership with the comparison group of white lawyers. Indeed, both sets of attorneys' engagement in civic life is high by any measure and is comparable to Heinz et al.'s research on attorneys' civic engagement rates in Chicago, as discussed in Chapter 1. Latino attorneys participated in civic activities at higher rates than those recorded by the SCCBS. The survey data demonstrate that Latino attorneys use their newfound professional status to become civically engaged, mainly in the larger community. Considering Putnam's position that members of the community generate social capital through interactions with one another in various ways, especially in participating in civic affairs, one could argue that the civic and community activities of Latino lawyers serve to enhance social capital—particularly the kind that increases democracy: bridging social capital. The data reveal that Latino attorneys play an important role as generators of social capital, which serves to diversify American professional society and politics. Most importantly, these data demonstrate the key role of education—the difference in trust and civic engagement comes after the benefits of higher education and specifically, a legal professional education.

BALANCING CIVIC COMMITMENTS TO BOTH CULTURES

One of the themes that came out of the Latino focus groups was that while Latino attorneys are embracing new civic opportunities to become involved in their communities, they are also in a new position, as professionals from a racial and ethnic community, to contribute to positive change in the Latino community at large. This is both good and bad. This group of Latino professionals clearly understand that there are many needs facing the Latino community; however, they are often pulled in many directions with their professional responsibilities, their civic commitments, and the pressing needs of the Latino community at large. *The issue of how to balance participating professionally in both the Latino world and the mainstream world is a difficult one for many Latino attorneys.* Though some of the focus-group participants quoted in Chapter 3 vocalized that they were weary from fighting for acceptance and had decided to retreat from mainstream organization participation, many of the Latino respondents recognized that they had an important role to play in *both* communities. This focus-group participant represents these views with the following comments:

I work a lot with Hispanics, and part of my work is working with people who are only Spanish speaking and assisting them—so it's very important to me to do that. But I'm also interested in getting into mainstream organizations, and they are welcoming me because they see me as bringing this diverse viewpoint and trying to—I try to go both ways. I try to bring Hispanics to mainstream things. I try to get those mainstream things to promote Hispanic goals, and I guess, at this point, I see it as part of my identity. I'm an American and I'm also Hispanic, and I think they go together well. So, I do Hispanic organizations, but I have a lot of others too.

This respondent felt positively about her work in both mainstream groups and with Latino organizations. Her role as a bridge to both communities was one she was not only proud of but saw as her responsibility as a Latina professional. However, another focus-group member talked about how community involvement often became a difficult balance:

I think that another factor that goes into involvement or lack of involvement—certainly can play into it—is where you are working and what kind of support you're getting. . . . I mean, at my previous firm, I can tell you that there would have been *no support* whatsoever for even me having this kind of discussion . . . as you're sitting there as an associate and you're moving up, trying to get to that magical carrot of partnership, there's a lot of pressure to play the game and rock the boat selectively. And it's really a tough one, but I mean you know it was tough enough that I left the firm over it! But it's just a piece of it that becomes a constant conflict that becomes: *"I do this, I'm jeopardizing my career. I don't do this, I'm not being true to myself. I do this, I'm pissing off all sorts of people. How do I reconcile all these things within my life and make it work?"* . . . I have to work, so how do I make all these choices and keep the balance and be true to myself and moving forward? And I think it is a really tough one.

Clearly, this focus-group respondent had experienced the pressure of trying to conform to unreasonable standards and left the first firm. This is not uncommon for first-generation Latino professionals, who often change positions in search of an environment that honors their values and commitments, as well as their contributions to the organization.

Focus-group participants were asked which way was the best to address Latino-specific needs—by defining them as part of the broader public interest through mainstream issues or by framing an issue as a "Latino issue." Most of the focus-group participants responded that it was definitely best to define or frame the issue as part of the broader public interest. However, there were disagreements. There were those who argued for a

Latino-focused perspective. Some participants, however, responded that balancing between both positions was ultimately the best way to go. Here is an illustration of the belief that the best way to address Latino issues and concerns is through a Latino-defined policy:

> It is important to address issues that are unique to the Latino community, to recognize that they exist in order to start figuring out ways to improve them. . . . I find that a lot of the mainstream community doesn't recognize what are the issues involving the Latino community—what are the needs of Latino children in education, what are the needs to bring the Latino community out of poverty here—so, I think it is important to focus on what are the issues unique to the Latino community.

This statement shows a recognition that there is a lack of information about Latino issues such as poverty rates or low educational attainment by mainstream white society. According to this respondent, the only way to counter this is by directly addressing the policy issues facing Latinos. But this statement also shows that this lack of knowledge is not simply a lack of facts but rather that "the mainstream community *doesn't recognize* what are the issues." This lack of recognition by many white Americans is intentional. As Ana Castillo pointed out, "The ignorance of white dominant society about our ways, struggles in society, history, and culture is not an innocent and passive ignorance, it is a systematic and determined ignorance. . . . We exist in a void, en *ausencia*, and surface rarely, usually in stereotype."[32] And the only way to deal with this lack of recognition is by addressing Latino needs directly, as this respondent argued.

Below is a good representative statement by the Latino respondents who believe it is important to balance between both positions but who also articulate the difficulty in doing so:

> I think there's a really delicate balance between the two. . . . [A]s Latino professionals, I think it's really important that we are, you know, kind of the cream of the crop, if you want to call it—there's so few of us. . . . It's really important to be in those broader, bigger schemes as well because they need to hear us for who we are and what our specific needs are, but also we can never forget that we need to be part of the [Latino] community so that we keep in touch with those topics and never lose sight of what's important to the [Latino] community, because I think if we go way too far away from that, we ourselves get lost in whatever everybody else thinks are our needs.

Staying connected to the Latino communities needs, especially as pro-fessionals, is a high priority for this group of Latino professionals, espe-cially when they have overcome many of the struggles still faced by the majority of Latinos in America. As this respondent emphasized, because "there are so few of us," it becomes even more important for them to never forget where they come from and to never get "lost in whatever everybody else thinks are our needs."

Finally, the majority of the Latino attorneys interviewed believed the best way to address Latino needs is through the broader public interest—or in another words, through mainstream civic and professional organiza-tions. The following statement from one of the respondents during the focus-group interview in Seattle is a good illustration of the many senti-ments behind this position:

> I think you have to get societal buy-in. I mean, widespread buy-in. It's just, how do you initiate that buy-in? And I think sometimes it does take folks' organizations, specific topics, whether it be the Hispanic groups' or whether it is a specific health issue. You need to get societal buy-in too so that ev-erybody sees that it's a problem of everybody, it's a problem that everyone needs to be solving. . . . If you don't get that buy-in, it could be: "Well, that's not really my problem. That's your problem. You guys have your own little group to figure it out. Just do it yourself." So, if it's truly a societal problem, you have to get that buy-in.

In agreement, another focus-group participant stated strongly that "I think it is wrong to segregate our issues, segregate our concerns." Indeed, this participant felt that most of the pressing Latino issues such as educa-tion were class issues, as opposed to specific ethnic or racial issues. Because he argued they were class issues, he felt the issues are equally important to *all* poor communities regardless of their race. As a consequence, he argued that the best way to address them is through economic policies that promote greater social equity and to stay away from focusing on race. It is understand-able that most of the respondents would want to get societal buy-in or that they would want to shy away from discussions of race. However, one need only examine the current immigration debate to see that the issues facing the Latino community go far beyond class. They go to the heart of American identity, and no amount of class talk changes this point.

The last question the focus-group participants were asked (for all ques-tions see Appendix B) included reading them this statement from Bowen and Bok's *The Shape of the River*:

Discussing black professionals, Bowen and Bok wrote, "This group of well-educated individuals is charged, in effect, with twin responsibilities: not only to help build a more integrated American society, but to strengthen the social fabric of the black community."[33] Do you believe this sentiment expressed in this quote by advocates of affirmative action in higher education applies to Latino professionals as well? Do you think that Latinos have an obligation as members of a historically disadvantaged minority group to use their training and skills to contribute to the improvement of the Latino community—or is this an unfair burden on persons such as yourself?

The reactions among the respondents were mixed. Most participants felt that it is definitely a burden but one they must gladly take on. Others, however, believed that giving back to the community is all about individual choice. The following is an exchange that took place at the Seattle focus group after I asked the group if anyone thought giving back to the Latino community was an unfair burden:

S3: I think it's an unfair burden for us as a group. I think it's a burden that a lot of us as individuals . . . I think it is put on us as a group, and I don't think that's a fair burden. I think a lot of us, including myself, take it on as a burden because we want it, not because it feels imposed.

S7: I think the characterization that it's unfair is to me almost irrelevant, I mean, because it has to be done. And I don't know if you'd call it fair or unfair, but it's there and it's kind of difficult to say. What would be fair? That we didn't have the burden? Then the work would not be done. You know. So, I don't know that I would say that it's unfair.

S2: I think it's kind of interesting because then it begs the question "How do you feel about people that are not involved that are Hispanic?" I mean, do you blame them, I mean maybe you should be doing something—or do you say, well that's your choice. I choose to be active. So, that's kind of interesting. I feel some sense of obligation, but I think it's also something that I want to do. I mean, if I picked another cause or something, it's because it's something that I want to change. I do have a general sense of giving back to the community, giving something back that I received. And I chose to do it with the Hispanic population—especially with kids and get them educated and get them through. But I can see myself picking other things and not feeling like an obligation to have to do it but just a sense that I want to do it—a sense that I really need to do it, you know, for myself.

S4: I would agree that I'm not sure that I would say it's an unfair or fair burden. I think we're privileged to have the ability to give to our community, and I think it's necessary too or else the only thing that separates me from someone who's just snuck across the border is my education and my income. If you take off my suit and you don't know where I live, I would be discriminated against just like that other person. So, unless I personally want to continue to be discriminated against, I have to improve the situation for all Hispanic people. You can call it self-preservation if you want, but we all have an obligation to each other if we have the ability to do so to make life more bearable, to raise the standard for everybody. And some people don't have that ability or the inclination, and that's just their choice for life, and I don't feel like I can say you must, you're educated and that's an obligation. I just feel like that's their personal decision, and I feel fortunate that I can, so I do.

This exchange among the Latino focus-group participants in Seattle about whether it was their obligation as Latino professionals to use their position and status in efforts that improve the Latino community was insightful. There was a strong view that if their energies are used in this manner, it is because of personal choice, because they want to, and because it helps them in the long run. However, the idea that it was an obligation is also present, because the work must get done. Another point made during the same Seattle focus group stresses the personal choice aspect again:

Yeah, I found that question interesting because I don't think they've ever posed it directly but they asked the same questions for example, of Michael Jordan as opposed to Magic Johnson. You know, Magic Johnson has really gotten involved and Michael Jordan obviously doesn't. And also was asked of Pele, you know, as to why he doesn't get more involved in social changes. And I don't know if they ever give an answer. But it's just a choice, a personal choice. . . . That one has different dynamics because they definitely have the ability to obviously make social changes.

Similarly, when the Latino focus-group participants in Yakima were asked the same question, most agreed that while it is a burden to participate civically, it is also a responsibility to give back to the Latino community, even if it is at times very uncomfortable, as the following exchange demonstrates:

Y10: I think certain groups are really hard to break into, and then other sort of groups where you really feel welcomed and you're more willing to open up—and I think that's where you can *feel the vibes* and you can tell which group is going to be more friendly to you and more understanding, and then you find your commonalities. I mean, a lot of us, especially in our profession, have a common lifestyle. But one group in particular is the women of the bar here. I think I can speak for myself, and I know participant number nine being a fairly new attorney, we have the same vibes. I've been here sixteen years. I still feel the negativity; it's very cliqueish, and it's really hard to break in.

Y3: With the women of the bar?

Y10: Yeah.

Y9: It's hard to deal with, oh yeah. It's very hard to deal with.

Y3: These are women's issues.

Y10: No, no, but in the court, same thing.

Y9: But you do have, it is a responsibility to be there, but it is hard to integrate to create more integration with the, like the women of the bar, so it's just not an all-white group, even though it's uncomfortable you still go, but at the same time you also like it says here, you have the obligation to help the Latino community as well.

Y4: I do feel that's a burden, and I mean that's something that's always in the back of my mind.

Y2: Exactly.

Y4: But, I mean, if I'm not going to do it, if we're not going to do it, who is?

Y11: Nobody.

Y4: Yeah. We have to do it. I have to do it.

Despite the fact that there are "negative vibes" in mainstream professional groups such as the Women's Bar, the Latino participants in Yakima believe they should be involved anyway. However, clearly the lack of acceptance in that organization has been long-standing. One Latina attorney has been experiencing the tension for over sixteen years. As she stated, "It's very hard to deal with."

For some Latino focus-group participants, the value of giving back to the Latino community is intertwined with family and the values with which they were raised, as the following Latina respondent noted:

I would say that, you know, my mother is also a lawyer and she's a Latina, and she raised us with the very strong impression that you have to be involved—that it is a priority that, you know, you just didn't make it where you are on your own. You have to give back to your community in whatever way you feel.

This is an important sentiment by this Latina respondent, but it eventually takes its toll as she also expressed in a smaller group, women-only interview that sometimes she wishes she had chosen another career. Her life feels out of control, and she does not feel supported in her profession.

LATINO ATTORNEYS WHO DOWNPLAY THEIR CIVIC ENGAGEMENT

What about Latino attorneys who do not participate in any civic organizations? This chapter began with a quote from Gabe Ibarra, who did not feel he could identify with mainstream organizations such as the Rotary. At the same time, though, he viewed Latino civic organizations as being perhaps too political and his "protest politics" days were over as an undergraduate. In addition to not being able to relate to either mainstream or Latino-specific civic groups, the following comments shed some light on some of the reasons the Latino respondents gave for not participating at all. Participants in both the Seattle and Yakima focus groups gave lack of time as a reason for their lack of civic involvement, as participants from the Seattle focus group stated:

> [W]hen I was first practicing, I was a member of the Mexican American Bar Association, and that was maybe two or three years of the early years of my practice, and I did some outreach work. But unfortunately, I had to focus more on earning money, and I did some family law stuff . . . but then because the focus was building the practice, I didn't have as much time to devote to outreach kind of services, and now I don't do anything focus[ing] on either the Latino community [or mainstream community] since I've been transplanted up here in Washington.

One woman from the Seattle focus group explained that it was difficult to balance demands at work with family responsibilities:

> I just do what, as I go about my day, what is sort of there to me. As a family law practitioner, what is most pressing for me are family law issues, so my early involvement—actually I did run the bilingual legal clinic when it first started in 1987 or '88. I did actually coordinate that for the first four years because it just landed on my lap—but after, really what was pressing to me was the family law arena 'cause that's where I worked. And so that's my involvement professionally within the family law arena. And with my kids, you know what's pressing in school, you know the PTA. So when you finish taking

care of those issues and because there's not a big Hispanic population around me, it's you know, to go seek out the Hispanic population takes a lot of effort.

This respondent minimized her civic engagement by discounting her participation in the local Parent Teacher Association as a civic engagement activity. Unlike the previous respondent whose civic participation declined throughout his career, this same participant then went on to explain that in addition to her PTA work, her civic engagement also includes ongoing activities within the Latino community:

I [currently] do chair the Judicial Screening Committee for the Hispanic Bar Association. But that really came about more because I did it for the King County Bar Association, participated on the committee, and it just seemed logical to me that if I'm doing all this work and the Hispanic Bar Association has a need for what I'm doing, I should help and participate in that. So, it is kind of a logical, but it's more what's around me because I don't live in a Hispanic community, it is harder to go, you know, find those activities and participate for me, to find them that are relevant to my existence. I know they're relevant and they're important, but you figure someone else will take care of it. . . . [I] do what seems more relevant to my actual day-to-day stuff.

The comments from this respondent are once again similar to what Gabe believed when he expressed that his involvement in the Yakima City Basketball League did not count as civic engagement. Although many of the Latino respondents stated that they were not too civically involved, once they went beyond the superficial level of a survey questionnaire and started having conversations about their activities, they would mention participation in the Parent Teacher Association, the King County Bar Association, and even the Judicial Screening Committee for the Hispanic Bar Association.

Some respondents in the Yakima focus group were not as tolerant of the "lack of time" justification for noninvolvement as their Seattle counterparts were, as the following discussion with the Latino attorneys in Yakima revealed:

Y5: I think that time availability has a lot to do with it, and it's hard being a new lawyer to begin with—and we're having to do all kinds of things associated with work and after hours, much less trying to get involved with other things. . . . I did get asked to be on the planning commission in the lower

valley. And only because I was asked. I don't go, I don't really assert myself to
get involved 'cause I just don't feel like I have the time, but since I was asked
I gave it a shot. And I mean, I was on the board for a year, and I just found
that you know even just that one meeting per month was, it was just getting
to be a little much. And so I got off the board, and mostly now I just stick to
work-related events and trying to promote things in that area, whether it's
Spanish presentations for work after hours and stuff like that. But beyond
that, I just don't think—I think there's a constraint in time.

It should be noted that this respondent works in the capacity of providing free legal services through one of the largest public interest law groups
in the area. Consequently, through the nature of her work, she is still engaged in outreach efforts to the Latino community. This did not, however,
keep others in the group from challenging her position. Here are two of
the replies she received for her comments:

Y10: *I think it is priorities!* [Stated quite firmly.] It's whether you think it's
important or not, whether you like doing it or not, and for myself, I think it's
my responsibility to be visible in as many organizations as I like to be visible
in and that I like to do that type of work, and I am very fortunate that I do
like to do this kind of stuff. Otherwise, I probably wouldn't be as involved
as I am. And I come and go. You get tired of it. You get burnt out because
you're the only one that's there trying to make a difference, trying to get
other people in. They don't want to because "I don't have time, I have kids."
Everybody in general has kids, different ages. So, it just depends on your
priorities.
Y8: I mean, I was raised and maybe it was my college experience. I was very
involved in school, and I too feel that I didn't get here by myself and I had
a lot of help—not only my family but all these other organizations that I
belonged to, and I feel, you're right. A priority and a responsibility to give
back and for me, women's issues, Latina women's issues are very important.
. . . Time constraints, everyone's got them. I mean, you know, I know some
people have family and have children and stuff, and that is a big part of who
they are. But I think you just, you're right, you just have to make time. And
that's how I feel.

Still another reason given for lack of participation by a few focus-group
participants in both the Yakima and the Seattle focus groups was that
oftentimes, people are simply not aware of the issues or have not found
organizations that deal with the issues. This participant became involved

in Latino community-building efforts after he became more aware of them as an undergraduate:

> [Y]ou know people who are not aware of issues, because I know for me I became aware of issues and what was relevant to the Hispanic community and things like that in college. . . . I got more educated because of the people that you know, that I was introduced [to]. . . . But otherwise, I mean, that's exactly how I became active. So that's kind of [being] oblivious and I put myself [in] that I was oblivious. . . . I kind of woke up.

CONCLUSION

In many ways, the Latino professionals in this study are a success story, despite the obstacles they continue to encounter. The statistics show how often and in what associations they are involved. However, this chapter goes beyond the statistics. Rather, the patterns in the numbers are combined with the personal narratives to highlight some of the thoughts behind their civic involvement, including their motivation and what they perceive as important about their civic participation. Both through the survey findings and the insightful discussions in the focus groups and interviews, one can see how much Latino professionals make a difference in their communities through their civic activities, even when they do not believe they are doing very much at all!

Their participation increases diversity not only in the professional work environment but also in other areas of civic life such as the Parent Teacher Association or the local basketball leagues that used to be predominately white. However, based on their experiences, one could argue that social capital is a concept that works better for white people than for racialized groups. Many of the respondents' experiences in mainstream organizations are negative and unpleasant. Regardless of the negative "vibes" however, they are still participating and still active in professional organizations and in their local community. The negative vibes are the reality of what it is for Latinos to live in the United States, even for professionals.

Most importantly, this chapter illustrates how important education is for civic engagement among previously marginalized communities such as blacks, as researched by Bowen and Bok, and the Latinos in this research. The Latino respondents' civic activities demonstrate that the benefits of higher education go well beyond private individual gains, extending to community gains. Based on these findings, one can make the case that high levels of formal education increase civic engagement among Latinos. Latino professionals have significantly higher levels of trust and civic participation when compared to Latinos nationally. This increase comes once they have received the benefits of college and a legal education. It is important to remember that, as we saw in Chapter 2, the Latino respondents in this study originally came from similar socioeconomic backgrounds as those seen in the overall U.S. Latino population. Forty-three percent of Latino attorneys' mothers did not even finish high school, lacking what Bowen and Bok referred to as inherited intellectual capital. Access to higher education changed their lives, and they in turn, are changing their community, despite the fact they often sell themselves short believing that their involvement does not really count. The lives of this group of Latino professionals are excellent examples of how Latinos from very modest backgrounds and a culture that has struggled for acceptance in a white dominant society are now for the most part—despite the obstacles they encounter in their new profession—deeply involved and committed members of their communities and their professions.

As we have seen in this research, improving the educational rates among Latinos is more meaningful than trying to deny them citizenship or access to America's civic, educational, and political institutions through negative immigration policies. For example, compared to previous generations, third- and fourth-generation Latinos participate in politics at lower rates.[34] Research shows that economically speaking, compared to previous generations of Mexican immigrants, third-generation Mexican Americans earn less.[35] As mentioned in Chapter 1, a little over half of Latinos have a high school diploma.[36]

This latest round of American anti-Latino, anti-immigrant sentiment has gone so far as to include mainstream discussions among policy makers and the media concerning the merits of repealing the citizenship clause in the Fourteenth Amendment of the Constitution for children born of undocumented immigrants. Rather than discussing who should be allowed to become citizens, the findings from this research suggest that it would be better if we were discussing ways we could get more Latinos to exhibit the type of civic and political behavior this group of Latino professionals exhibit. To do this requires that we shift the conversation from finding ways to continue to exclude Latinos and instead focus on ways to welcome them into society. As we see from the Latino lawyers' civic behavior, higher levels of formal education produce positive changes in civic and political participation. In this case, the opportunities to become involved in the community provided by a legal education truly do open doors for political and civic engagement by Latino lawyers, while at the same time improving our democracy through greater involvement of Latinos in all aspects of society, even if it is simply by "somebody whose civic involvement consists of being in the Yakima City Basketball League."

6

EDUCATION MATTERS

Eva was raised in a family that was plagued by alcoholism and domestic violence. Her mother managed to send her to a prestigious all-girls private school from elementary through high school. Eva went on to the University of Washington (UW) for her undergraduate studies. And so did her mother. While Eva attended UW, her mother began studying at UW law school. Her mom graduated from law school in 1994, and Eva earned her bachelor's degree in philosophy in 1997. Following her mother's footsteps, she too began studying at UW law school. By this time, Eva was a single parent of a two-year-old girl. However, she managed to graduate from law school in June 2000 and passed the bar that same year. Eva and her daughter moved to Yakima, where she began practicing law.

Eva opened up her own law firm after years of struggling in firms or working for other people. It is now one of the largest and most successful law firms in Yakima owned by a woman, and the largest one owned by a woman of color. In 2009, she was appointed to the Yakima City Council, the first Latino/a member in city history, even though Yakima is composed of more than 50 percent Latinos. She quickly became respected for her ideas on how to deal with the city's gang problems but lost re-election by 3 percent to a conservative radio talk show host. In Yakima, a Latino has never been able to win a local contested election for public office other than school board president. Eva remains active on boards and has started a neighborhood association in a gang-entrenched area.

Her daughter is now fifteen years old and is doing well in school. Eva considers herself to be very fortunate, in large part, because of her belief in the power of education to change a life. She understands that education is not always encouraged for Latinos by the community and even by teachers. Her efforts to combat gang violence are mostly to turn Latinos toward education and away from the streets.

The majority of the Latino respondents in this study are second-generation Americans who have had to balance two worlds. They pursued membership in one of the most prestigious and powerful professions in America and simultaneously tried to maintain their cultural roots by speaking Spanish and helping out in the Latino community. The majority of their parents lacked high levels of formal education—many didn't even have a high school diploma. Most of their fathers came to the United States to work as manual laborers or blue-collar workers. Given where they started, it is no wonder they have a strong desire to help other Latinos in their communities. They understand that education changes lives. This quote from one of the Latina respondents is very representative of the experiences of the Latinos interviewed:

> I made it to an elite college because I was intellectually curious and knew that education would open up a world of possibilities for me—would provide me with opportunities and information that my parents had not had. My mother only has a fifth-grade education. My father never attended school at all. I was adventurous and ambitious, and I had no idea that I would be in competition with middle-class and wealthy classmates who had been preparing for elite universities since they were five. I had never heard of the elite prep schools from which of my classmates at Yale graduated, and I had no idea that high school students actually took courses to improve their SAT scores. I also had no idea how much money elite education would cost. Paradoxically, my family's poverty worked to my advantage. As a consequence of generous financial aid—for which I will always be grateful—I was able to graduate from college with virtually no debt.

This Latina acknowledges how much her education changed her, but she was also politically astute enough to know that as a Latina, if she was going to make a difference, she would have to have the right credentials: She stated:

By the time I applied to law school, I had become highly politicized. I wanted to use law to make a difference in the world, and I knew that I [as a Latina] would not be taken seriously unless I attended a top law school.

Because of this extremely personal understanding and commitment to "make a difference in the world," one can argue that the benefit of increasing educational outcomes among Latinos has a ripple effect throughout the entire Latino community. Very few people know what these Latino respondents have been through to get to where they are as lawyers. This is especially significant considering what happens to second-generation Latinos who rebel against society in a pattern of downward assimilation, as Alejandro Portes and Rubén Rumbaut found in their research.[1] Latino youth who reject society and their immigrant parents' way of life, often find themselves severely limited in their educational and life opportunities. This is all too common.

The Latino respondents in this study were asked the following open-ended question on the survey: "What do you believe are the two or three most important issues facing the Latino community in Washington?" They were given three lines to list any answer they wanted. The most frequent response was education, which was noted fifty-four times. (The top ten issues and the number of times they were mentioned are listed in Table 6.1 in Appendix A.) Perhaps this is because most of the Latinos in this study had to face many challenges in order to enter the world of professionals.

The study participants participate in mentoring programs, speak at local high schools that have high numbers of Latinos, participate in educational outreach programs, and provide pro bono services (recall Anna from Chapter 2, who won the 2009 King County Bar Association Award). They work for the poor at nonprofit law firms that target the larger Latino community.[2] Their commitment to giving back to their communities, especially through educational improvement efforts, is aimed at keeping the pipeline of future Latino professionals flowing (for percentages, see Figure 5.1 in Appendix A). Witness what this Latino lawyer had to say:

I want to help get people to finish school and get into the ranks of maybe lawyers, doctors, etcetera. I mean, I love doing leadership conferences here because we talk to the high school kids, and although they may not be going to law school, you just want to get them to finish—to finish school. I was reading this article in *The Wall Street Journal* many years ago that really just shocked me, and that's how come I've continued working with kids whenever

I can, even through law school. When they showed statistics from Texas that showed that less than 50 percent of Latinos graduated from high school, I really thought it was a typo. That could not be true. It's just unbelievable. It affects how far these kids go—how far the community advances. So definitely, people like me and other people who have made it in the lawyer ranks etcetera, you know, are fortunate to have made it that far. You know everybody's worked hard etcetera, but definitely because other people have done this work before. But secondly, there is an obligation to somehow help people or provide the opportunity for others to actually advance, and that is just key. And my role, mostly because I love kids, is focusing through high school and being a mentor when I can. But that is just unacceptable that we have those graduation levels so . . . I want to teach high school sometime before I stop working.

At an individual level of analysis, this respondent understands the value of education. He paid his own way through Catholic high school, then university and law school. The mixture of personal effort and a deep understanding that education is crucial for one's future success, especially for Latinos, provides a guide to acting for him.

Educational opportunities for successive generations only work because others have paved the way. For example, Paul Attewell and David Lavin studied the impact of higher education on the next generation of "nontraditional" students (mostly poor and minority), who attended the eighteen-campus City University of New York, which guaranteed enrollment to New York City high school graduates beginning in the 1970s. Attewell and Lavin convincingly documented that the "democratization of public higher education . . . is the first step up the ladder of social mobility and . . . generates an upward mobility" for the children of college educated mothers.[3] Education becomes a community resource for people of color. As this Latino respondent said, education "affects how far these kids go—how far the community advances." As the previous chapter pointed out, education also impacts civic activity levels. The sense of "obligation to somehow help people or provide the opportunity for others to actually advance" is an integral piece of self-narratives of success among the Latino lawyers in this study.

At a policy level of analysis, this chapter points to the wisdom of improving educational outcomes among disenfranchised communities such as Latinos, particularly when Latinos encounter barriers in an educational system that often segregates them into a lower tier in the educational curriculum and school system.[4] The experience of most Latinos shows a lack of supportive educational policies or environments. Professor Rodolfo Acuña poignantly detailed this in a newspaper article titled, "Mexicans Are Not Dumb; The Schools Fail."[5] Acuña began by reminding readers of John Dewey's claim "that students did not fail, schools failed students." Acuña argued this has been the experience of Latinos for generations. He stated:

> For the most part, the American public schools wrote them off as failures, blaming it on their culture—called them culturally deprived or culturally disadvantaged. . . . The National Education Association came out with a study, "The Invisible Minority," part of its findings were based on a survey of the Tucson Schools. Aside from the teaching of bilingual education, the report recommended the building of pride in Mexican American students. It quotes an essay of a 13-year old eighth grade Chicana: *"To begin with, I am a Mexican. That sentence has a scent of bitterness as it is written. I feel if it weren't for my nationality I would accomplish more. My being a Mexican has brought about my lack of initiative. No matter what I attempt to do, my dark skin always makes me feel that I will fail. Another thing that 'gripes' me is that I am such a coward. I absolutely will not fight for something even if I know I'm right. I do not have the vocabulary that it would take to express myself strongly enough."*

Acuña argued that these attitudes about failure and lack of worth are self-fulfilling barriers. He used them to explain the high dropout rate among Mexican Americans. Acuña contended that the process starts with stripping Latinos of their cultural worth, which in turn, strips them of their self-worth: "Americanize them and take their identity away from them. . . . Mexican-Americans were schooled to fit a stereotype. It ingrained a negative self-image that produced the haunting words '*I feel if it weren't for my nationality I would accomplish more.*'"

This is a Latino and particularly Mexican-American story since the 1848 Treaty of Guadalupe Hidalgo, which ended the war between the United States and Mexico. Within a generation of the official end of the war, the use of the Spanish language, the practice of the Catholic religion, and diverse combinations of indigenous and Spanish customs were in sharp conflict with the Anglo culture and customs.[6] In many locations, parallel and segregated societies were established, and discriminatory laws and practices became commonplace.[7] In many instances, restricted covenants were written into real estate transfers. Mexicans could not eat at local restaurants and could not shop at local drug stores or be seen in town after sunset.[8] It was not un-common for Mexican children who could not speak English to be placed in classrooms for the mentally retarded.[9] Indeed, some schools openly denied Mexican children more than an elementary education, using "scientific rac-ism" arguments that they were inferior and should not be mixing in the same schools with Anglos.[10] Thus, in many regions of the Southwest, Latinos were segregated in schools, accorded unequal economic opportunities, kept from having an independent political voice, forced to live in conditions of extreme poverty, and blamed for many of society's problems, ranging from crime to communicable diseases.

Other ethnic and racial groups had similar experiences.[11] The other side of this second-class status for Latinos is that they were needed and used as a source of cheap labor, ultimately posing a major dilemma for agribusi-ness. In Texas, "Mexicans were attached to the new agricultural society through the construction of separate and subordinate institutions that rigidly defined their position as farm laborers."[12] The legal declarations of second-class status are largely gone, but powerful social practices that en-force the status differences remain. Some of these were described in ear-lier chapters. In this chapter, the emphasis is on educational institutions. American schools have failed Latinos, as they are failing so many others.[13]

This chapter examines some of the reasons why improving educational attainment among Latinos is important for the entire community—Latino and non-Latino alike. Among the important benefits are increasing social capital and diversifying the professions by increasing the numbers of edu-cated Latinos. It discusses some policy ideas for improving educational outcomes among Latinos. The chapter reviews literature on Latino experi-ences in educational institutions. One promising approach emerges from the story of how Jews in nineteenth-century America used education as a way to improve their quality of life. Through sound public policy commit-ments aimed at increasing the educational levels of Latinos, it is possible to increase the numbers of Latino professionals.

We should note that the discipline of political science discourages policy advocacy in scholarship. Political scientists commonly focus on the distinction between *what is* and what *ought to be*, or the "facts and values" perspective,[14] which basically argues that social scientists should remain "skeptical," "neutral," and "dispassionate" observers, who limit themselves to reporting their findings. However, Lisa García Bedolla argued, "It is imperative that social scientists make their work politically relevant, as well as constructive . . . [and that] sometimes missing from political behavior studies is a reminder of why scholars do this work in the first place, why we care about democracy or about participation in a democracy."[15] Professor García Bedolla pointed out that political scientists have a long tradition of describing what *ought to be*, going back to the motivation of John Locke and the Enlightenment thinkers.[16]

When recommendations are centered on ways to increase access, rights, or opportunities for marginalized communities, social science will unavoidably challenge dominant narratives, opening them to charges of being "too polemical" or not "objective and scientific enough." Where race and gender define social hierarchies, methodological discussions will approach contested subjects. Professor Robert Jensen, of the University of Texas at Austin, described this link between authority and identity in the academy: "My voice gets heard in large part because I am a white man with a Ph.D. who holds a professional job with status. In most settings, I speak with the assumption that people not only will listen, but will take me seriously. I speak with the assumption that my motives will not be challenged; I can rely on the perception of me as a neutral authority, someone whose observations can be trusted."[17] This is often not the case for "experts" of color, who are seen as having biased, unscientific agendas.

The current discipline of political science is very uncomfortable with making value judgments. However, in his book, *The Essentials of Political Analysis*, Philip Pollock argued, "To the extent that a value judgment is based on empirical evidence, political analysis can affect opinions by shaping the reasons for holding them."[18] Eugene Meehan demonstrated that empirical and normative claims are both knowledge-based and inherently testable. Given scarce resources devoted to social science, it is irresponsible to pursue work that does not contribute knowledge that might improve human well-being.[19] Because political science is a discipline that examines aspects of the human experience, facts can—and should—shape opinions. It is for these reasons that I argue we ought to examine ways to improve the educational outcomes for Latinos in America: (1) value judgments have been part of what political scientists have done from at least the Enlightenment period, and certainly from the founding of America; (2) the topics covered by the discipline necessitate tapping into the "human-sense" part of what we do; and (3) ideas of what should be done, or "value judgments," are based on the empirical evidence from this study. It is a value judgment based on solid evidence, and it is in line with long-standing political science disciplinary traditions interested in having practical relevance, improving democracy, and focusing on civil rights issues among a marginalized community in America. Furthermore, according to the American Political Science Association, the boundaries of the field of political science include concerns with "how power and resources are allocated in society"[20] and "critical issues such as . . . civil rights."[21] Therefore, policy ideas of what "ought to be" with regard to improving educational policy for Latinos are perfectly justifiable within the discipline and are especially important for a community that has many needs.

BENEFITS OF INCREASED EDUCATION AMONG LATINOS

We have discussed some of the many benefits Latino attorneys enjoy due to their increased levels of education. They are far more politically and civically active than Latinos who do not have law degrees. They also enjoy the economic security and professional status that neither their own parents nor most Latinos share. As a group they remain marginalized. Because of their professional status, they are now part of society in ways that most Latinos could never imagine. Latino lawyers are now in a position to choose their own life plan, one of the basic tenets of liberal societies. Political theorist Will Kymlicka argued that achieving the "good society" requires treating people with equality and autonomy. Sometimes, though, this includes protecting and promoting minority cultures, particularly when those cultures are disadvantaged and when the protection seeks to improve that disadvantage.[22] In other words, Kymlicka argued for the recognition of *difference* in contrast to a "color-blind" society and that group rights and protections ultimately lead to a good society with greater inclusiveness. This leads to the first reason for recommending public policies that improve educational attainment in the Latino community—increased social capital.

Increased Social Capital

As Chapter 5 demonstrated, improving educational attainment among Latinos in America is important in increasing bridging social capital and thus, improving our civic health as a nation. The Latino lawyers in this study have high levels of civic engagement tied to identity, as one participant described: "There is an obligation to somehow help people or provide the opportunity for others to actually advance, and that is just key." Latino lawyers are involved in many organizations, from city sports leagues to professional groups, because they feel a sense of giving back to the communities around them based on their new status as lawyers. One respondent said, "People like me and other people who have made it in the lawyer ranks, et cetera, you know, are fortunate to have made it that far." Their civic engagement is creating bridging social capital, which Putnam argued improves the civic health of communities. Their status as lawyers affords them a certain measure of legitimacy and respect that many Latinos in America do not have. Thus, expanding educational opportunities among Latinos is the key to not only improving the quality of life of Latinos but also to improving the civic health of our communities in America. Latino lawyers have demonstrated that they are on the cutting edge of bridging social capital, so the societal benefits from increased levels of educational attainment among the largest ethnic and racial group in America are far reaching.

Diversifying the Legal Profession

From the perspective of social capital, the legal profession is insufficiently diverse. Having greater numbers of Latino lawyers promotes increased social capital not just in the community but also in the legal environment. This study reveals that Latino lawyers face many challenges in the legal profession. Other attorneys of color face similar obstacles. According to the report, *Miles to Go*, and the U.S. Equal Employment Opportunity Commission's October 2003 Diversity in the Law Firms report, as reported by Molly McDonough, only 4 percent of partners are members of racialized groups.[23] The negative professional experiences described throughout this book are direct consequences of this lack of diversity. Increasing the numbers of women and racialized groups in the legal profession will eventually contribute to changing the legal environment in a number of positive ways, as the activities of the Latino attorneys in this study demonstrate. The place to start is with promoting public policies that increase the number of people of color graduating from college and then law schools.

Because Latino lawyers represent only about 2 percent of attorneys in the state of Washington, too much of their energy is expended fighting barriers to acceptance and recognition. With greater numbers, the likelihood is that the professional legal environment will have greater acceptance and understanding, as working alongside people of color becomes the norm. In turn, Latino lawyers will experience a more positive professional life and give more to their firms. But when the numbers are so low, the burdens of any change are one-sided. This is what Richard Zweigenhaft and G. William Domhoff discovered when they examined diversity in the power elite. They found that while women, minorities, and gays have made some progress in elite professions, because their numbers are so few and because the top of powerful organizations are still controlled by white Anglo-Saxon Protestant males, the impact of minorities has been limited. Usually minorities are the ones to make the most changes and sacrifices rather than white males in the organizations.[24]

Diversity is an important stated goal in the legal profession, and having more Latinos graduate from colleges and law schools will further this goal. The legal profession—including law firms—is now recognizing the importance of diversity beyond the social justice arguments. Corporate legal chiefs from companies such as Sara Lee and Shell Oil are actively seeking law firms with greater diversity because this diversity contributes to new ideas and perspectives.[25] The fact that "corporate pressure is changing the racial mix at some law firms"[26] is an example of the goal of diversity in the legal profession. McDonough stated, "Diversity is no longer just the right thing to do. It's an essential factor to compete in today's business climate."[27]

Both national and regional bar associations have adopted diversity policies. In the April 2005 issue of *Bar News*, Washington State Bar Association president Ron Ward wrote that:

> For the legal profession, diversity serves our present and future enlightened self-interest. For our country, it is the key to our continued societal viability, or our inevitable decline. In a global multinational community in which economic evolution is moving with laser-like speed, it is the test and the determinant factor as to whether we will become obsolete, or remain competitive. That inexorable fact applies to law firms and the legal community in the Northwest.[28]

Beyond the competitive edge and corporate demands to improve creativity, innovation, and new ideas by hiring attorneys with different backgrounds, Ward asked this question of the legal community, "Why Diversity?" and answered it by stating, "Because all segments of society have a right to representation by a profession that includes their peers, to have the adjudication of their legal affairs presided over by a judiciary of their peers, and to be judged by a jury of their peers."[29] For these reasons, the legal profession is committed to the goal of diversity. Having more Latinos make it through university and law school will help them reach that goal.

Diversity is increasingly recognized as an important goal in other important professions as well. For example, the Association of American Medical Colleges (AAMC) has devoted a lot of time and energy to diversifying the medical profession, including the publication of numerous reports on the status of ethnic and racial groups in the medical profession. These reports include a 2006 AAMC study called, "Diversity in the Physician Workforce: Facts and Figures 2006" and "Finishing the Bridge to Diversity." According to AAMC, Latinos comprise 2.8 percent of physicians, and African Americans comprise only 3.3 percent of physicians.[30] The AAMC also has a website called aspiringdocs.org, designed to provide outreach and recruitment for individuals from ethnic and racial minority groups interested in attending medical school.[31] As Dr. Jordan J. Cohen argued in "Finishing the Bridge to Diversity," there are important historical, practical, and moral reasons for increasing diversity in the medical profession. Like the legal profession, many in the medical profession are committed to making their profession reflect the larger population.

AFFIRMATIVE ACTION: A NEW LOOK AT AN UNPOPULAR POLICY

So how can diversity in the legal profession be achieved? This will require improving the education rates among Latinos. When only 57 percent of Latinos aged twenty-five or older have even graduated from high school, this is a huge challenge. [32] With these exceptionally low figures, there are many challenges to overcome in order to get Latinos through high school, and then on to university, and finally on to law school. This requires some difficult and often unpopular public policy approaches. Most people are in favor of social equity and diversity until it comes down to deciding on how to accomplish it. One of the most controversial public policies aimed at improving educational outcomes among disenfranchised groups is affirmative action in college admissions programs. Although it is beyond the scope of this book to discuss all the arguments (whether legal, academic, or those found in popular politics) surrounding affirmative action, it is a policy that the majority of Americans have apparently rejected, even those who have benefited from it.

For example, Michelle Alexander argued that civil rights groups and organizations have erroneously put their energy and resources into defending public policies such as affirmative action and, in the process, have lost touch with more pressing needs of people of color such as the crisis in mass incarceration of black men as a result of the Reagan Administration's War on Drugs.[33] She maintained that affirmative action not only becomes a distraction for civil rights leaders, but it also makes things worse for people of color at the very bottom of society. Affirmative action creates examples of "black exceptionalism," which whites can point to as examples of "good" choices made in life rather than bad ones by people of color, thus preventing us all from seeing the racial caste system we live under in America. Alexander described affirmative action as a "racial bribe," which people of color need to relinquish in order to begin the real work of dismantling our racial caste system, wherein our criminal justice system has one in three black men in its grips. Even the Latino attorneys interviewed were highly divided on this issue.

Despite the controversy over affirmative action and the growing shift to "color-blind" admissions in universities, the example provided to us by the Latino attorneys in this study demonstrates that affirmative action policies are needed now more than ever. However, affirmative action should be implemented differently in order to be truly effective. In short, it should begin long before disadvantaged youth are about to be considered for college admission.

The experiences of Latino lawyers teach us that race and ethnicity remain heavy obstacles in American society. Nevertheless, their success stories also demonstrate that education makes all the difference in whether one will become an active, committed member of the community. Therefore, the larger benefits of a public policy such as affirmative action are felt at many levels of society. Finding different methods to implement it will not only make the policy more effective, but more fair as well.

Why argue for the modification of an unpopular policy? In agreement with Garth Massey, based on the reality of discrimination and exclusion in America, affirmative action policy can be viewed as a requirement for a good society and for justice. Massey pointed to three strong arguments in favor of the policy, which provide for "both a logical and moral imperative" to support it.[34] They are Community Choice, Rawlsian Fairness, and the Good Society. The experiences of Latino lawyers teach us that discrimination is not gone. Massey highlighted that 97 percent of Fortune 500 companies are still headed by men, most of them white. Zweigenhaft and Domhoff found that during the last decade, there were seventy-five women and people of color heading Fortune 500 companies. However, this number is still very low. When over 90 percent of the legal profession is made up of white people, legislation to provide entry is imperative. He argued that fairness must be "guaranteed by building into laws, procedures, guidelines, and organizational practices that explicitly prohibit consumer, worker, and statistical discrimination."[35] Furthermore, we can use John Rawls's theory of justice to give voice to ethnic and racial minorities, in which society's laws are designed under a "veil of ignorance"—not knowing whether one will be poor, rich, male, female, black, Asian, Latino, white, gay or straight. Under this theory of justice, society is designed to include a fair and level playing field for all, despite differences. Massey contended that these types of protections or laws for society are exactly what affirmative action represents. He argued that by thinking of the type of future society one wants for one's children and grandchildren, such thinking would lead to supporting affirmative action. He stated, "Support for affirmative action rests, in part, on the view that different cultures enrich a society, that women's experiences are as valid as men's, that vital imagination and creativity have many sources, and that a society can be richer, more resourceful, and more at peace with itself when everyone is included, when everyone can make a contribution."[36]

Massey believed it is important to ask the question *What kind of America do we want in the future?* He pointed out that despite our history of legal discrimination—based on race, ethnicity, nationality, gender, or sexual orientation—and a "mountain of data" demonstrating that affirmative action works not only for the individual who benefits but also for the community in which they participate, most people still find it very difficult to support affirmative action.

With Massey's arguments for affirmative action in mind, one could improve upon this controversial public policy in its implementation. For example, some have argued that for affirmative action to be truly fair, it should be based on class status rather than race regarding college admission. The problem with this approach, as pointed out by William Bowen and Derek Bok, is that this view would still leave many people of color out of major institutions of higher education.[37] Others contend that by the time one gets to the point of college entrance, affirmative action is too little too late. To benefit those who truly need it, affirmative action must come far before the point of college admissions.[38]

Affirmative action in education admissions should be modified to include a combination of the two criteria used to determine whether a person should qualify for affirmative action policies for entrance into the university system: (1) In addition to race and ethnic background, affirmative action policy should be implemented in a way that will give additional consideration to children who lack inherited intellectual capital; and (2) marginalized students should be identified and assisted far earlier (in elementary school) for guidance and direction to college, in order to not lose the majority of ethnic and racial minority students, who by twelfth grade, will have been "tracked" out of college preparatory programs by educators and, thus, will be ineligible to even apply to universities.

There are many arguments against affirmative action policy—that it is reverse discrimination, that it was intended for blacks as a remedy for past racial injustice, that it stigmatizes people of color and prevents us from achieving a "color-blind" society, and so on.[39] Again, while it is beyond the scope of this book to address these issues, it is important to acknowledge them, particularly the most recent critique by Michelle Alexander, which espouses that affirmative action amounts to racial bribery that people of color should relinquish. While Alexander convincingly demonstrated that the current mass incarceration of people of color is a shame on our nation and a tragedy occurring right in front of us, she failed to show that ending attention on affirmative action will provide the motivation, reflection, and resources to shift directions and begin a movement to end mass incarceration. It is not a zero-sum proposition.

Efforts to eliminate racial injustice should be made at all levels of society. That is one of the points of this book—that even those who have "made it" face limits based on our racism. While the obstacles professionals of color face are very different from the obstacles faced by those imprisoned, this does not necessarily mean that energies do not belong in both areas. There are more than enough people committed to making this a better country for all people of color so that we don't have to choose only one area on which to focus. Furthermore, as Zweigenhaft and Domhoff demonstrated in *The New CEOs*, there is still so much inequality based on race, class, and gender among the economic power elite in America that we cannot give up diversity programs that alleviate some degree of inequality, even if they undermine other forms.[40]

Regarding the first point that along with race and ethnicity, affirmative action in higher education should reach out to minorities whose parents do not have a university education, the commonly held argument that affirmative action policy unfairly benefits people of color from the most privileged backgrounds would be addressed. Giving a slightly higher preference to individuals whose parents do not hold a college education is important for many reasons. Children who need educational guidance the most are those whose parents do not know how to help them navigate the confusing system of college education entrance requirements. This includes information about applying for scholarships and financial aid, knowing which standardized exams to take and when, and making a decision about which universities to apply to. These are just a few of the many choices that are difficult or impossible to make if one comes from a family who has never been faced with these questions or is unaware of which options are available. These are the students who need the most assistance. Affirmative action programs should target these children.

However, this is not to say that affirmative action should be limited to only those whose parents lack a formal education. Why? Because too often for people of color, there will be racial and ethnic obstacles for the children of minority professionals as they travel on their journey through America's professional circles. The example of Latino lawyers demonstrates that time and again, race and ethnicity are factors *at every stage* in their professional experiences. Therefore, until American society comes to terms with its discriminatory past and present, all people of color will need public policies that provide them with some protections against the unfair discrimination they encounter and will continue to encounter. Arguing for some type of color-blind notion of fairness is to live in denial.

One need only examine power dynamics in any large private corporation; news organization; political or government organization at the local, state, or national level; or university institution to see that the social stratification of American institutions is overwhelmingly held in the hands of white people. Pointing to the handful of minorities in any of those circles as examples of how America has now gotten beyond racism and discrimination is to prove that America is structured by and for white Americans. Until institutions are representative of *all* Americans, if we are interested in a just society, there must be public policy protections for individuals from groups largely left out of the political, professional, and financial power circles in America. However, there should also be a slightly greater preference for those ethnic and racial minority members who are also first-generation college students.

The second policy criterion is to reach out to ethnic and racial minority students early on, perhaps as early as the sixth grade (due to the fact that the majority of these students are steered away from taking the right courses to be eligible to apply to university in the first place). Educators track minorities at a national level.[41] So, by reaching out to them early, affirmative action policy would be far more inclusive and help the students who really need it, those who are systematically kept out of the college pipeline. If students are not targeted at an earlier age, many will not even take the appropriate college preparatory courses in high school that would allow them to apply to university once they are seniors. There are successful models of education programs that target minority students early on in their education. Zweigenhaft and Domhoff highlighted examples in *The New CEOs*. They stated, "Corporate-mediated educational networks . . . seek out promising students of color as early as kindergarten. . . . Without these programs, the statistics for African Americans completing post-graduate business degrees, law degrees, and master's and doctorates . . . would be even lower than they are now."[42]

Targeted efforts early on are necessary because the opposite is happening for Latinos and other people of color. It is a well-known and documented fact that Latinos are often "tracked" into vocational programs very early on. There is a vast literature documenting the barriers and unequal access to educational opportunities placed before Latinos in the elementary and secondary education system that often keep them from entering college in the United States.[43] One example of the detrimental effects of educators' tracking of Latino students, conducted by Harriet D. Romo and Toni Falbo, found that Latinos have experienced and continue to experience unequal access to education. Their book, *Latino High School Graduation: Defying the Odds*, looks at the obstacles that 100 Hispanic high school students in Texas had to overcome to earn a high school diploma. These case studies provide valuable insights into how Hispanics are too often negatively impacted by school policies such as tracking and low teacher expectations. Romo and Falbo stated:

> Our position is that the goal of public education should be to educate *all students* [emphasis in original] so that they can be productive adults and good citizens. . . . While some of the students we studied could have ob-

tained bachelor's degrees, none of them succeeded in four-year universities after high school graduation. *Their underachievement was due in part to the schools' tracking of Mexican American* [emphasis added] students into general or vocational coursework that did not train them to have the skills they needed to get a bachelor's degree or a job that offered future mobility. Most of our students did not even make it to community college.[44]

They added, "Indeed, some very bright students we studied were unable to graduate from high school because *school policies* [emphasis added] were not responsive to their needs, as children of uneducated Mexicans."[45]

The situation is worse for Latinas, who are underrepresented in the college prep track and overrepresented in vocational preparation in high school, and frequently do not complete high school. In "Slipping Through the Cracks: Dilemmas in Chicana Education," Denise Segura conducted in-depth interviews of Chicanas from mostly working-class and low-income backgrounds in the San Francisco Bay Area who have "slipped through the educational cracks." All the Latinas she interviewed were U.S. citizens—half were second generation and half were third generation—with both of their parents born in the United States as well. Segura's interviews revealed some of the injustices found in our educational system and how they affected these Latinas. With only 45 percent of Mexican-American students completing high school, she argued that the reasons underlying the poor completion rate go beyond individual successes or failures to systemic causes. According to Segura, the "personal failure" explanation is the view predominately held among educators. Segura's paper revealed a multifaceted set of barriers for Chicanas. The need to maintain traditional female roles, the legacy of a working-class background, the lack of teacher accountability, and the experience of racial harassment are just a few of the barriers with which this group of Chicanas interviewed by Segura had to deal. In the end, however, she concluded by stating:

> Within schools, teachers and counselor actions channeled Chicanas into non-academic programs offering a lower quality of instruction. Their placement into general education curriculum tracks effectively restricted their early life chances, and neither teachers nor counselors encouraged the Chicanas to attend or prepare for professional careers. Diffident instruction, lack of teacher caring, and inadequate counseling constrained the educational chances of the respondents.[46]

Until teachers, administrators, school board members, and other policy makers are sensitive and knowledgeable to the systemic ways educational policies and practices present barriers for Latinos, they will continue to "slip through the cracks" of the American educational system. Currently, the literature reveals the pattern that "if a poor female student of color remains in school, she is typically tracked in vocational, general, or special education programs without regard to her ability or potential."[47] Romo and Falbo found that parents did not know how to change the situation for their children. They stated: "We learned from the families we studied that parents of 'at risk' students were reluctant to demand that the schools take action to prevent school failure for their children. Most of the parents were demoralized by their feelings that they had failed in public schools. They also believed that they were powerless to make the schools work for their children."[48]

This is why it is so crucial to reach out to Latino students *early on*—before they are tracked out of college by educators who have systematically treated Latinos as "nobodies,"[49] and by an educational system that often focuses more on indoctrination and assimilation rather than intellectual development.[50] One can only imagine how quickly the educational rates for Latinos would increase if the same energy and resources used by educators to track Latinos away from college were used to help them get into college. But until that happens, affirmative action policy for university admissions must be targeted to Latino youth much earlier in order to make sure that the dreams they have for themselves do not get squashed by the educational system that is supposed to help those dreams be realized.

It is unlikely that affirmative action will be embraced wholeheartedly, no matter what the data show and no matter how it is implemented. However, implementing these two criteria of targeting minority children, particularly those who lack inherited intellectual capital, and helping to track them into college starting in elementary school, in combination with Massey's emphasis on thinking of the type of society we want in the future, would certainly lead to much greater access and opportunity for people like the Latino lawyers in this study. They are now contributing, productive, successful members of their communities and of their professions because of their high levels of formal education. What a country this would be if most of the largest ethnic and racial group could follow this example through the benefit of reasonable, fair, and just public policies such as affirmative action. It would keep the American dream alive for the largest ethnic and racial group in the country. Latino attorneys in Washington State currently represent only 1 percent of the legal profession, despite being the largest minority group in the state. Unless there are public policies to provide access for entrance into the profession, these numbers will not improve. However, improved educational attainment among all Latinos is what is greatly needed, or there will not be enough Latinos in the pipeline who are eligible to apply to and attend law school.

A MODEL OF HOPE: THE JEWISH EXAMPLE

Current education rates among Latinos may lead some people to believe that the situation is hopeless. However, there is a group who can provide a model for Latinos to follow. Jewish communities in America in the early twentieth century experienced many similarities to Latino communities today. They were part of a close-knit family and community who helped them survive the lack of acceptance they experienced in America; they grew up speaking a language other than English in the home (they spoke Yiddish as a first language and English as a second language); and they obviously had a different religion from the dominant Protestant belief system. Similar to Latinos today, Jews in America experienced discrimination based on language, religion, culture, and ethnicity, yet today as a group, they have achieved an excellent quality of life and have been extremely successful by most measures. Latinos nationwide have much to learn from Jews about how to improve their quality of life through an emphasis on education. In a similar vein, Zweigenhaft and Domhoff argued that Jews who successfully assimilated into the top levels of Fortune 500 companies have a lot to teach "the new CEOs" of today: blacks, Latinos, Asian Americans, and women.[51] They stated, "Much can be learned about what makes newcomers acceptable (and unacceptable) in the halls of power by studying how Jews, and which Jews, made it into the higher circles."[52]

This argument is not to suggest that one can compare the American historical experience or even current circumstances of these two groups *precisely*. Obviously, there are many fundamental differences in the historical experiences and current situation of Jews and Latinos in the United States. Nor is this to suggest that Jews currently experience complete acceptance.

First, Latinos cannot as easily follow the traditional white ethnic immigrant assimilation model that many Jews have followed during the last two generations. This included changing one's name slightly to sound less "ethnic," not identifying with one's culture, forgetting one's first language, and not practicing one's religion. In short, because of discrimination and lack of acceptance in America, many Jews have chosen to assimilate after a couple of generations by camouflaging themselves in the hopes of acceptance and equal treatment. As discussed through the experiences of Latino lawyers, the reality for racialized communities such as Latinos in America is quite different.

For communities of color, the white ethnic narrative of hard work and assimilation is held up as a model of the American dream. However, the problem with this is that certain groups have additional barriers because of their different visible physical racial characteristics, "foreign" names, and non-English language barriers that cannot as easily be overcome due to racial and ethnic differences. As the nation's largest ethnic and racial group, Latinos have not been politically and socially incorporated as easily as other white ethnic immigrants have in the past.[53] Some of the Latino lawyers' experiences described in this book demonstrate just how incomplete and inaccurate the white ethnic immigrant myth is, even for the most privileged members of the Latino community. Latinos are a racialized group in America, and the ethnic immigrant narrative is not open to them in the same way.[54]

Another important difference between the two immigrant communities is that when Jews arrived in America, it was, for most, considered a one-way trip. This is not necessarily true for Latino immigrants. Connections between home and the new country are often maintained through remittances, improved technology and communication, and even the dream of retiring back in the "old country."[55] While it is common for Latino immigrants to consider the possibility of returning to their countries of origin, in fact, most do not. In a survey of 555 migrant seasonal farmworkers in Idaho, over 70 percent planned on staying in the United States permanently.[56] Despite these caveats, there are enough important lessons that Latinos can learn from the path that Jewish communities have taken in achieving the American dream.

In *Studying the Jewish Future*, Calvin Goldscheider's demographic description of Jewish life in America in the early twentieth century is very similar to Latinos' circumstances today. Goldscheider's account revealed just how similar Latinos are today to Jewish communities around 1910. These similarities included high immigration levels, concentration in urban centers, most Jews having only a primary education, and most being trapped in occupational semiskilled to skilled factory jobs. They lived in similar circumstances to Latinos today, and their way out of their circumstances was through education. As Goldscheider noted, "Jews in the United States have become the most highly educated of all American ethnic and religious groups, of all communities in the world, and of all Jewish communities ever in recorded history."[57] However, he argued, this was not the case just four generations ago. Four generations ago, he stated, Jews, like Latinos today, faced discrimination, concentration in the cities, low levels of education, labor segregation in hard labor in factories or blue-collar work, with very few professionals. As Russ Lidman pointed out, "Jews were regarded as factory fodder in the nineteen hundreds."[58] Similarly, Latinos are predominantly engaged in manual labor in America, including slaughterhouses, construction, and in the fields—today's equivalent of factory fodder.

Goldscheider's assessment of the Jewish future described that education (always an important aspect of Jewish culture) became an important and highly emphasized Jewish value, especially in twentieth-century America. As Goldscheider stated, "When children and grandchildren became doctors and lawyers, skilled businesspeople and teachers, it was thought that this was the 'Jewish' thing to do."[59] It was their way out, but it was not always easy. Goldscheider mentioned that Jews paid a price during the transitional years. One of the costs he mentioned were the sacrifices made in families, especially between the generations with a formal education and those without one.

When one comes from a close-knit culture such as Latino or Jewish culture, even the act of moving away from home to a place that does not accept you is difficult. Not only can it damage one's relationship with one's immediate family, but it can also be a very isolating and lonely experience. Goldscheider stated, "Although parents encouraged their children to obtain a high level of education, the lifestyle associated with higher education often meant disruption and conflict between parents and children who had different educational levels and between siblings and peers who had different access to educational opportunities."[60]

Goldscheider noted that over a couple of generations, these sacrifices were well worth it, with now over 90 *percent* of Jews attending college. Similarly, the quality of life among Latinos would be very different—even if acceptance were not complete or total as is the case with Jews or the

Latino lawyers examined—if in four generations, 90 percent of Latinos obtained a college education. *Political and social incorporation and acceptance become less important if an entire community has real access to the American dream.*

This is why arguing for public policies that help improve the education rates among Latinos becomes so important not only to improving the quality of life in Latino communities, but also because by increasing the educational rates among Latinos, it keeps the hope that the American dream remains viable for all.

CONCLUSION

This chapter reviewed some of the reasons education is key in improving the quality of life in Latino communities. Although some studies showed how education is failing the Latino community, Latino lawyers' stories show us that by increasing the educational rates among Latinos, social capital is increased, diversity in the legal professions can be achieved, and most importantly, hope remains that the American dream can be vibrant and strong for communities largely lacking in inherited intellectual capital and wealth. The Jewish model provides an example of this hope. However, this cannot be done without a commitment to politically unpopular educational policies such as affirmative action and an acceptance of Latinos as deserving and full members of American society.

⑦

CONCLUSION:
LATINO PROFESSIONALS IN AMERICA

In telling the story of Latino lawyers, we find that despite the respondents' professional and economic successes there are plenty of examples of discrimination and racism within their lives. This is a finding that people do not want to hear. The "let's get beyond race" mantra of the general public is found everywhere. "When are you going to get over your 'race' thing?!" an irritated professor in graduate school asked a student who commented that a book discussed in a seminar on the civic behavior of Americans was "incomplete because it was missing the civic experiences of people of color." His tone made it perfectly clear that her observations were not welcomed and that she had better change her tune if she wanted to succeed in his class. He was clearly not open to discussions about the "race thing" in his graduate seminar in political science. The rest of the class got the message. Race was not to be discussed in his political science seminar.[1] He is not alone. Like this professor, most Americans want to get beyond discussions of race. Many white Americans are tired of it and see it as pointless and unproductive, a distraction from "real" material issues like the economy. Some even go so far as to see it as unpatriotic.

This chapter summarizes the key points of the book and discusses their significance for Latinos in America today. Having listened to the stories from the diverse group of Latino lawyers in this study, their experiences with racial hostility and discrimination suggest that despite our progress with race relations, we still have a long way to go. We may not be the society we were in the 1950s, but as Joe Feagin argued in *The White Racial Frame*, racism is still a central aspect of American society and culture. It has been this way from our nation's birth, and its basic features remain resilient.[2]

As most women's lives are shaped through gendered experiences, the experiences of most people of color center on obstacles around race, even for professionals. In our segregated society, race often determines where we go to school, whom our friends are, whom we marry, where we live, where we work, how successful we are with promotions in the workplace, how much money we make, the quality of (and access to) our medical care, and who goes to prison for using drugs and who gets probation. The list goes on. These are just some of the reasons people of color cannot get over the "race thing." No one wants to get over this "race thing" more than people of color, who continually experience the discrimination. Racism is not just (or even most importantly) a situation among individuals—it is systemic, permeating our institutions, ideology, history, and current culture.[3]

Recall in Chapter 1, the elements of Feagin's theory of the white racial frame. Feagin's extensive research showed that white Americans engage in negative beliefs about people of color or racial stereotypes. They rationalize these beliefs through narratives and interpretation. They incorporate racial images, which lead to emotional feelings about people of color—what Feagin called "racialized emotions." This results in inclinations to discriminate against people of color.[4] The current immigration debate surrounding Latinos, and specifically undocumented immigrants, as "not quite like us," "criminal," "lawbreakers," "culturally too different" from mainstream Americans and society is an example of the white racial frame. Feagin noted that the degree of oppression each immigrant group has faced has historically varied. Yet one common element is the abhorrence expressed toward each group. Feagin stated:

> From the time of their first entry into the new United States in the mid-nineteenth century, Latin American and Asian immigrants and their children have been positioned . . . somewhere on the racialized ladder below whites—with a substantial negative evaluation on the social dimensions of superior/inferior and insider/foreigner. Thus Latin American and Asian immigrants and their children, unlike earlier European immigrants by the second or third generation, have not been allowed by whites to assimilate structurally and completely into the extant white society.[5]

This is key to understanding why anti-Latino sentiment in this country runs so deep. Without this context, it would not make sense for Americans to continue to promote the tremendous suffering[6] and criminalization of people because of America's vacillating immigration policies over the decades.[7] Feagin and other scholars demonstrated that Latinos are racialized as non-white and thus experience discrimination in countless ways.

The stories from the Latino professionals surveyed and interviewed in this study provide examples of the white racial frame. They also provide examples of counterframes, such as their motivation to become lawyers to combat discrimination for Latinos and the type of law practice chosen. However, not many scholars research the experiences of the most advantaged members among Latinos.[8] Their experiences are not as well known as the circumstances in which the majority of Latinos live.

Although statistics on the well-being of blacks and Latinos have been mentioned throughout this book, it is important to reiterate the following relevant information: "Blacks earn 62 cents for every dollar of white income, and Latinos earn 68 cents for every dollar of white income; Blacks and Latinos are 2.9 and 2.7 times as likely, respectively, to live in poverty than whites; Black and Latino children are 3.3 and 2.9 times as likely, respectively, to live in poverty than white children."[9] More specifically, an examination of median net worth reveals that Latino households are worth around $8,000 compared to non-Hispanic white households, which are worth close to $90,000, and more than a quarter of Latinos have either a zero or negative net worth compared to 13 percent of white households.[10]

Regarding educational levels, current census data indicate that only 57 percent of Latinos aged twenty-five or older have graduated from high school compared to 88.7 percent of the non-Hispanic white population;[11] only 12.1 percent of Latinos have a bachelor's degree or more compared to 30.6 percent of non-Hispanic whites;[12] only 5 percent of Latinos nationally have achieved master's and professional degrees; and only around 3 percent have achieved doctoral degrees.[13] It is important to mention these statistics again to underscore that the Latino respondents in this study have "made it" according to most measures of success.

The group of highly accomplished Latino professionals documented in this book have a lot to teach us about America, education, and race relations today. A better understanding of the experiences of Latino professionals yields valuable insights and lessons for how to improve the difficult circumstances of all Latinos and underscores how important it is to get beyond our current racial hierarchical structure in America.

THE WHITE RACIAL FRAME, SOCIAL CAPITAL, AND LATINO PROFESSIONALS

The Latino professionals highlighted in this study teach us three main lessons about race in America today, particularly for people of color who are "in between" the historically predominant "Black-White Paradigm."[14] Feagin's white racial frame theory helps us understand the first two lessons, and the social capital theory, made popular by Robert Putnam, helps us understand the third key point. The major findings from this study are as follow: (1) Latinos remain marginalized, even as they gain educational and economic parity with white professionals; (2) popular notions of a color-blind society and the push for color-blind public policies do not work in a society that remains racially unequal; and (3) despite these circumstances, Latino professionals use their expertise and training in the law to become civically, professionally, and politically engaged in ways they could not have been without their professional credentials and status.

The Marginalization of Latino Professionals

It is my hope that the stories documented throughout this book can help Americans be more accepting of Latinos in this country. As the stories demonstrate, becoming a lawyer clearly does not mean one is accepted into the world of legal professionals. They are not the only minority group to experience such marginalization. Chou and Feagin demonstrated with their data on Asian Americans that ethnic and racial groups cannot expect to be treated better by whites even once they are professionals.[15] This is true for African Americans as well. Jennifer Hochschild's findings were paradoxical but revealed that middle-class success for African Americans correlates with their growing disbelief in the reality of the American dream.[16] Feagin also found this to be the case for Latino professionals. Discrimination permeates Latino professional environments. He stated:

> Well-educated Mexican American and other Latino workers also report
> discrimination. In Silicon Valley, some Latino employees have recently

filed lawsuits to fight the discrimination they encounter in high tech firms. Indeed, even in the humanities, social sciences, and professional schools in institutions of higher education, there are many cases of routine discrimination, in both hiring and promotion. A distinguished professor at the University of Texas (Austin), Enrique Trueba, has recounted numerous cases of Latino/a faculty who have faced discrimination in higher education.[17]

The fact that the Latino professionals in this study are doing very well—at least as measured by their professional status, income, and professional satisfaction and engagement—paradoxically demonstrates how deep racism and discrimination run in America. We know Latinos are racialized in this country when the most successful members of the Latino community, those who have "done everything right," regularly experience discrimination. The evidence highlighted throughout this book shows that Latino lawyers face constantly challenging experiences as members of an ethnic and racial minority. As the experiences of these Latino professionals demonstrate, prejudice and discrimination are still real issues with which they must contend.

This can be seen in the comments the Latino attorneys make, such as stating they are often mistaken as "court clerks, bailiffs, or interpreters" rather than as the representing counsel. Other statements they make address having to deal with people's prejudice or societal stereotypes. Some of the Latino respondents point out that they receive belittling treatment from their colleagues. All these examples point not only to the marginalization of Latinos in firms and courtrooms but also to the larger issue of systemic racism in the legal environment.

The typical firm is still stratified by race and class, to the exclusion of Latino attorneys. Statements the Latino respondents made about not fitting in with the "big firm culture" or not being contacted by Anglo clients, or being viewed as "threatening," "unqualified," or "undesirable" in firm environments, coupled with the low rates of people of color making partner, demonstrate racial and ethnic inequality in our legal institutions.

The situation in law firms illustrates how institutional racism operates, whether in private firms or in government organizations and programs. In Robert Lieberman's book regarding the history of race and the welfare state, he explained how the New Deal policy of Social Security originally excluded blacks from receiving any benefits because it excluded occupations in which blacks were heavily concentrated. This institutional exclusion was not due to the blatant exclusion of blacks but rather because of institutional structures that restricted black access to benefits.[18]

Restriction of benefits occurs with these Latino lawyers, who tell us they do not "fit in" with the firm environment. The fact that they are not making partner both at the national level or in Washington State law firms points to the importance of examining the institutional structure of law firms, which may be keeping Latinos from making partner. How? Latino lawyers are most likely being excluded from insider referrals or other important information by their predominately white colleagues. In addition, Latino lawyers may be experiencing psychological warfare within their firms—making the road to partner almost impossible.[19] Lieberman argued that the premise of institutional racism is that racial inequality is *built into structures* of American politics and that citizens do not necessarily have to be racist or even have racist intentions to perpetuate systemic racism in institutions.[20] Based upon the stories that the Latino respondents shared in this study, the same can be said of law firms. Too many of the Latino respondents had these experiences for them to be considered individual anomalies.[21] That people because of their race and culture remain vulnerable to discrimination or mistreatment by their colleagues or clients, after having acquired skills and expertise and educational and professional credentials, points to the power of systemic racism in America today.[22]

Political theorists K. Anthony Appiah and Amy Gutmann illustrated the depth of racial injustice in America with an excerpt from an interview of famous tennis player, Arthur Ashe, in which the interviewer asked him if AIDS was the worst burden he had had to deal with. Ashe responded, "Being black is the greatest burden I've had to bear."[23] Ashe died of complications related to AIDS in 1993 at age fifty. This speaks volumes about the experiences of marginalization for people of color, even for those who are rich and famous tennis players like Arthur Ashe and those who are educated professionals from racial and ethnic groups such as Latinos, African Americans, Asian Americans, or from other racialized groups in America today.[24] As Appiah and Gutmann argued, "Racial injustice may be the most morally and intellectually vexing problem in the public life of this country."[25] If racial injustice is unethical and immoral, then why are white people reluctant to change this system, particularly in a society in which the values of equality, justice, and freedom are our foundational principles? It is not from lack of knowledge or awareness about the problem. As Feagin stated:

Today, in the United States there are too many people who know the white racist framing and the racial hierarchy with its extreme inequalities are quite immoral and need to be systematically and rapidly replaced, yet remain at a distance as passive bystanders and do not object to even the more overt aspects of racist performances and other racist actions by whites around them.[26]

Why is this? Is this because of a lack of empathy for people of color? One answer lies with Michelle Alexander's assertion of racial indifference. Alexander argued that racial indifference has been an important and over-looked concept found in every era of racial oppression, from slavery, to the Jim Crow era, to what she contends is our current racial caste system. Alexander argued that the War on Drugs has created a new caste system resulting in the mass incarceration of black and brown men.[27] And we are indifferent to it. Rather than deal with the root problems for people of color such as inadequate educational opportunities or poverty, we crimi-nalize them through a racially biased drug sentencing system. So when "those children" grow up and use or deal drugs, we can then focus on their "bad choices" and forget about them. Whatever the reasons for this indifference, Alexander argued that anti-racist struggles must begin with a discussion of how to change the problems found in the criminal justice system in America.

There are abundant societal benefits to ending racism, as Feagin outlined in his concluding chapter of *The White Racial Frame.* These include eco-nomic gains for society as a whole when marginalized groups such as African Americans, or in this case, Latinos can "come out from under the shroud of racism and gain much new energy for seeking their broader group and soci-etal goals."[28] Also, democracy would improve when people of color are fully welcomed and included in all of America's institutions, including political ones. Feagin argued that one of the costs of excluding and marginalizing eth-nic and racial minority groups is losing the valuable contributions they could bring to improving our society: contributions in art, knowledge, creativity, and so on. Feagin stated, "All Americans will benefit from the inclusion of new knowledges in the public and private spheres. . . . A great expansion of social and political democracy will make much essential knowledge *finally available* for the long-term development and improvement of what is still very much a democracy 'under construction.'"[29]

There are three ways this can be accomplished. First, Feagin con-tended we must begin enforcing our civil rights laws, which have never

been seriously enforced in many policy areas, from housing to employment. Second, Feagin believed we need real diversity in this nation's
political leadership. Congressional scholars Roger H. Davidson, Walter J.
Oleszek, and Frances Lee stated, "There is no substitute for having a
member of one's own group in a position of influence, and many groups
do not receive representation commensurate with their presence in the
population."[30] What does it mean with regard to the white racial frame
when less than 20 percent of Congress is female, less than 10 percent is
black, and less than 5 percent is Latino? Do our representative institutions need to exhibit what is known as descriptive representation, where
representatives look like their constituents? Or are our policies best made
with what is known as substantive representation, where representatives
need not represent the descriptive characteristics of their constituents
but can in theory still represent their points of view?

One quick look at our nation's public policies easily answers this question.
Finally, we can change racism in society through our educational institutions
and through the mass media. According to Feagin, doing these three things
would change the white racial frame to a liberty and justice frame. According to him, though, first we need to acknowledge how we all benefit from
dismantling racial hierarchies. He optimistically argued, "Systemic racism
can and will eventually be replaced with a more humane and just political-
economic system, or U.S. society will not likely survive in the long term.[31]
Unfortunately, today the continued marginalization of Latinos and other
people of color in America goes far beyond the low visibility of Latino faces
in education, popular culture, mainstream media, and political representation and leadership at all levels of government. As the experiences of the
Latino respondents in this study show, marginalization is pervasive in our
professional environments as well.

FAR FROM A COLOR-BLIND SOCIETY

In a related point, the experiences of the Latino lawyers in this study
demonstrate that we are far from a color-blind society. Ultimately, their
experiences teach us that race is an ongoing process in America.[32] It may
change and evolve, but discrimination based on race, ethnicity, and culture
has certainly not been eliminated from our society. If we desire to build
a more cohesive, less "disunited" America and we believe that a liberty

and justice frame—as Feagin called it—should be available to everyone, regardless of race, ethnicity, or culture, then there is much to be learned from studying the experiences and behaviors of Latino lawyers—both positive and negative. Race is experienced by Latino lawyers at each step along the way, from the interview process to the "systemic and long-held racial discrimination" practices in the profession. The notion that "people don't take you seriously," or the "presumption of incompetence" and the "negative stereotypes" of being "lazy" or having benefited from "affirmative action" all highlight how we are far from the color-blind society people would like to believe that we live in.

This point is made by many scholars of race such as Feagin, Omi and Winant, Cobas, Duany, Bonilla-Silva, and others.[33] A color-blind society sounds appealing because it plays on historical concepts of the American foundational ideology of the United States as a land of equality and opportunity; however, this is fiction. Eduardo Bonilla-Silva observed in his book *Racism Without Racists* that many Americans sincerely believe we are living in a post-racial society, particularly with the election of our first black president. Bonilla-Silva argued that because most Americans believe we are living in a color-blind society, if minorities don't succeed, it is because they don't work hard enough or because of learned behavior from their dysfunctional culture(s). However, Bonilla-Silva painstakingly documented that along almost every measure of well-being, Americans are stratified by race. He demonstrated that "racial considerations shade almost everything in America."[34] His research documented the following areas where Americans are still impacted by race:

> Blacks and dark-skinned racial minorities lag well behind whites in virtually every area of social life; they are about three times more likely to be poor than whites, earn about 40 percent less than whites, and have about an eighth of the net worth that whites have. They also receive an inferior education compared to whites, even when they attend integrated institutions. In terms of housing, black-owned units comparable to ones owned by whites are valued at 35 percent less. Blacks and Latinos also have less access to the entire housing market because whites, through a variety of exclusionary practices by white realtors and homeowners, have been successful in effectively limiting their entrance into many neighborhoods. Blacks receive impolite treatment in stores, in restaurants, and in a host of other commercial transactions. Researchers have also documented that blacks pay more for goods such as cars and houses than do whites. Finally, blacks and dark-skinned Latinos are

the targets of racial profiling by the police that, combined with the highly racialized criminal court system, guarantees their overrepresentation among those arrested, prosecuted, incarcerated, and if charged for a capital crime, executed.[35]

From this list of examples by Bonilla-Silva, it is clear we have a long way to go with regard to race in America. If we did not possess the type of racial indifference that Alexander talked about we could not rationalize the mass incarceration of blacks and Latinos; we could not accept the current treatment of farmworkers, meat packers, and other laborers, which exposes them to dangerous pesticides, terrible working conditions, and inadequate health coverage; we would protest against legislation such as Arizona's SB 1070, which allows for the civil rights and civil liberties violations of Latinos; we would demand Congress pass the DREAM Act that would have allowed children brought to the United States by their parents but raised in the United States the opportunity to fulfill their human potential and one day be productive members of society; and we would not tolerate the separation of children from their parents as is done whenever an undocumented parent is deported. We clearly have a long way to go in order to achieve racial justice in America. And the white racial frame is a powerful tool for analyzing the inequitable circumstances and conditions of people of color in America.

Still, we have made progress with regard to civil rights since Jim Crow America. For example, Du Bois documented a time in American history when simply the education of a black man resulted in tragedy.[36] His essay called "Of the Coming of John" described the experience of a black man who grew up in the Deep South during Jim Crow. He left to be educated in the North, only to discover that the North was not the land of racial equality he hoped it would be. Now as an educated professional black man, John returns to the South, only to be considered "dangerous." It wasn't long before circumstances led to his lynching.[37] Yes, we have come a long way from the circumstances described by Du Bois.

However, we currently operate under different forms of racial injustice. Whether it is indifference to racial injustice, as Alexander argued; whether we are living with what Bonilla-Silva referred to as a "new racism," whereby racism is now "subtle, institutional, and apparently nonracial";[38] or whether we are caught up in a post-Obama color-blind way of thinking about racism, a lot of work remains to be done in order to be accepting and inclusive of all members of society. Amy Gutmann argued that the idea of color-blindness appeals to many because it makes us think of the "ideal America." However, this book adds to the conclusions reached by these scholars: It is inaccurate to believe in the concept of color-blindness. For example, just looking at one issue, the wealth gap between whites and blacks is so huge that Feagin argued it would take 634 years to close.[39] Rather than pretend we live in a color-blind society and should therefore be promoting class-based public policies instead of race-based policies to remedy our current inequality based on class and race, Gutmann's response is to argue for both. She stated, "Class conscious and color conscious policies are both necessary, neither is sufficient, to address racial injustice."[40] Both are needed because race and class are so closely linked, according to Gutmann. She contended that:

> Color consciousness . . . faces up to the fact that Americans today are still identified by their color and treated in distinct, often morally indefensible ways by virtue of it. Not to be color conscious is not to face up to this fact. The color of Americans significantly affects their life chances and experiences, not for any essentialist reasons but for no less significant historical and social reasons, which no single individual is sufficiently powerful to change.[41]

The development of Latino professionals—and other communities of color—who become active members of both the mainstream white community and their own communities must be nurtured and expanded through color-conscious public policies.[42] Relevant to this research, it includes public policies that promote a growing middle class among other ethnic and racial communities so that when Asian professionals, black professionals, Latino professionals, Indian professionals, and others try to address the multiple needs in their communities, they will not be as isolated as most of the Latino professionals in this study are.

CIVIC ENGAGEMENT AMONG LATINO PROFESSIONALS

Despite the struggles the Latino respondents experience in their communities and in their careers, they continue to participate in professional and civic arenas unheard of for generations of Latinos before them. This participation promotes what Robert Putnam referred to as "bridging" social capital, which can be the foundation of a liberty and justice frame for America, if it is to be inclusive and open. This is in part because research demonstrates that contact between Latinos and whites reduces prejudice among both groups, *but especially among whites.*[43] The participation or "contact" among Latinos in arenas previously closed to them is creating a more tolerant, less prejudicial society. This we have seen from the high degree of civic engagement, professional success, and commitments to bridging social capital among Latino professionals and is one of the reasons why the civic and professional behavior among Latinos is so important.

First, it is important to highlight the significance of the Latino lawyers' civic contributions. Much of what is known about Latinos and politics is focused primarily on electoral behavior, representation, ideology, and interest group politics. While those aspects are important, there is a lot less known about civic engagement and community connectedness beyond mainstream political topics. This study reveals a tremendous diversity of involvement, rich personal experiences, and complex reasons behind civic engagement efforts among a highly engaged group of Latino professionals. They are active in a variety of civic endeavors as well as professional organizations. Their reasons for their professional and civic activism are as diverse as their chosen civic commitments, from volunteering on campaigns and giving money to charities, to participating in city basketball leagues.

The Latino respondents' commitments to civic engagement benefit the communities in which they live and foster democracy for the larger society through their dedication and participation, both of which are strongly motivated by their ethnic identity. As highlighted in Chapter 2, over 47 percent spoke Spanish as their first language, and over half (53.6 percent) indicated that they currently speak Spanish for work. Furthermore, 38.6 percent indicated that they currently speak both Spanish and English socially, and 54.9 percent celebrated Latino holidays while growing up. Yet, over half have chosen marriage partners from other racial and ethnic groups. These findings demonstrate how truly bicultural these Latino professionals can be. The importance of one's racial and cultural identity to one's sense of value and self-worth clearly impacts one's political and civic commitments.[44] In addition, the freedom to choose what one believes is the "good life" is intimately tied to one's culture and self-identity.[45]

Perhaps how well these Latino attorneys are doing—at least as measured by their professional status, income, and civic engagement behaviors—paradoxically demonstrates the power of the barriers to assimilation.

Societal exclusion, not lack of effort on the part of Latinos, is a very real roadblock. One need only look at the persistent inequality and exclusion of Latinos by measuring current levels of education attainment, lack of health care, numbers in the criminal justice system, and levels of poverty to see that Latino communities still face barriers and obstacles to political and social incorporation in America.

Because Latino professionals are engaged in their profession, involved in the communities in which they live, and very committed to the Latino community as well, one can argue that they are promoters of "social capital." Their commitments are a testament to the richness, tenacity, and perseverance of Latinos in American society, despite the fact they are not welcomed or accepted in many arenas.

KEY IMPLICATIONS

The three main points from this study—that Latino professionals remain marginalized, that notions of color-blindness are misguided, and that Latino professionals are highly engaged in their professions and in their communities—lead to some key implications to consider as some final thoughts. These include implications for the legal profession to consider, increasing awareness of gender issues, and political implications for Latino professionals of all kinds in America.

First, there are important implications for the legal profession. The American Bar Association has long been concerned with the nature of the civic activities of the legal profession, as reviewed in Chapter 1. The results of this study regarding Latinos are consistent with Brint and Levy's[46] and Heinz et al.'s conclusions[47] that lawyers are highly committed to civic activities and contribute to increased levels of social capital in their communities. Heinz et al. found that over 70 percent of the lawyers they surveyed in Chicago are involved in at least one type of civic association.

The data in this study had similar findings. For example, Washington lawyer rates of participation showed that 86.9 percent of the comparison group was involved in one or more types of civic associations, and 80.4 percent of the Latino attorneys were engaged in one or more civic activities. Furthermore, Latino attorneys are very satisfied with both the law school education they received (with close to 50 percent indicating that they

were "Very Satisfied" with their law school education) and their choice
of profession (84.2 percent indicated that they were also "Very Satisfied"
with their jobs as lawyers). This set of observations raises another important question: If Latino attorneys are so well socialized by their law school
education, and if they feel so positive about their career choice, then why
are they not making it to the ranks of partner in law firms? A June 4, 2001,
article in *The Seattle Times*, "Diversity Lacking in the Legal Profession,"
by Alex Fryer, highlighted this point. He also brought attention to the fact
that "the lack of diversity will become even more pronounced in the next
few years" due to I-200. An August 7, 2001, *New York Times* article, "Few
Minorities Rising to Law Partner," by Jonathan Glater, also revealed that
this is not a phenomenon unique to Washington State, as does the American Bar Association report *Miles to Go*.[48]

The experiences of Latino attorneys highlight that there is a widespread
sense of isolation and at times, even open hostility, in the legal profession
toward attorneys of color.[49] Their negative experiences require a lot of effort to deal with, going above and beyond their daily professional responsibilities and commitments. Such commitments and responsibilities are
already taxing for many ethnic and racial professionals, who are typically
first-generation professionals trying to maintain a balance between pursuing their new roles as professionals and maintaining their connections to
their communities of origin. The extra burden of having to "prove oneself"
again and again often creates oversensitivity and self-doubt on the part
of Latinos, feelings that contribute to many Latino attorneys questioning
why they should participate in professional and civic associations and community outreach. As one Yakima Latina attorney mentioned, "You get cut
down; you get cut down." Or worse yet, as another focus-group participant
commented, "It's like putting yourself on the fire front to be a target."
Perhaps this pervasive notion of having to be many times better than
non-Latino attorneys to succeed and get professional respect is one of the
reasons why Latino lawyers have transferred out of law firms or lessened
their civic engagement efforts over the years or why, as one focus group
participant claimed, "I don't want to do the Bar Association. I don't want
to do all the [mainstream organizations]. I just don't want to do it," and has
decided to completely leave mainstream association interactions entirely.

This marginalization is so great that some of the respondents have opted
out of mainstream civic and professional organizations all together. On the
other hand, other Latino lawyers argue that the discrimination they experi-

ence in their profession is all the more reason to keep on trying. Other Latino attorneys interviewed argued forcefully that neither lack of time, nor
discomfort, nor any other reasons constitute sufficient excuses to opt out
of using their newfound professional status and privilege to both educate
their non-Latino colleagues on Latino life and work toward advancement
in the Latino community. However, an insightful finding is that the majority of Latino lawyers in these focus groups, especially the one conducted in
Yakima, maintained that participating in broad mainstream associations is
indeed the way to help the Latino community, no matter how uncomfortable it may be at times. Therefore, regardless of the barriers placed before
them, they continue to be involved in mainstream activities and efforts, as
this quotation from a longtime attorney in Yakima revealed:

> I believe also that we should be involved in the general community, and I try
> to be as much as I can. Sometimes, it's very difficult because of the "vibes"
> that I feel, or sometimes when I speak up about a Latino issue, you can just
> feel the tension, "Oh, there they go again complaining about whatever." *But
> I think it is really important for us as attorneys to participate in just the
> general community as well. I think that does help the Latino community all
> by itself.*

Therefore, this study has clear implications for the professional legal
community, but it also has implications for every professional group who is
hoping to diversify, such as the medical field, the corporate world, government, or academia. Given the fact that the Latinos in this study are highly
satisfied with their choice of profession and are civically engaged in comparable ways to the comparison group of non-Latino attorneys, it is essential
that professions take the steps required to ensure that more Latinos and
other minorities make it in their chosen professions, whether that includes
tenure at universities or partners at law firms. If professions do not provide
the mentoring and support needed to do this, then we will have increased
marginalization in the professions and will lose an opportunity to promote
social cohesion among an increasingly diverse country—especially in light
of the history of exclusion in the legal field, in this case.[50]

Although one may argue that professionals of color are well aware that
they will have to work harder than white Americans, this does not ease the
feelings of exhaustion, doubt, bitterness, and resentment associated with
continually having to prove themselves. This is all energy that could better
be placed, in terms of serving as role models to youth and in other ways to

improve their communities. Most white colleagues and clients do not understand that Latinos and other people of color (especially those who are from working-class backgrounds and are lacking in inherited intellectual capital) feel this way. This gulf between white and non-white groups is a barrier to understanding.

Second, there are some essential findings based on gender to address. As discussed in Chapter 4, women of color encounter additional unique obstacles in the legal profession. For example, there are persistent problems such as being "pigeonholed" in family law positions, low representation in law school faculty positions, a high attrition rate at law firms (close to 86 *percent* of minority women leave law firms within seven years), and minority males vastly outnumbering minority females in the areas of law firm partners, patent lawyers, and judges. The combination of race, class, and gender exacerbates inequality, even for lawyers. In addition, some of the main findings, specifically on Latina lawyers in this study, indicate that an amazing 87.8 percent of Latinas were either "Very Satisfied" or "Moderately Satisfied" with the type of law they currently practice compared to 82.8 percent of females from the comparison group and 81.6 percent of Latino attorneys. This study found that Latina attorneys faced additional challenges from the Latino culture, the legal profession, and the community.

The Latina respondents in this study are often caught between unreasonably rigid gender roles in Latino culture and stereotypes and limitations from mainstream white society. As one attorney from Seattle stated, "I think people need to understand the challenges of becoming a lawyer in spite of our culture that expects different from us, from our families that expect less from us, from our husbands that are not always supportive. The fact is that in our culture humbleness is a virtue, but not in American culture. That culturally, we sometimes feel caught between acting as advocates for Latinos in an American system or acting as Americans representing foreigners." In addition, not only did these Latina lawyers feel they had to "work twice as hard," but in addition, Latina lawyers faced situations such as dealing with comments from their colleagues like "What do I have to do to get a date with you?" Finally, an important and unexpected finding was the community challenges Latina lawyers face. When asked, "Do you feel part of the local geographic community where you work?" just over half (53.8 percent) of the Latina attorneys agreed. This was one of the greatest gender differences between the male and female Latino attorneys. These are some of the gender differences found in this study and confirmed by the survey and testimonials from the Latina attorneys interviewed. Clearly, if we only examine the issues around race and ignore obstacles and oppression based on how gender intersects with race, we have not done the work that needs to be done to ensure our professional environments are equitable for everyone.

Finally, it is important to examine the political implications for Latino professionals in America. For example, Luis Fraga and collegues documented the experiences of Latinos in America in *Latino Lives in America: Making It Home.* Fraga et al. convincingly documented the experiences of Latino respondents in fifteen states and Washington, D.C., to determine how successful Latinos are in making a home for themselves in America. The authors found that as a marginalized community, Latinos' process of assimilation and acculturation to America is not so simple.[51] After examining six topics, including notions of the American dream and assimilation, education, discrimination, new settlement patterns, transnationalism, and identity, Fraga et al. stated:

> [I]t is not a question of whether Latinos see themselves as wishing to or try-ing to make America their home but rather how and how quickly they are doing so and the impediments they encounter. . . . Their progress is clearly affected by Latinos' unique situations . . . as well as broader social factors associated with socioeconomic inequality and prevailing norms about what it means to be American.[52]

The experiences detailed in this book support Fraga et al.'s findings. The Latino lawyers in this study are trying to be part of their profession and their community. They are doing what other Americans are doing. They work hard, and they believe that education is the key to improvement for themselves, as evidenced by their successful completion of a bachelor's degree and then a legal education, but also as evidenced in their commit-ment to helping other Latinos achieve higher education. They participate in their profession, their community, and politics. However, investigating the professional, civic, and political experiences of Latino professionals through quantitative and qualitative data sources provides an incontrovert-ible example that supports how the theory of the white racial frame oper-ates and how Latinos are still not accepted in America.

Similar to the findings from Fraga et al., the Latino lawyers in this study have found that acceptance into mainstream American political and professional life is not so simple. Looking at individuals in one of the most powerful professions coming from one of the most disadvantaged and historically marginalized communities in America provides important information about how much anti-racist work still needs to be done. As political theorist Will Kymlicka maintained, respecting and protecting unique and diverse cultures is the true work of creating social integration. These Latino professionals are doing precisely that.

However, in today's anti-immigrant, anti-Latino climate, energy is once again spent on trying to convince Americans that Latinos will not destroy Western civilization, that they will not culturally divide the country, and that they are not here to *"reconquistar"* America. These are cyclical, old arguments that need to be put to rest. In fact, a quick glance at American history demonstrates their cyclical nature. If they were not so damaging to the Latino community, this latest round of anti-Latino sentiment would be intellectually boring. How often can Latinos be scapegoated? Why does it return every couple of decades? We have been down this road so many times that it is amazing it continues to work. Latinos have not destroyed American culture thus far, so the country needs to get over its defensiveness and scapegoating of Latinos and deal with the real reasons behind our economic, social, and political problems.

If we care about expanding and strengthening our democracy and improving the civic health of our society, would it not make sense to find a way to incorporate the largest ethnic and racial group into American society at all levels? This is in America's national self-interest as well as in keeping with her ideals of equity, liberty, and freedom of opportunity. For Latinos, particularly dark-skinned Latinos, the lack of acceptance is palpable in the grocery stores (especially during the harvest season in many farming communities around the country) by the looks received by and treatment from other customers, as well as by store employees. It is evident in the inner-city stores, such as standing in line at a Wal-Mart and overhearing an angry customer complaining that all the clerks are "Hispanic." It is evident driving home every day after work when someone is harassed repeatedly by the same police officer on the same highway for "driving while brown." It is evident on the facial expressions of people in churches in areas like Siler City, North Carolina, which has only recently experienced the increased arrival of Mexican migrants to their community. And it is evident by the experiences of Latino professionals highlighted in this study that they are not welcomed into the full range of what it means to be an American.

These are just some of the ways that life is experienced by Latinos in the United States. This lack of acceptance as full and equal citizens has carried over into not only professional environments but also into American universities, where there has been a growing backlash and resentment toward multicultural centers and affirmative action policies. This lack of acceptance of Latinos in America goes far beyond the low visibility of Latino faces in popular culture and mainstream media, or lack of political representation and leadership at all levels of government. This lack of acceptance is pervasive across America.[53]

The findings from this study raise a few questions as well. Given that Latino professionals are engaging in both mainstream and Latino community-building efforts, research questions to consider in future studies should include: How can more Americans begin to see Latinos as a most welcome part of American society and culture, rather than as perpetual foreigners and outsiders? How can more white people in American society begin to value the contributions from all people of color, particularly given the fact that demographic changes are inevitable and having a large group of people of color and a defensive minority white group portends for a sad future for this country? This is not to discount the point that white people have struggles as well, but it is to point out that in most circumstances, Latinos and other people of color encounter *additional and completely unnecessary obstacles that are unique to their racial status*. We would all benefit from research that exposes our faults along issues of social justice, race, and equality because we all benefit from finding solutions that address these issues.

In this conclusion, consider that elite white groups need to relinquish the system of racial hierarchy and see the benefits of having a truly multiracial society, without asking people of color to "sell out" and act, talk, think, and try to be like white people in order to succeed. Elite white groups need to make a place at the table for people of color in this democracy, without imposing absurd notions such as the "model minority," which seeks to benefit some people of color who "behave," without being truly open to *all* people of color. Everyone needs to participate in this country so our principles of justice and liberty can finally match our racial reality. As the participants in this study plainly show, Latino professionals are doing their part. Now it is time for others to do their part as well.

If people do not care or are not committed to changing the white racial frame that we all live under, we will all lose. What is the cost to society at large if public policies that have demonstrated widespread benefits in increasing educational outcomes, social capital, and economic parity among diverse communities are discontinued? What is the cost to America's civic, social, and economic health of the dismantling of educational policies that promote access to higher education and result in the kinds of community commitments across the board that these Latino professionals exhibit? As Michele Moses argued in defense of race-based educational policies, without them America is seriously lacking in fundamental fairness and equality. She stated: "Ultimately, if we do nothing and we say nothing to protest the move away from race-conscious educational policies, then we will be left with nothing but the empty and meaningless rhetoric of democracy and opportunity."[54] All these questions become especially timely now that Latinos are the largest racial and ethnic community in the country and are still racially and socially marginalized. Their ongoing struggle for acceptance and integration will test just how democratic, open, and free America truly can be. It is my hope that learning about the professional, civic, and community experiences of Latino professionals will help bring us closer to welcoming all Latinos as full and equal members of American society.

FIGURES AND TABLES

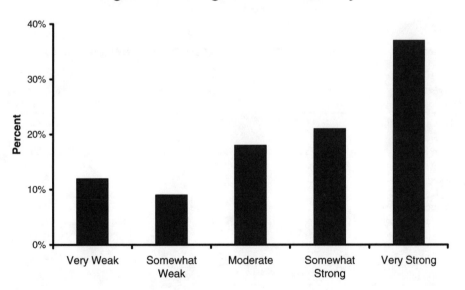

Figure 2.1 Strength of Latino Identity

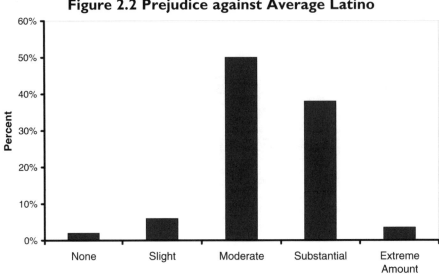

Figure 2.2 Prejudice against Average Latino

Table 2.1. Level of Educational Attainment of the Parents of Washington Lawyers

Highest Grade Completed	Mother's Educational Background		Father's Educational Background	
	Latinos (n = 99)	Comparison Group (n = 739)	Latinos (n = 99)	Comparison Group (n = 739)
Not a High School Graduate	43.4%	5.4%	38.4%	7.6%
High School Graduate	22.2%	34.6%	24.2%	24.8%
Some College (no degree)	5.1%	10.7%	6.1%	8.0%
Associate Degree	5.1%	7.3%	4.0%	4.1%
Bachelor's Degree	15.2%	27.5%	15.2%	24.4%
Some Graduate Work (no degree)	—	0.3%	—	0.1%
Graduate Degree	8.1%	13.1%	10.1%	21.9%
Law Degree	1.0%	1.1%	2.0%	9.0%

Table 2.2. Occupation of Lawyers' Parents While in K-12 Grades

| | Mother's Occupational Background | | Father's Occupational Background | |
Occupational Category	Latinos (n = 101)	Comparison Group (n = 722)	Latinos (n = 98)	Comparison Group (n = 733)
Farmer, rancher	—	0.4%	1.0%	2.6%
Professional (lawyer, teacher, doctor)	13.9%	22.9%	29.6%	45.0%
Business owner	2.0%	3.5%	7.1%	10.6%
Manual worker/ blue collar	21.8%	4.7%	44.9%	20.2%
Office worker/ white collar	16.8%	15.2%	12.2%	16.6%
Executive (management, director)	1.0%	0.6%	1.0%	3.3%
Homemaker	40.6%	51.5%	—	—
Student	—	0.1%	—	0.1%
Unemployed	4.0%	1.1%	4.1%	1.5%

Table 3.1. Type of Law Practice for Washington Attorneys

Type of Practice	Latinos (n = 97)	Comparison Group (n = 711)
Solo practice	22.7%	22.4%
Small firm	16.5%	21.7%
Middle-sized firm	10.3%	10.7%
Large firm	9.3%	13.5%
City or county government	10.3%	8.7%
State government agency	2.1%	5.2%
Federal fovernment agency	8.2%	3.8%
House counsel for a firm	1.0%	3.8%
Judge or magistrate	3.1%	2.4%
Other (write-in category)	16.5%	7.9%

Table 3.2.   Obstacles to Law School Education of Washington Lawyers: Family Obligations

Scale	Latinos	Latinas	Comparison Males	Comparison Females
1. None	45.0%	33.3%	62.3%	53.3%
2. A little	11.7%	23.8%	16.3%	17.1%
3. Uncertain	1.7%	4.8%	1.3%	0.8%
4. Somewhat	18.3%	11.9%	17.7%	14.4%
5. Substantial	23.3%	26.2%	8.4%	14.4%

Table 3.3.   Obstacles to Law School Education of Washington Lawyers: Knowledge

Scale	Latinos	Latinas	Comparison Males	Comparison Females
1. None	41.7%	33.3%	63.3%	50.4%
2. A little	28.3%	21.4%	22.4%	28.1%
3. Uncertain	0.0%	4.8%	3.4%	3.9%
4. Somewhat	16.7%	31.0%	8.8%	11.3%
5. Substantial	13.3%	9.5%	2.1%	6.3%

Table 3.4.   Obstacles to Law School Education of Washington Lawyers: Cost

Scale	Latinos	Latinas	Comparison Males	Comparison Females
1. None	16.7%	14.3%	24.7%	17.6%
2. A little	11.7%	21.4%	23.7%	22.3%
3. Uncertain	3.3%	2.4%	1.9%	0.4%
4. Somewhat	33.3%	21.4%	29.1%	28.1%
5. Substantial	35.0%	40.5%	20.5%	31.6%

Table 3.5. Demographic Distribution of Samples

	Latino Lawyers (n = 102) (%)	Comparison Lawyers (n = 757) (%)
Gender		
Female	41.2	34.3
Male	58.8	63.9
Current Marital Status		
Married	68.0	73.2
Single	32.0	26.8
Partner's Ethnic / Racial Background		
Asian American/ Pacific Islander	6.3	3.6
Latino	22.1	3.9
Caucasian/White	47.4	68.4
Native American	1.1	1.1
African American/ Black	2.1	—
Other	1.1	1.1
Partner's Professional Background		
Yes	74.5	47.0
No	25.5	53.0
Family Status		
Children	64.7	67.4
No Children	35.3	32.6
Step-Children	14.7	12.3
No Step-Children	85.3	87.7
Income		
$30,000 or less	3.7	5.3
$30,000–$39,000	12.3	5.3
$40,000–49,000	8.6	8.7
$50,000–$59,000	12.3	9.4
$60,000–$69,000	12.3	12.7
$70,000–$99,000	12.3	20.1
$100,000–$149,000	23.5	22.1
$150,000 or more	14.8	16.3

Table 4.1. Civic Activities in Local Community among Latino Attorneys

	Latina Lawyers	Latino Lawyers
Volunteer in political campaign	42.9%	40.7%
Contribute financially to politics	66.7%	61.0%
Involved in political activity to promote Latino community	45.2%	40.7%
Contribute time to charities	58.5%	67.2%
Contribute financially to charities	90.2%	70.2%
Church attendance (monthly)	36.8%	50.0%
Other volunteer activities	16.7%	28.8%

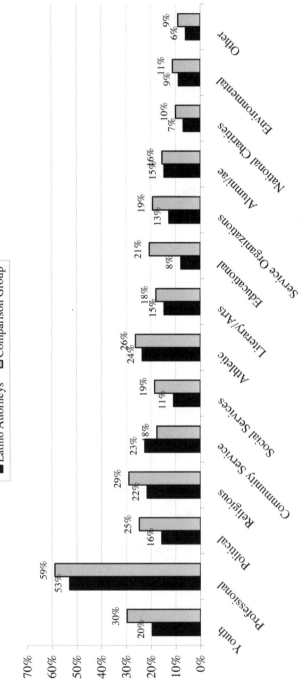

Figure 5.1 Membership in Civic Activities

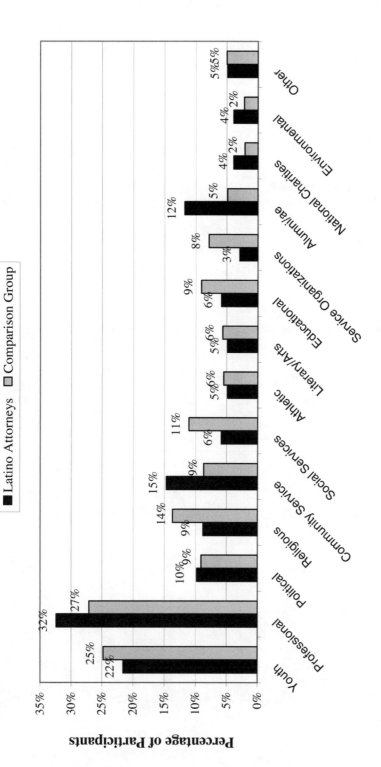

Figure 5.2 Leadership Role in Civic Activities

Table 5.1.   Sense of Social Trust for Washington Lawyers

Scale Point / Category	Trust in Others		Others Are Honest	
	Latinos	Non-Latino Lawyers	Latinos	Non-Latino Lawyers
1. Most people can be trusted / are honest	12.0%	16.7%	11.0%	15.9%
2. Some people can be trusted / are honest	55.0%	55.8%	62.0%	58.0%
3. Undecided	12.0%	13.1%	14.0%	17.3%
4. It's good to be careful / Some people are always cheating	18.0%	11.5%	12.0%	8.3%
5. You can't be too careful / People are always cheating	3.0%	2.8%	1.0%	0.5%

Table 5.2.   Lawyers' Ideological Views on Economic and Social Issues

Ideological Scale	Economic Issues		Social Issues	
	Latinos	Comparison Group	Latinos	Comparison Group
Very conservative	7.1%	7.2%	4.0%	5.8%
Somewhat conservative	20.2%	25.4%	8.1%	13.3%
Moderate	28.3%	29.3%	7.1%	18.1%
Somewhat liberal	22.2%	25.7%	34.3%	32.5%
Very liberal	22.2%	12.4%	46.5%	30.4%

Table 5.3.   Summary of Civic Activities

	Latino Lawyers	Comparison Group Lawyers
Voting	97.3%	96.0%
Interest in local politics	79.2%	81.9%
Read newspaper daily	84.7%	87.5%
Volunteer in politics	41.6%	57.9%
Contribute financially to politics	63.4%	71.4%
Boards and commissions	23.8%	15.5%
Discuss local politics	41.8%	44.8%
Volunteer activities	63.6%	71.0%
Contribute financially to charities	78.6%	89.8%
Church volunteer activities	23.5%	30.2%
Church attendance	44.6%	46.2%

Table 6.1. Most Important Issues Facing the Latino Community in Washington

Issue Listed	Occurrence of Listing
1. Education/educational opportunities	54
2. Employment opportunities	19
3. High poverty	16
4. Lack of political representation / political power	15
5. Facing prejudice or racism / discrimination	14
6. Immigration issues	13
7. Lack of unity / community cohesion among Latinos	11
8. Housing	8
9. Adequate health care	7
10. Farmworker rights	7

(B)

SURVEY QUESTIONNAIRES AND INTERVIEW PROTOCOLS

CIVIC ENGAGEMENT AMONG MEMBERS OF THE WASHINGTON STATE BAR, 2001

You are among a group of randomly selected members of the Washington State Bar Association participating in a survey being conducted by the Division of Governmental Studies and Services in the Department of Political Science at Washington State University. This research is intended to enhance our understanding of the contributions made to civic affairs and community service by Washington attorneys. It examines the "public aspect" of lawyers' activities in the state of Washington by exploring whether recent changes in the legal profession—ranging from a move away from the traditional tenure system, to the creation of numerous categories of partners, to changes in the compensation system—have adversely affected participation in voluntary associations and other forms of community service. This survey asks you about your professional activities, about your background, about your legal education, and about your current degree of civic engagement and community involvement. The questionnaire should take **under one hour** to complete. Please skip over any questions that you do not wish to answer, and feel free to write additional comments in the margins and at the end of the survey instrument.

This request is for completely **voluntary** participation. Your responses will remain totally confidential. This research project was reviewed and approved by the WSU Institutional Review Board, assuring that all proper procedures will be followed to insure the confidentiality of your responses. Your name and address will NOT BE CONNECTED to your answers. All survey data will be identified only by the mail tracking number recorded at the bottom of this page. That number is used for coordinating mailings exclusively; no permanent record of this number will be retained after the survey is completed. You have been provided with a pre-addressed, postage-paid envelope for your convenience.

Thank you in advance for taking part in this important research project. If you have any questions please call either of us at (509) 335-3329 [Lovrich] or (360)

570-8674 [Chávez-Pringle]. If you would like to receive a summary of the survey results please check this box. ❏

Please return the completed form in the pre-addressed postage-paid envelope provided. If you have misplaced the envelope, the return address is:

Division of Governmental Studies and Services
c/o Maria Chávez-Pringle and Nicholas P. Lovrich
Department of Political Science
P.O. Box 644870
Washington State University
Pullman, WA 99164-4870

Mail tracking # _____

SECTION A: EDUCATIONAL EXPERIENCE AND BACKGROUND

A1. When did you complete law school? Year _____

A2. Overall, how satisfied have you been with the professional law education that you received?

❏ Very satisfied
❏ Moderately satisfied
❏ A little dissatisfied
❏ Very dissatisfied
❏ Neither satisfied nor dissatisfied

Comments: _____

_____

A3. In your community, who inspired you to go to law school? (Check all that apply.)

❏ Parent(s)
❏ Other family member
❏ College dean or other administrator
❏ Teacher
❏ Counselor

❏ Resident or academic advisor
❏ Others: _____

A4. How big of an obstacle to your law school education was each of the following:

Family obligations:

❏ None
❏ A little
❏ Uncertain
❏ Somewhat
❏ Substantial

Knowledge about how to get into law school:

❏ None
❏ A little
❏ Uncertain
❏ Somewhat
❏ Substantial

Cost of a law school education:

❏ None
❏ A little
❏ Uncertain
❏ Somewhat
❏ Substantial

A5. What level of education was attained by your parents?

Mother: _____
Father: _____

A6. Please indicate the occupation of both your parents while you were in elementary and secondary school (K-12). (If more than one occupation, choose the predominant occupation.)

Mother: _____
Father: _____

A7. If applicable, list your siblings' ages, sex, level of education (highest degrees), and current occupations.

Age	Gender (M/F)	Education Level	Current Occupation

A8. As an undergraduate, did you participate in any student organizations, clubs, athletics, or other extracurricular activities?

❑ Yes
❑ No

If yes, please specify:

_____

_____

_____

_____

A9. While in law school, did you participate in student organizations, clubs, athletics, or other extracurricular activities?

❑ Yes
❑ No

If yes, please specify:

_____

_____

_____

_____

A10. Upon reflection, what are the one or two most important considerations that caused you to want to go to law school?

_____

_____

_____

A11. Upon reflection, what were one or two of the greatest challenges you faced in law school?

_____

_____

_____

A12. Imagine that you had your life to live over again and were just graduating from college. Knowing what you know now, how likely is it that you would choose to go to law school all over again?

- ❑ Very likely
- ❑ Moderately likely
- ❑ Uncertain
- ❑ A little unlikely
- ❑ Very unlikely

A13. On the whole, how satisfied are you with the work you currently do?

- ❑ Very satisfied
- ❑ Moderately satisfied
- ❑ A little satisfied
- ❑ Neither satisfied nor dissatisfied
- ❑ Very dissatisfied

Comments:

_____

_____

_____

SECTION B: PROFESSIONAL WORK BACKGROUND

B1. Do you currently practice law?

- ❑ Yes
- ❑ No

If yes, what are your primary areas of practice?

_____

_____

_____

B2. How long have you been practicing in Washington? _____ **(in years)**

B3. What type of law do you practice?

❑ Solo practice
❑ Work in small firm of five or fewer attorneys
❑ Work in middle sized firm of six to twenty attorneys
❑ Work in large firm of twenty-one plus attorneys
❑ Work for city or county government
❑ Work for a state government agency
❑ Work for a federal government agency
❑ Work as the house counsel for a firm
❑ Serve as a judge or magistrate
❑ Other _____

B4. List up to five of the professional organizations of which you are a member.

_____

_____

_____

_____

_____

_____

B5. Does your firm have a pro bono policy? If so, briefly explain the policy and the areas of practice it covers.

_____

_____

_____

B6. Do you personally provide any pro bono legal services?

❑ Yes
❑ No

If yes, specify roughly how many hours per month, and in what areas:

_____

_____

_____

B7. During an *average week*, how would you describe your schedule of professional activities? Please allocate your professional obligations—including work responsibilities, organizational or associational responsibilities, *pro bono* services, and any community involvement related to your legal skills and training—so that the total equals 100%.

Average Week	Work Responsibilities	Associational Responsibilities	Community Involvement	Pro Bono Services
% of time				

B8. During any time in the past, did you have a mentor?

❑ Yes
❑ No

If yes, (a) what was your mentor's gender (M/F): _____
and (b) how did your mentor help you?

_____

_____

_____

_____

SECTION C: PERSONAL DEMOGRAPHIC INFORMATION

C1. Birthdate: _____

C2. Gender (M/F): _____

C3. Place of Birth (city, state, country): _____

If non-U.S.: How long have you lived in the U.S. (in years): _____

C4. What is your religious preference, if any?

- ❑ Protestant
- ❑ Catholic
- ❑ Jewish
- ❑ Muslim
- ❑ Other: _____
- ❑ No religion

C5. Current Marital Status

- ❑ Single, never married
- ❑ Married
- ❑ Separated
- ❑ Divorced

C6. Family Status

Number of Children: _____
Number of Step-Children: _____

If no children, do you plan to have children in the future?

- ❑ Yes
- ❑ No
- ❑ Uncertain

C7. Spouse/Partner's Ethnic Background (or n/a for not applicable): _____

C8. Spouse/Partner's Occupation (or n/a for not applicable): _____

C9. Approximate annual salary: _____

SECTION D: CIVIC ACTIVITIES

D1. While you were growing up, did your parents participate in community-based social and/or civic activities outside the home (e.g., clubs, unions, church organizations, sports teams, community groups, etc.)?

Mother (yes/no): _____
Father (yes/no): _____

D2. Did your parents participate in political activities outside the home (e.g., political campaigns, party caucuses, political conventions, etc.)?

Mother (yes/no): _____
Father (yes/no): _____

D3. Thinking about your *local* community, how interested are you in local community politics and local community affairs?

- ❏ Very interested
- ❏ Moderately interested
- ❏ Uncertain
- ❏ Slightly interested
- ❏ Not interested at all

D4. How often do you discuss local community politics or local community affairs with others?

- ❏ Every day
- ❏ Nearly every day
- ❏ Once or twice a week
- ❏ Less than once a week
- ❏ Never

D5. To what extent have you participated as a volunteer (non-employee participation) in *each* of the following activities since you became an attorney? Mark (√) for all that apply.

	Volunteer Activities	Member/ Participant	In Leadership Role	Indicate hours per month (if applicable)
A	Youth organizations (Little League, coaching, etc.)			
B	Professional or trade associations			
C	Political clubs, government organizations, or local government activities			
D	Religious activities (not including worship services)			
E	Community centers, neighborhood improvement groups, civil rights, social-action associations			

	Volunteer Activities	Member/ Participant	In Leadership Role	Indicate hours per month (if applicable)
F	Social services (hospital planning board, hospital volunteer, etc.)			
G	Sports teams/clubs			
H	Literary, art, music, cultural, or historical societies			
I	Educational organization (PTA, school board, trustee)			
J	Service organization (Rotary, Veterans, Chamber of Commerce)			
K	Alumni activities— fund raising, student recruitment, etc.			
L	National charities			
M	Environmental activities			
N	Any other group in which you participate as a volunteer (specify): _____			

D6. Over the last four years have your volunteer activities been:

❑ Increasing
❑ Staying the same
❑ Decreasing

D7. Did you vote in the 1996 Presidential election?

❑ Yes
❑ No

D8. Did you vote in the 2000 Presidential election?

❑ Yes
❑ No

D9. Have you ever worked as a volunteer (non-employee participation) for a candidate running for national, state, or local office?

❑ Yes
❑ No

D10. In the last four years have you contributed money to an individual candidate, a party group, a political action committee, or any other organization that supported candidates?

❑ Yes
❑ No

D11. In the past two years have you served in a voluntary capacity (non-employee participation) on any official local governmental board or council that deals with community problems and issues such as a town council, a school board, a zoning board, a planning board, or the like?

❑ Yes
❑ No

D12. Thinking about a time that you decided to participate in a political activity (campaigning, contacting politicians, making campaign contribution, protesting, community board, etc.), which of these lists of reasons bests describes your motivations for your activity (Check all that apply.):

❑ I found it exciting.
❑ I wanted to learn about politics and government.
❑ The chance to work with people who share my ideals.
❑ The chance to meet important and influential people.
❑ The chance to influence government policy.
❑ My duty as a citizen.
❑ I am the kind of person who does my share.
❑ The chance to further my job or career.
❑ The chance for recognition from people I respect.
❑ I might want to run for office someday.
❑ The chance to be with people I enjoy.
❑ I did not want to say no to someone who asked.
❑ I might want to get help from an official on a personal or family problem.
❑ The chance to make the community or nation a better place to live.
❑ The chance to further the goals of my political party.
❑ Add your own reason that is not included in this list: _____

D13. Thinking of political activities in which you have participated, which of these categories best describes who was usually most affected by the issue or problem:

❑ Other people
❑ Myself/family and other people

❑ All people in local community
❑ All people in nation

D14. Aside from attending your church or synagogue, in the past twelve months, did you spend any time on charitable or voluntary service activities?

❑ Yes
❑ No

D15. Aside from contributions to your church or synagogue, did you contribute any money to charitable or voluntary service activities and organizations?

❑ Yes
❑ No

D16. Aside from attending services, in the past twelve months have you been an active member of your church/synagogue in the capacity of serving on a committee, giving time for special projects, and/or helped organize meetings?

❑ Yes
❑ No

D17. Thinking about your views concerning *economic issues* (such as taxes, government spending) where would you place yourself on the scale below:

❑ Very conservative
❑ Somewhat conservative
❑ Moderate
❑ Somewhat liberal
❑ Very liberal

D18. Thinking about your views concerning *social issues* (such as women's rights, gay rights) where would you place yourself on the scale below:

❑ Very conservative
❑ Somewhat conservative
❑ Moderate
❑ Somewhat liberal
❑ Very liberal

D19. How would you label yourself in terms of *political preferences*:

❑ Strong Republican
❑ Republican
❑ Independent
❑ Democrat
❑ Strong Democrat
❑ Other: _____

D20. In regard to *following public affairs* and being engaged in civic activities in the area where you reside, which of the following are typical of your activity (check all that apply):

❑ Read newspaper daily
❑ Do volunteer work in the community
❑ Am interested in politics
❑ Attend church regularly (at least monthly)

D21. In the area of *general outlook on life*, please place yourself on the following five-point scales by drawing a circle around the number that best represents your own beliefs:

Most people can be trusted		Undecided		You can't be too careful in dealing with people
1	2	3	4	5

Most people are honest		Undecided		People are always cheating to get ahead
1	2	3	4	5

If you have any further comments or thoughts that you would like to add, please feel free to do so here or an a separate sheet of paper; we are very interested in your views.

_____
_____
_____

_____

_____

_____

_____

_____

_____

_____

THANK YOU VERY MUCH for completing this survey questionnaire!

WASHINGTON STATE
LATINO/A ATTORNEY
SURVEY QUESTIONNAIRE, 2001

You are among a group of Latina/o lawyers in the state of Washington participating in this survey. It is part of an on-going research project being conducted in connection with a doctoral dissertation project supported by the Division of Governmental Studies and Services in the Department of Political Science at Washington State University. This research is intended to lead to improvements in our understanding of the experiences and contributions of a very important segment of the Latino professional middle class in the state of Washington. The survey asks you to indicate your background, identify some of the obstacles you had to overcome to become a lawyer, and to describe your current degree of civic engagement. The questionnaire should take under one hour to complete. Please skip over any questions which you do not wish to answer, and feel free to write comments in the margins and at the end of the survey instrument.

*This request is for completely **voluntary** participation. Your responses will remain totally confidential. This research project was reviewed and approved by the WSU Institutional Review Board and my dissertation committee, who require that all necessary procedures will be followed to insure the confidentiality of your responses. Your name and address will NOT BE CONNECTED to your answers. All survey data will be identified only by the mail tracking number recorded at the end of this survey. That number is used for coordinating mailings only; no permanent record of this number will be retained after the survey is completed.*

Thank you in advance for your participation in this important research project. You have been provided with a pre-addressed, postage-paid return envelope for your convenience. If you have any questions please call me at (360) 570-8674 or (509) 335-3329. If you would like to receive a summary of the survey results please check this box. ❏

If you would consider being a participant in a focus group to be conducted after the survey is completed, please check this box. ❏

Thank you again for your participation.
Maria Chavez-Pringle

SECTION A: EDUCATIONAL EXPERIENCE AND BACKGROUND

A1. When did you complete law school? Year: _____

A2. Overall, how satisfied have you been with the professional law education that you received?

❏ Very satisfied
❏ Moderately satisfied
❏ A little dissatisfied
❏ Very dissatisfied
❏ Neither satisfied nor dissatisfied

Comments: _____
_____
_____

A3. In your youth, who in your community inspired you to go to law school? (Check all that apply.)

❏ Parent(s)
❏ Athletic coach
❏ Other family member
❏ Administrator
❏ Teacher
❏ Counselor
❏ Resident or academic advisor
❏ Others: _____

A4. What presented the biggest obstacle to the completion of your undergraduate education?

❏ High school preparation
❏ Cost of college education
❏ Knowledge about how to get to college

❑ Fear of leaving home
❑ Other _____

A5. In your community, who inspired you to go to law school? (Check all that apply.)

❑ Parent(s)
❑ Other family member
❑ College dean or other administrator
❑ Teacher
❑ Counselor
❑ Resident or academic advisor
❑ Others: _____

A6. How big an obstacle to your law school education was each of the following:

Family obligations:

❑ None
❑ A little
❑ Uncertain
❑ Somewhat
❑ Substantial

Knowledge about how to get into law school:

❑ None
❑ A little
❑ Uncertain
❑ Somewhat
❑ Substantial

Cost of a law school education:

❑ None
❑ A little
❑ Uncertain
❑ Somewhat
❑ Substantial

A7. What level of education was attained by your parents?

Mother: _____
Father: _____

A8. Please indicate the occupation of both your parents while you were in elementary and secondary school (K-12). (If more than one occupation, choose the predominant occupation.)

Mother: _____
Father: _____

A9. If applicable, list your siblings' ages, sex, level of education (highest degrees), and current occupations.

Age	Gender (M/F)	Education Level	Current Occupation

A10. During the course of your college and/or law school studies, did you receive scholarships or other assistance specifically intended to enhance the presence of Latinos earning a college degree and/or pursuing a professional degree?

❑ Yes
❑ No

A11. Did you receive any honors, awards, or other types of academic and/ or professional recognition while in college or in law school?

❑ Yes
❑ No

If yes, please specify:

_____

_____

_____

A12. As an undergraduate, did you participate in any student organizations, clubs, athletics, or other extracurricular activities?

❑ Yes

❑ No

If yes, please specify:

_____

_____

A13. While in law school, did you participate in student organizations, clubs, athletics, or other extra-curricular activities?

❑ Yes

❑ No

If yes, please specify:

_____

_____

_____

A14. Upon reflection, what are the one or two most important considerations that caused you to want to go to law school?

_____

_____

_____

A15. Upon reflection, what were one or two of the greatest challenges you faced in law school?

_____

_____

_____

A16. Imagine that you had your life to live over again and were just graduating from college. Knowing what you know now, how likely is it that you would choose to go to law school all over again?

❑ Very likely
❑ Moderately likely
❑ Uncertain
❑ A little unlikely
❑ Very unlikely

A17. On the whole, how satisfied are you with the work you currently do?

❑ Very satisfied
❑ Moderately satisfied
❑ A little satisfied
❑ Neither satisfied nor dissatisfied
❑ Very dissatisfied

Comments:

_____

_____

_____

A18. Do you feel that being Latino/a has caused you difficulties in your profession as a lawyer?

❑ Yes
❑ No

If yes, please explain:

_____

_____

_____

SECTION B: PROFESSIONAL WORK BACKGROUND

B1. Do you currently practice law?

❑ Yes
❑ No

If yes, what are your primary areas of practice?

_____

_____

_____

B2. How long have you been practicing in Washington? _____ (*in years*)

B3. What type of law do you practice?

- ❏ Solo practice
- ❏ Work in small firm of five or fewer attorneys
- ❏ Work in middle sized firm of six to twenty attorneys
- ❏ Work in large firm of twenty-one plus attorneys
- ❏ Work for city or county government
- ❏ Work for a state government agency
- ❏ Work for a federal government agency
- ❏ Work as the house counsel for a firm
- ❏ Serve as a judge or magistrate
- ❏ Other _____

B4. List up to five of the professional organizations of which you are a member.

_____
_____
_____
_____
_____

B5. Does your firm have a pro bono policy? If so, briefly explain the policy and the areas of practice it covers.

_____
_____
_____
_____

B6. Do you personally provide any pro bono legal services?

- ❏ Yes
- ❏ No

If yes, specify roughly how many hours per month, and in what areas:

_____
_____
_____

B7. What would you consider to be the one or two greatest challenges in your profession?

_____

_____

_____

_____

B8. During an _average week_, how would you describe your schedule of professional activities? Please allocate your professional obligations—including work responsibilities, organizational or associational responsibilities, _pro bono_ services, and any community involvement related to your legal skills and training—so that the total equals 100%.

Average Week	Work Responsibilities	Associational Responsibilities	Community Involvement	Pro Bono Services
% of time				

B9. During any time in the past, did you have a mentor?

❑ Yes
❑ No

If yes, (a) what was your mentor's gender (M/F): _____
and (b) how did your mentor help you?

_____

_____

_____

_____

SECTION C: PERSONAL DEMOGRAPHIC INFORMATION

C1. Birthdate: _____

C2. Gender (_M/F_): _____

C3. Place of Birth (city, state, country): _____

If non-U.S.: How long have you lived in the U.S. (in years): _____

C4. Where were your parents born? (city, state, country):

Mother: _____

Father: _____

C5. What is your religious preference, if any?

❑ Protestant
❑ Catholic
❑ Jewish
❑ Muslim
❑ Other: _____
❑ No religion

C6. Current Marital Status

❑ Single, never married
❑ Married
❑ Separated
❑ Divorced

C7. Family Status

Number of Children: _____

Number of Step-Children: _____

If no children, do you plan to have children in the future?

❑ Yes
❑ No
❑ Uncertain

C8. Spouse/Partner's Ethnic Background (or n/a for not applicable):

_____

C9. Spouse/Partner's Occupation (or n/a for not applicable): _____

_____

C10. Approximate annual salary: _____

SECTION D: LANGUAGE AND CULTURAL BACKGROUND AND EXPERIENCES

D1. What was the first language you learned to speak?

❑ Spanish
❑ English
❑ Other: _____

D2. What language(s) did you speak when you started school?

❑ Spanish
❑ English
❑ Both
❑ Other: _____

D3. What language(s) do you presently speak with your own immediate family?

❑ Spanish
❑ English
❑ Both
❑ Other: _____

D4. What language(s) do you presently speak? (Check all that apply.)

At work:

❑ Spanish
❑ English
❑ Both
❑ Other: _____

Socially:

❑ Spanish
❑ English
❑ Both
❑ Other: _____

D5. Rate your Spanish-speaking fluency:

❑ None
❑ Poor

❑ Fair
❑ Moderate
❑ Fluent

D6. What languages were usually spoken in your home while you were in school (K-12)?

❑ Mostly Spanish
❑ Mostly English
❑ Both equally
❑ Other: _____

D7. What languages were spoken in the community where you were raised?

❑ Mostly Spanish
❑ Mostly English
❑ Both equally
❑ Other: _____

D8. How would you describe (in cultural terms) the people with whom you associate regularly?

❑ Mostly Anglos
❑ Mostly Latinos
❑ A diverse set of persons

D9. List any special events, celebrations, or national holidays that your family celebrated while you were growing up (e.g., Cinco de Mayo, Quinceneras, Diesiseis de Septiembre, etc.):

_____

_____

_____

D10. How would you characterize your personal lifetime experience with prejudice—that is, prejudice suffered by you personally in the past?

❑ None
❑ Slight
❑ Moderate
❑ Substantial
❑ Extreme

D11. How would you characterize the personal lifetime experience with prejudice of the average Latino in Washington?

- ❑ None
- ❑ Slight
- ❑ Moderate
- ❑ Substantial
- ❑ Extreme

D12. How would you characterize your personal experience with prejudice in your professional career?

- ❑ None
- ❑ Slight
- ❑ Moderate
- ❑ Substantial
- ❑ Extreme

D13. How would you characterize the prejudice experienced in their legal professional careers by Latino/a lawyers in Washington?

- ❑ None
- ❑ Slight
- ❑ Moderate
- ❑ Substantial
- ❑ Extreme

D14. Did your parents participate in community-based social and/or civic activities outside the home (e.g., clubs, unions, church organizations, sports teams, community groups, etc.)?

General Community Orientation:

Mother:

- ❑ Yes
- ❑ No

Father:

- ❑ Yes
- ❑ No

Specifically Latino Orientation:

Mother:

- ❏ Yes
- ❏ No

Father:

- ❏ Yes
- ❏ No

D15. Did your parents participate in political activities outside the home (e.g., political campaigns, party caucuses, political conventions, etc.)?

General Community Orientation:

Mother:

- ❏ Yes
- ❏ No

Father:

- ❏ Yes
- ❏ No

Specifically Latino Orientation:

Mother:

- ❏ Yes
- ❏ No

Father:

- ❏ Yes
- ❏ No

D16. When asked to describe your ethnic identity, which term would you be most likely to use?

- ❏ American
- ❏ South American
- ❏ Mexican American/Chicano
- ❏ Central American
- ❏ Puerto Rican
- ❏ Dominican

❑ Cuban
❑ Other: _____

D17. How would you rate your sense of Latino identity?

❑ Very strong
❑ Somewhat strong
❑ Moderate
❑ Somewhat weak
❑ Very weak

Comments: _____

_____
_____

SECTION E: LATINO COMMUNITY IN WASHINGTON

A note on terms: "Community" will refer to a group of people sharing similar characteristics and common interests (e.g., minority communities) that may or may not include a specific geographic neighborhood.

E1. What do you believe are the two or three most important issues facing the Latino community in Washington?

_____
_____
_____

E2. In your opinion, who are some key people and/or organizations working to address public policy issues affecting the Latino community in Washington?

_____
_____
_____

E3. To your knowledge, how well do institutions of higher education do in helping to improve community among Washington's Latino residents?

❑ Poor job
❑ Fair job
❑ Uncertain/don't know
❑ Good job
❑ Excellent job

E4. Do you take part in any Latino community-building efforts?

❏ Yes
❏ No

If yes, please describe these efforts:

_____

_____

_____

E5. How serious do you think the impact of I-200, which ended state affirmative action programs in Washington, will be on the Latino community? What are your comments?

_____

_____

_____

E6. Thinking about your *local* community, how interested are you in local community politics and local community affairs?

❏ Very interested
❏ Moderately interested
❏ Uncertain
❏ Slightly interested
❏ Not at all interested

E7. How often do you discuss local community politics or local community affairs with others?

❏ Every day
❏ Nearly every day
❏ Once or twice a week
❏ Less than once a week
❏ Never

E8. In your opinion, what does the future hold for the Latino community in Washington?

❏ It will lose ground over the next decade.
❏ It will stay at its present level of accomplishment.
❏ It will make some degree of progress.
❏ It will make significant progress over the next decade.

SECTION F: CIVIC ACTIVITIES

F1. Are you currently registered to vote?

❑ Yes
❑ No

F2. Did you vote in the 1996 presidential election?

❑ Yes
❑ No

F3. Did you vote in the 2000 presidential election?

❑ Yes
❑ No

F4. Have you ever worked as a volunteer (non-employee participation) for a candidate running for national, state, or local office?

❑ Yes
❑ No

If yes, please specifiy: _____

_____

F5. In the last four years have you contributed money to an individual candidate, a party group, a political action committee, or any other organization that supported candidates?

❑ Yes
❑ No

F6. In the past two years have you served in a voluntary capacity (non-employee participation) on any official local governmental board or council that deals with community problems and issues such as a town council, a school board, a zoning board, a planning board, or the like?

❑ Yes
❑ No

F7. Have you taken part in any political activities (e.g., political campaigns, initiative campaigns, legislative lobbying, political protests, etc.)

specifically designed to promote the advancement of the Latino community?

❑ Yes
❑ No

F8. Thinking about a time that you decided to participate in a political activity (campaigning, contacting politicians, making campaign contribution, protesting, community board, etc.), which of these lists of reasons best describes your motivations for your activity (check all that apply):

❑ I found it exciting.
❑ I wanted to learn about politics and government.
❑ The chance to work with people who share my ideals.
❑ The chance to meet important and influential people.
❑ The chance to influence government policy.
❑ My duty as a citizen.
❑ I am the kind of person who does my share.
❑ The chance to further my job or career.
❑ The chance for recognition from people I respect.
❑ I might want to run for office someday.
❑ The chance to be with people I enjoy.
❑ I did not want to say no to someone who asked.
❑ I might want to get help from an official on a personal or family problem.
❑ The chance to make the community or nation a better place to live.
❑ The chance to further the goals of my political party.
❑ The chance to further the goals of the Latino community.
❑ Add your own reason that is not included in this list: _____

F9. Thinking of political activities in which you have participated, which of these categories best describes who was usually most affected by the issue or problem:

❑ Other people
❑ Myself/family and other people
❑ All people in local community
❑ All people in nation

F10. Aside from attending your church or synagogue, in the past twelve months, did you spend any time on charitable or voluntary service activities?

❑ Yes
❑ No

If yes, specify: _____

F11. Aside from contributions to your church or synagogue, did you contribute any money to charitable or voluntary service activities and organizations?

❑ Yes
❑ No

If yes, specify: _____

F12. Aside from attending services, in the past twelve months have you been an active member of your church/synagogue in the capacity of serving on a committee, giving time for special projects, and/or helped organize meetings?

❑ Yes
❑ No

If yes, specify: _____

F13. To what extent have you participated as a volunteer (non-employee participation) in *each* of the following activities since you became an attorney? Mark (√) for all that apply.

	Volunteer Activities	Member/ Participant	In Leadership Role	Indicate hours per month (if applicable)
A	Youth organizations (Little League, coaching, etc.)			
B	Professional or trade associations			
C	Political clubs, government organizations, or local government activities			
D	Religious activities (not including worship services)			
E	Community centers, neighborhood improvement groups, civil rights, social-action associations			

	Volunteer Activities	Member/ Participant	In Leadership Role	Indicate hours per month (if applicable)
F	Social services (hospital planning board, hospital volunteer, etc.)			
G	Sports teams/clubs			
H	Literary, art, music, cultural or historical societies			
I	Educational organization (PTA, school board, trustee)			
J	Service organization (Rotary, Veterans, Chamber of Commerce)			
K	Alumni activities—fund raising, student recruitment, etc.			
L	National charities			
M	Environmental activities			
N	Any other group in which you participate as a volunteer (specify): _____			

F14. Over the last four years have your volunteer activities been:

❑ Increasing
❑ Staying the same
❑ Decreasing

F15. How would you label yourself in terms of *political preferences*:

❑ Strong Republican
❑ Republican
❑ Independent
❑ Democrat
❑ Strong Democrat
❑ Other: _____

F16. Thinking about your views concerning *economic issues* (such as taxes, government spending) where would you place yourself on the scale below:

❑ Very conservative
❑ Somewhat conservative
❑ Moderate

❑ Somewhat liberal
❑ Very liberal

F17. Thinking about your views concerning *social issues* (such as women's rights, gay rights) where would you place yourself on the scale below:

❑ Very conservative
❑ Somewhat conservative
❑ Moderate
❑ Somewhat liberal
❑ Very liberal

F18. In regard to *following public affairs* and being engaged in civic activities in the area where you reside, which of the following are typical of your activity (check all that apply):

❑ Read newspaper daily
❑ Do volunteer work in the community
❑ Am interested in politics
❑ Attend church regularly (at least monthly)

F19. Do you feel part of the local geographic community where you work?

❑ Yes
❑ No

F20. In the area of *general outlook on life*, please place yourself on the following five-point scales by drawing a circle around the number that best represents your own beliefs:

Most people can be trusted		Undecided		You can't be too careful in dealing with people
1	2	3	4	5

Most people are honest		Undecided		People are always cheating to get ahead
1	2	3	4	5

If you have any further comments or thoughts that you would like to add, please feel free to do so here or an a separate sheet of paper; we are very interested in your views.

_____
_____
_____
_____
_____
_____
_____
_____
_____
_____

THANK YOU VERY MUCH for completing this survey questionnaire!

Please return the completed form in the pre-addressed postage-paid enve-lope provided. If you have misplaced the envelope, the return address is:

Division of Governmental Studies and Services
c/o Maria Chávez-Pringle and Nicholas P. Lovrich
Department of Political Science
P.O. Box 644870
Washington State University
Pullman, WA 99164-4870

Mail tracking # _____

KEY INFORMANT INTERVIEW QUESTION GUIDELINE FOR LATINO/A LEADERS IN THE WASHINGTON STATE LEGAL COMMUNITY, AUGUST THROUGH OCTOBER OF 2000

Former Washington State Supreme Court Justice Charles Z. Smith provided the names of key contacts who could provide historical and cultural context on the Latino legal community in Washington. I contacted each of the names provided by Justice Smith and scheduled interviews with the people who consented to my request for a total of seven key informant interviews.

1. What is your connection to the Latino legal community (for example: involvement in the Washington State Hispanic Bar Association)?
2. How would you describe the Latino legal community in Washington?
3. What is your background (e.g., where you grew up, neighborhood, schools, etc.)?
4. Tell me about how you got to where you are today as a Latino professional? Where did you go to college; what were your experiences in college, law school, or as a professional lawyer? How did being Latino shape or impact these experiences and efforts, if at all?
5. Thinking about your involvement in the Latino community, were there any issues or problems ranging from public policy issues to community, family, or personal concerns that led you to become involved? What were they? Who was most affected by the problems?
6. Here is a list of potential questions that I have developed for the focus groups of volunteers of the WSHBA. Do you think they make sense? What in your opinion is missing?

LATINO ATTORNEY FOCUS GROUP DISCUSSION GUIDE

November 7, 2001 (Seattle), and November 8, 2001 (Yakima)

[5 minutes] Introductions:

Greetings:

Facilitator Maria
Good evening. Thank you for taking time out of your busy schedules to meet with us tonight. My name is Maria Chávez-Pringle and I am a doctoral candidate at

Washington State University finishing up my dissertation, which as you well know focuses on Latino lawyers in Washington.

Purpose of Study: The information collected in this study, both from the surveys and from focus groups like the one being held here tonight, will reveal some important insights about the civic lives of Latino professionals in our state. Latinos represent the nation's fastest growing minority community, and Latino lawyers are a critical group within that community. Few others know the justice system, the political system, and what it is like to be a member of a disadvantaged minority community as well as Latino lawyers. I'm very glad you could make it here tonight, and I appreciate your participation greatly. Thank you.

Facilitator Dr. Lovrich

Hello and welcome. My name is Nicholas Lovrich . . . As Maria said, we are here tonight to ask for your insights into civic engagement and public affairs relating to the Latino community of Washington. I am Maria's dissertation committee chair, and am here to assist her with the facilitation of this focus group.

Role of Facilitators: Our roles as facilitators here tonight will be to ask you a few questions and keep the discussion focused and on track. We have six questions to go over and only a little over an hour to do this. Your perspectives, attitudes, and insights are crucial to this study and we want to make sure we get through the questions.

[5 minutes] Brief Get Acquainted Period

Facilitator Maria

Before we begin, we would like to go around and introduce each other by briefly stating your first name and sharing your favorite hobby or what you most enjoy doing or something you do very well.

[5 minutes] Ground Rules

Facilitator Dr. Lovrich

Before we start we need to lay out the ground rules for tonight's discussion. We want to make sure that everyone has the opportunity to share their perspectives, and also go "off the record" if they wish to do so. Please be assured that there will not be a single name, address, or any other identifying information recorded in the transcription of this session. We will use "participant #1" to tag comments made for later analyses. So, for those of you who have not taken part in a focus group before, we will pass out a few ground rules for focus groups [below] for you to read over quickly. [Because this is a group of highly trained lawyers, I will not read the ground rules to them, rather just hand them out and give them a few minutes to go over them.] Does anyone have any questions? Is there anything about the study you would like me to tell you before we begin?

LATINO ATTORNEY FOCUS GROUP GROUND RULES

November 7, 2001

Confidentiality

- Please be assured that there will not be a single name, address, or any other identifying information recorded along with the comments made here tonight.
- Because your comments are very important, I will be taking notes. I won't be writing down any names, however. Your comments will be kept anonymous. In the dictation, I will identify the main themes and ideas expressed here, as well as some quotes that speak to those themes.
- If at any time you would like to say something but do not want it recorded, you may ask to have the tape recorder turned off during the discussion to express that view.
- No one will be listening to the tapes except me. I will also be the one transcribing them, and they won't be released to anybody under any circumstances.

Respect

- There are **six specific questions** to discuss tonight, and about 90 minutes in which to discuss them. It is important that everyone has a chance to speak on each question. If I have moved on to a new question and you would like to say more on the previous topic, just let me know and we'll get your comments for the record.
- **No personal attacks** on other group members. Some of the questions are controversial and it is important that everyone respect the perspectives expressed.
- It is very important that each of you voice your opinions and views **CANDIDLY**. We are not attempting to reach consensus or general agreement. Your views and feelings may be very different from other group members, so group agreement is not the goal.
- There are no right or wrong perspectives. Everyone is encouraged to express their own ideas and opinions without feeling that others will be disrespectful.

Respect

- **Please speak clearly** so that a complete record of the focus group is captured. It is important to speak clearly and one at a time for everyone to hear and respond to comments. In addition, your comments are picked up on the recorder better. The transcripts from the session will be used along with the notes to make a summary of the common themes and key insights emerging from our discussion.

Need for Active Participation

- **Your interaction and input on the questions is very important** to the understanding of Latino professionals' patterns of civic engagement for this study. You are encouraged to speak to each other about each question and issue raised here tonight.

Note: Direct any questions concerning this study to:
Professor Nicholas P. Lovrich, Director
Division of Governmental Studies and Services
Washington State University
PO Box 644870
Pullman, WA 99164-4870
Phone (509) 335-3329, Fax: (509) 335-2362
Or you may email Maria Chávez-Pringle at mlchavez@wsunix.wsu.edu

We hope you will enjoy this discussion and will now begin our conversation with the first question.

[60 –70 minutes] Focus Group Questions

- The survey indicated that Latino lawyers here in Washington are civically engaged at comparable rates to those of non-Latino attorneys overall, but in categories such as community service Latino lawyers are civically engaged at higher rates. In addition, it revealed that Latino lawyers are civically engaged at much higher rates than Latinos nationally. The survey showed that Latino lawyers are mainly generating their civic concerns and activities by getting involved within the broader civic community rather than in civic associations and activities that are Latino-focused. Why do you think this is the case?
- In a related question, the survey indicated that as involvement in mainstream community and political activities increased, involvement in Latino-specific activities actually decreased. In other words, there are two groups of Latino lawyers with regards to civic engagement: one group with a strong commitment to specifically improving the Latino community, and the other group who focuses their civic efforts exclusively on the broader community. Given that, what do you believe is the best way to address issues facing the Latino

community in Washington—(1) by framing them as part of the broader public interest, or (2) by defining them as unique Latino interests and concerns?

- When Latino attorneys were asked if they take part in any political activities designed to specifically promote the advancement of the Latino community, the survey indicated that 57 percent of respondents do not, and 43 percent do. What factors or reasons do you think make a difference in whether someone engages in Latino community-building efforts or not?

- The survey included an open question that asked Latino attorneys to write their comments about Initiative 200. The answers were coded into whether they believed the impact would be positive, have no impact, or would be negative on the Latino community. Seventeen percent feel that I-200 would have a positive impact on the Latino community, 23% indicated they were undecided, and 60% felt it would have a negative impact. What do you think the effects of I-200 will be on the Latino community?

- How much do you believe you have benefited professionally from affirmative action?

- Discussing black professionals, Bowen and Bok wrote: "This group of well-educated individuals is charged, in effect, with twin responsibilities: not only to help build a more integrated American society, but to strengthen the social fabric of the black community" (1998, p. 169). Do you believe this sentiment expressed in this quote by advocates of affirmative action in higher education applies to Latino professionals as well? Do you think that Latinos have an obligation as members of a historically disadvantaged minority group to use their training and skills to contribute to the improvement of the Latino community—or is this is an unfair burden on persons such as yourself?

- Are there any additional comments? Does anyone have any final questions?

LATINA LAWYER INTERVIEWS, DECEMBER 2004

1. What is or are some of the most important aspects of being a lawyer to you? Discuss your identity as a person of color and as a professional.

_____

_____

_____

2. How does being a Latina impact your work as a lawyer? For example, did it affect the type of legal path chosen?

_____

_____

_____

3. Thinking about your individual journey, what would you say are or have been your greatest challenges and/or successes?

With home and family?

_____

_____

_____

At work and in your profession?

_____

_____

_____

In your community or neighborhood?

_____

_____

_____

4. What kinds of social support and networks do you utilize to overcome some of the obstacles just discussed or to celebrate some of the successes?

_____

_____

_____

5. If you were given the chance to live your life over, would you become a lawyer? Would you encourage (or have you encouraged) your own daughter to pursue a career in law?

_____

_____

_____

6. What do you think is important to add in a book that discusses the experiences of Latina lawyers? Is there anything that I haven't asked that tells your stories to others, so that they really understand your experiences as Latina attorneys?

_____

_____

_____

NOTES

FOREWORD

1. Southern Poverty Law Center, *Under Siege: Life for Low-Income Latinos in the South.* Montgomery, AL: SPLC (2009), p. 4.

CHAPTER I

1. Jennifer L. Hochschild, *Facing Up to the American Dream: Race, Class, and the Soul of the Nation* (Princeton, NJ: Princeton University Press, 1996).

2. Hochschild, *Facing Up to the American Dream.*

3. Mia Tuan, *Forever Foreigners or Honorary Whites?: The Asian Ethnic Experience Today* (New Brunswick, NJ: Rutgers University Press, 1999).

4. Luis Ricardo Fraga, John A. Garcia, Rodney E. Hero, Michael Jones-Correa, Valerie Martinez-Ebers, and Gary M. Segura, *Latino Lives in America: Making It Home* (Philadelphia: Temple University Press, 2010), p. 5.

5. Fraga et al., *Latino Lives in America*, 179.

6. José A. Cobas, Jorge Duany, and Joe R. Feagin, *How the United States Racializes Latinos: White Hegemony & Its Consequences* (Boulder, CO: Paradigm, 2009).

7. Cobas et al., *United States Racializes Latinos*, 1.

8. Ibid., 7.

9. Ibid.

10. Arizona State Legislature, Committee on Military Affairs and Public Safety. SB 1070 summary. Accessed June 14, 2010, www.azleg.gov/FormatDocument.asp?inDoc=/ legtext/49leg/2r/summary/h.sb1070_04-15-10_houseengrossed.doc.htm

11. For example, see "Immigrants Push State Initiative Targeting Those Here Illegally," Washington State Initiative 1056, accessed June 14, 2010, http://seattletimes. nwsource.com/html/localnews/2012110918_immigration14m.html.

12. For the full story, see www.npr.org/templates/story/story.php?storyId=6196755.

13. For example, see Ronald T. Takaki, *A Different Mirror: The Making of Multicultural America* (Boston: Little, Brown and Company, 1994).

14. *Time* Online, www.time.com/time/nation/article/0,8599,1135872,00.html

15. Joe, "Land Mines to Stop Mexican Immigrants?: The Radical White Right," *Racism Review*, June 15, 2010, www.racismreview.com/blog/2010/06/15/land-mines-to-stop-mexican-immigrants-the-radical-white-right

16. For example, during the 2004 presidential election, vigilantes patrolled voting stations to make sure "illegals" did not try to vote in Arizona. During the 2006 midterm election, a letter was sent to naturalized immigrants telling them not to vote. This type of voter intimidation is nothing new. Voter intimidation of people of color has a long history, especially in the South and Southwest toward African Americans and Latinos. For many new citizens of Hispanic origin for whom 2004 was to be their first presidential election, this type of political rejection was a grave injustice in the country they had formally accepted as their own. Other examples include vigilante groups who, armed and dangerous, are patrolling the Arizona/Mexico border trying to catch "illegals." For example, during a documentary interview, "Broken Border," which aired on April 25, 2005, on the Canadian Broadcasting Corporation (CBC), the leader of one vigilante organization said he was not against Mexicans coming here to work legally; rather he was against them coming to the United States the "wrong way." However, when asked if he would support President Bush's Guest Worker Program, which would allow Mexican laborers to work in the United States *legally* for up to three years at a time, he responded with an emphatic no. This is an excellent example of symbolic racism, in that people who harbor racist views against people of color in America today do not state their hostility toward members of other ethnic and racial groups outright. Rather, they code their rejection and racism toward ethnic and racial groups under various arguments.

17. Her full article can be found at www.stopthenorthamericanunion.com/Roots.html.

18. Mingying Fu, "Diverse Campus, Polarized View: The Controversy over Affirmative Action in a Multi-ethnic Environment." Paper presented at the annual meeting of the Western Political Science Association, Oakland, CA, March 17–19, 2005, 6–7.

19. Eduardo Bonilla-Silva, *Racism Without Racists: Color-Blind Racism and Racial Inequality in Contemporary America* (New York: Rowman & Littlefield, 2010).

20. Bonilla-Silva, *Racism Without Racists*, 3.

21. Ibid., 4.

22. For example, see Samuel Huntington, "Hispanic Immigrants Threaten the American Way of Life," *Foreign Policy*, March/April 2004, www.foreignpolicy.com/ story/cms.php?story_id=2524.

23. For a complete analysis of Huntington's arguments, see his book, *Who Are We? The Challenge to America's National Identity*, published in 2004 by Simon & Schuster, which expands upon his original article.

24. Jack Citrin, Amy Lerman, Michael Murakami, and Kathryn Pearson, "Testing Huntington: Is Hispanic Immigration a Threat to American Identity?" *Perspectives on Politics* 5:1 (March, 2007), 47.

25. Kevin R. Johnson and Bill Ong Hing, "National Identity in a Multicultural Nation: The Challenge of Immigration Law and Immigrants," *Michigan Law Review* 103:6 (May 2005), 1380.

26. Lisa García Bedolla, *Fluid Borders: Latino Power, Identity, and Politics in Los Angeles* (Berkeley: University of California Press, 2005), 65.

27. Luis R. Fraga and Gary M. Segura, "Culture Clash? Contesting Notions of American Identity and the Effects of Latin American Immigration," *Perspectives on Politics* 4:2 (June 2006), 283–284.

28. Kevin R. Johnson, *How Did You Get to Be a Mexican? A White/Brown Man's Search for Identity* (Philadelphia: Temple University Press, 1999), 152.

29. Johnson, *How Did You Get to Be a Mexican?*, 154.

30. Ibid., 88.

31. George Lipsitz, *The Possessive Investment in Whiteness: How White People Profit from Identity Politics* (Philadelphia: Temple University Press, 1998), 3.

32. Bill Ong Hing, *Defining America Through Immigration Policy* (Philadelphia: Temple University Press, 2004).

33. García Bedolla, *Fluid Borders*, 5.

34. Ibid.

35. Ibid.

36. Melissa R. Michelson, "The Corrosive Effect of Acculturation: How Mexican Americans Lose Political Trust," *Social Science Quarterly* 84:4 (2003), 918–933.

37. Teresa A. Sullivan, "A Demographic Portrait," *Hispanics in the United States*, ed. Pastora San Juan Cafferty and David W. Engstrom (Piscataway, NJ: Transaction Publishers, 2000), 1–30.

38. Richard L. Zweigenhaft and G. William Domhoff, *The New CEOs: Women, African American, Latino, and Asian American Leaders of Fortune 500 Companies* (New York: Rowman & Littlefield, 2011).

39. Christine M. Sierra, "The University Setting Reinforces Inequality," *Chicana Voices: Intersections of Class, Race, and Gender*, ed. Teresa Cordova, Norma Elia Cantú, Gilberto Cardenas, Juan García, and Christine M. Sierra (Albuquerque: University of New Mexico Press, 1993).

40. María de la Luz Reyes and John J. Halcón, "Racism in Academia: The Old Wolf Revisited," *Latinos and Education: A Critical Reader*, ed. Antonia Darder, Rodolfo D. Torres, and Henry Gutiérrez (New York: Routledge, 1997), 424.

41. Ibid., 426.

42. Ibid.

43. Stephen Macedo et al., *Democracy at Risk: How Political Choices Undermine Citizen Participation, and What We Can Do About It* (Washington, DC: Brookings Institution Press, 2005), 71.

44. García Bedolla, *Fluid Borders*, 190.

45. This claim relies on the criteria for improving theory in qualitative methods proposed by Gary King, Robert O. Keohane, and Sidney Verba in *Designing Social Inquiry: Scientific Inference in Qualitative Research* (Princeton, NJ: Princeton University Press, 1994).

46. Joe R. Feagin, *The White Racial Frame: Centuries of Racial Framing and Counter-Framing* (New York: Routledge, 2010), vii.

47. Feagin, *The White Racial Frame*, viii.

48. Ibid., 10 and 11.

49. Ibid., 16.

50. Ibid., ix.

51. Ibid., 116–120.

52. See Richard Griswold del Castillo, *The Treaty of Guadalupe Hidalgo: A Legacy of Conflict* (Norman, OK: University of Oklahoma Press, 1990); David Gutiérrez, *Walls and Mirrors: Mexican Americans, Mexican Immigrants, and the Politics of Ethnicity* (Berkeley: University of California Press, 1995); and Rodolfo Acuña, *Occupied America: A History of Chicanos* (New York: HarperCollins, 1988).

53. Griswold del Castillo, *The Treaty of Guadalupe Hidalgo*.

54. David Montejano, *Anglos and Mexicans in the Making of Texas, 1836–1986* (Austin: University of Texas Press, 1987), 168.

55. García Bedolla, *Fluid Borders*, 37.

56. Abraham Hoffman, *Unwanted Mexican Americans in the Great Depression: Repatriation Pressures, 1929–1939* (Tucson: University of Arizona Press, 1974).

57. Hoffman, *Unwanted Mexican Americans*.

58. García Bedolla, *Fluid Borders*, 48.

59. Kitty Calavita, *Inside the State: The Bracero Program, Immigration, and the I.N.S.* (New York: Routledge, 1992).

60. Ronald Schmidt Sr., Yvette M. Alex-Assensoh, Andrew L. Aoki, and Rodney E. Hero, *Newcomers, Outsiders, and Insiders: Immigrants and American Racial Politics in the Early Twenty-first Century* (Ann Arbor, MI: University of Michigan Press, 2009), 67.

61. Schmidt et al., *Newcomers, Outsiders, and Insiders*, 84–85.

62. José Trías Monge, *Puerto Rico: The Trials of the Oldest Colony in the World* (New Haven, CT: Yale University Press, 1997).

63. Trías Monge, *Puerto Rico*, 50.

64. Roberto Suro, *Strangers Among Us: How Latino Immigration Is Transforming America* (New York: Vintage Books, 1998), 140.

65. Suro, *Strangers Among Us*.

66. Juan Gonzalez, *Harvest of Empire: A History of Latinos in America* (New York: Viking, 2000).

67. Suro, *Strangers Among Us*, 148.

68. Gonzalez, *Harvest of Empire*, 81.

69. Suro, *Strangers Among Us*.

70. Alejandro Portes and Alex Stepick, *City on the Edge: The Transformation of Miami* (Berkeley: University of California Press, 1993).

71. Portes and Stepick, *City on the Edge*, 102.

72. Gonzalez, *Harvest of Empire*, 109.

73. Suro, *Strangers Among Us*, 164.

74. Portes and Stepick, *City on the Edge*, 102.

75. Ibid., 140.

76. Schmidt et al., *Newcomers, Outsiders, and Insiders*, 68–69.

77. Ibid., 103.

78. U.S. Census Bureau, "The Hispanic Population in the United States: 2004—Detailed Tables," www.census.gov/population/www/socdemo/hispanic/cps2004.html

79. For more information on this report, go to www.pewhispanic.org/page.jsp?page=reports.

80. U.ß. Census Bureau, "The Hispanic Population in the United States."

81. Ibid.

82. Excelencia in Education, "Facts," June 29, 2006, www.edexcelencia.org/research/facts.asp

83. Robert D. Putnam, *Bowling Alone: The Collapse and Revival of American Community* (New York: Simon & Schuster, 2000).

84. Macedo et al., *Democracy at Risk*, 6.

85. Ibid., 4.

86. Ibid.

87. Ibid.

88. Putnam, *Bowling Alone*.

89. For example, see Everett Carll Ladd, *The Ladd Report* (New York: The Free Press, 1999) and Michael Schudson, *The Good Citizen: A History of American Civic Life* (New York: The Free Press, 1998). Schudson claimed that civic engagement is declining and argued instead, that American citizenship has simply evolved. He concluded that today's "monitorial citizen" is no better or no worse off than citizens of the past and that the predominant measures of civic health such as voting, trust in government and institutions, and social memberships should also include the quality of public discourse, the gap between the rich and poor, the ability of the least advantaged members of society to have their views heard, and finally the degree to which the state guarantees the rights of citizens. Ladd investigated the question of declining civic involvement through an examination of surveys, polls, membership rolls, census reports, and government files and concluded that Americans still maintain an exceptional and rich sense of civic involvement that may be varied and evolving but is definitely not on the decline as Putnam and others argued.

90. Robert D. Putnam and Lewis M. Feldstein, *Better Together: Restoring the American Community* (New York: Simon & Schuster, 2003), 2.

91. Putnam and Feldstein, *Better Together*, 3.

92. See, for example, Paula McClain, "Social Capital and Diversity: An Introduction," *Perspectives on Politics* 1:1 (2003), 101–102; Maria Chávez, Brian Wampler, and Ross Burkhart, "Left Out: Trust and Social Capital Among Migrant Seasonal Farmworkers," *Social Science Quarterly* 87:5 (2006), 1012–1029; Lisa Garcia Bedolla and Becki Scola, "Race, Social Relations and the Study of Social Capital." Paper presented at the annual meeting of the American Political Science Association, Chicago, 2004; Fredrick C. Harris, "Will the Circle Be Unbroken? The Erosion and Transformation of African American Civic Life," *Civil Society, Democracy, and Civic Renewal*, ed. Robert K. Fullinwider (Lanham, MD: Rowman & Littlefield, 1999), 317–338; Kent E. Portney and Jeffrey M. Berry, "Mobilizing Minority Communities: Social Capital and Participation in Urban Neighborhoods," *The American Behavioral Scientist* 40:5 (March/April 1997), 632–644; Gary M. Segura, Harry Pachon, and Nathan Woods, "Hispanics, Social Capital, and Civic Engagement," *National Civic Review* 90:1 (2001), 85–96; Rodney E. Hero, "Social Capital and Racial Inequality in America," *Perspectives on Politics* 1:1 (2003), 113–122; and Eric M. Uslaner and Richard S. Conley, "Civic Engagement and Particularized Trust: The Ties That Bind People to Their Ethnic Communities," *American Politics Research* 31:4 (2003), 331–360.

93. For example, one of the leading textbooks in this area is *Professional Responsibility: Ethics by the Pervasive Method*, by Stanford Law Professor Deborah. L. Rhode. It is divided into two parts: Professional Responsibility and Regulation, and Legal Ethics in Legal Context.

94. F. Raymond Marks, Kirk Leswing, and Barbara A. Fortinsky, *The Lawyer, the Public, and Professional Responsibility* (Chicago: American Bar Foundation, 1972).

95. John P. Heinz et al., "Lawyers' Roles in Voluntary Associations: Declining Social Capital?" *Law & Social Inquiry* 26 (2001), 626.

96. Steven Brint and Charles S. Levy, "Professions and Civic Engagement: Trends in Rhetoric and Practice, 1875-1995," *Civic Engagment in American Democracy*, ed. Theda Skocpol and Morris P. Fiorina (Washington, DC: Brookings Institution Press, 1999), 166.

97. Ryan Blaine Bennett, "Safeguards of the Republic: The Responsibility of the American Lawyer to Preserve the Republic Through Law-Related Education," *Notre Dame Journal of Law* 14 (2000), 652, accessed February 4, 2001, Lexis-Nexis.

98. "Washington State Court Rules: Rules of Professional Conduct" www.courts. wa.gov/court_rules/?fa=court_rules.list&group=ga&set=RPC.

99. Bennett, "Safeguards of the Republic," 659.

100. "Washington State Court Rules: Rules of Professional Conduct."

101. Macedo et al., *Democracy at Risk*, 119.

102. Ibid.

103. For example, see Sidney Verba, Kay Lehman Schlozman, and Henry E. Brady, *Voice and Equality: Civic Voluntarism in American Politics* (Cambridge, MA: Harvard University Press, 1995); and Raymond E. Wolfinger and Steven J. Rosenstone, *Who Votes?* (New Haven, CT: Yale University Press, 1980).

104. Macedo et al., *Democracy at Risk*, 119.

105. Other important institutions in developing and fostering civic engagement include the role religious institutions can play in increasing levels of political participation and civic activism (Verba et al. 1995); the civic engagement benefits of both partisan and nonpartisan political institutions (Brint and Levy 1999); the social connectedness stemming from involvement and membership in voluntary associations (Putnam 2000; Price 1998); civic duty within the institution of the family, particularly the role of the father (Eberly 1998); and finally, the interconnection between the individual, community, government, and business sector, and the voluntary nonprofit sector (O'Connell 2000). These numerous institutions are widely believed to be key to the civic health of a democratic nation. Efforts to maintain social trust, promote the development of social capital, sustain the operation of just societal institutions, and maintain a strong democracy through healthy levels of political participation and civic voluntarism are believed by many social scientists to depend largely on all of these aspects of society.

106. Brian O'Connell, *Civil Society: The Underpinnings of American Democracy* (Hanover, NH: University Press of New England, 1999).

107. Putnam, *Bowling Alone*, 145–147.

108. Ibid., 147.

109. This information was downloaded from the Washington State Bar Association's website: http://www.wsba.org/info/about/demographics.htm. It includes WSBA demographic information by ethnicity, age, practice, language, firm size, gender, disabled status, and sexual minority status.

110. It should be noted that some of the respondents reacted to these categories by marking up and crossing out the categories on the survey. For example, under the category "Mexican American/Chicano," of respondents who checked this category, 12 percent either crossed out the "Mexican American" or the "Chicano" part of the label, demonstrating that they did not identify as both labels together.

CHAPTER 2

1. National Center for Education Statistics, "Profile of Graduate and First-Professional Students: Trends from Selected Years, 1995–96 to 2007–08," U.S. Department of Education, NCES 2011-219, Tables 7 and S7, 22–23, nces.ed.gov/pubs2011/2011219.pdf.

2. Alejandro Portes and Rubén G. Rumbaut, *Legacies: The Story of the Immigrant Second Generation* (Berkeley: University of California Press, 2001).

3. Janet Bauer, "Speaking of Culture: Immigrants in the American Legal System," *Immigrants in Courts*, ed. Joanna I. Moore with Margaret Fisher (Seattle: University of Washington Press, 1999), 14.

4. Luis R. Fraga, John A. Garcia, Rodney E. Hero, Michael Jones-Correa, Valerie Martinez-Ebers, and Gary M. Segura, *Latino Lives in America: Making It Home* (Philadelphia: Temple University Press, 2010), 183.

5. Rosalind S. Chou and Joe R. Feagin, *The Myth of the Model Minority: Asian Americans Facing Racism* (Boulder, CO: Paradigm, 2010).

6. Bauer, "Speaking of Culture," 8.

7. Ron Schmidt, *Language Policy and Identity Politics in the United States* (Philadelphia: Temple University Press, 2000), 47.

8. Schmidt, *Language Policy*, 53.

9. Ibid., 179, originally quoted in the *Orlando Sentinel Tribune*, 1993.

10. Lisa García Bedolla, *Fluid Borders: Latino Power, Identity, and Politics in Los Angeles* (Berkeley: University of California Press, 2005).

11. Tamis Hoover Rentería, *Chicano Professionals: Culture, Conflict, and Identity* (New York: Garland Publishing, 1998).

12. Ibid., 11.

13. Ibid., 178.

14. Of the fathers who were born in another country, 24.5 percent are from Mexico, 7.8 percent from Cuba, and 6.9 percent from Puerto Rico. Other countries of origin for Latino lawyers' fathers include Bolivia, Colombia, Costa Rica, Ecuador, El Salvador, Peru, the Philippines, and Spain. Of the 40.3 percent of Latino lawyers' mothers who immigrated, 18.6 percent came from Mexico. Almost 5 percent (4.9 percent) came from Cuba, and 3.9 percent from Puerto Rico. Other countries of origin for Latino lawyers' mothers include Colombia, Costa Rica, El Salvador, the Philippines, and Spain, with one mother born in Japan and one in Africa.

15. Cornel West, *Race Matters* (New York: Vintage Books, 1994), 97.

16. West, *Race Matters*, 97.

17. Some of the respondents reacted to these categories by marking up and crossing off the categories on the survey. For example, under the category "Mexican American/Chicano," of respondents who checked this category, 12 percent either crossed out the "Mexican American" or the "Chicano" part of the label, demonstrating they did not identify as both labels together.

18. García Bedolla, *Fluid Borders*.

19. Lani Guinier and Gerald Torres, *The Miner's Canary: Enlisting Race, Resisting Power, Transforming Democracy* (Cambridge, MA: Harvard University Press, 2002), 75.

20. Guinier and Torres, *The Miner's Canary*, 11.

21. Ibid., 16–17.

22. Amy Gutmann, *Identity in Democracy* (Princeton, NJ: Princeton University Press, 2003), 2.

23. Gutmann, *Identity in Democracy*, 193.

24. Ibid., 9.

25. Ibid., 205.

26. Ibid., 204.

27. Joe R. Feagin, *The White Racial Frame: Centuries of Racial Framing and Counter-Framing* (New York: Routledge, 2010).

28. This information was obtained from the U.S. Census Bureau, Ethnicity and Ancestry Statistics Branch, Population Division, "Current Population Survey: Annual

Social and Economic Supplement," 2004, www.census.gov/population/www/socdemo/hispanic/cps2004.html

29. For more information on this report, go to www.pewhispanic.org/page.jsp?page=reports.

30. U.S. Census Bureau, "The Hispanic Population in the United States: Population Characteristics," *Current Population Survey* (Washington, DC: U.S. Census Bureau, 2002), 20–545.

31. This information was obtained from the U.S. Census Bureau, Ethnicity and Ancestry Statistics Branch, Population Division, "Current Population Survey, Annual Social and Economic Supplement," 2004, www.census.gov/population/www/socdemo/hispanic/cps2004.html

32. This information was obtained from Excelencia in Education Inc., June 29, 2006, www.edexcelencia.org/research/facts.asphttp

33. William Bowen and Derek Bok, *The Shape of the River: Long-Term Consequences of Considering Race in College and University Admissions* (Princeton, NJ: Princeton University Press, 1998).

34. For the complete demographic breakdown of all Washington State lawyers, see the Washington State Bar Association's website: www.wsba.org/lawyers/wlisessions.htm.

CHAPTER 3

1. Michele Wucker, *Lockout: Why America Keeps Getting Immigration Wrong When Our Prosperity Depends on Getting It Right* (New York: PublicAffairs, 2006), 224.

2. Wucker, *Lockout*.

3. Ibid., xiv.

4. Ibid., xv.

5. "The House We Live In," *Race: The Power of an Illusion, Episode III*, produced by California Newsreel, in association with Independent Television Service (ITVS).

6. Alejandro Portes and Rubén G. Rumbaut, *Legacies: The Story of the Immigrant Second Generation* (Berkeley: University of California Press, 2001), 217.

7. Ronald Schmidt Sr., Yvette M. Alex-Assensoh, Andrew L. Aoki, and Rodney E. Hero, *Newcomers, Outsiders, and Insiders: Immigrants and American Racial Politics in the Early Twenty-first Century* (Ann Arbor, MI: University of Michigan Press, 2010), 34.

8. Schmidt et al., *Newcomers, Outsiders, and Insiders*, 260–262.

9. Joe R. Feagin, *The White Racial Frame: Centuries of Racial Framing and Counter-Framing* (New York: Routledge, 2010).

10. Feagin, *The White Racial Frame*, viii.

11. Ibid., ix.

12. Joe Feagin and José Cobas, "Latinos/as and the White Racial Frame: The Procrustean Bed of Assimilation," *Sociological Inquiry* 78, no. 1 (February 2008): 39–53.

13. Feagin and Cobas, "Latinos/as and the White Racial Frame," 52.

14. Zulema Valdez, "Agency and Structure in Panethnic Latino Identity Formation: The Case of Latino Entrepreneurs," in *How the United States Racializes Latinos: White Hegemony & Its Consequences*, ed. José A. Cobas, Jorge Duany, and Joe R. Feagin (Boulder, CO: Paradigm, 2009).

15. Valdez, "Agency and Structure in Panethnic Latino Identity Formation," 211.

16. Teresa Sullivan stated, "Hispanics make up less than 3 percent of engineers, natural scientists, dentists, pharmacists, and speech therapists. About 3 to 4 percent of physicians, lawyers, and teachers are Hispanic. Hispanics are also generally underrepresented among technical workers, sales workers, and administrative workers." This quote is from her chapter, "A Demographic Portrait," in *Hispanics in the United States*, ed. Pastora San Juan Cafferty and David W. Engstrom (New Brunswick, NJ: Transaction, 2000), 1–30.

17. "The Status of Racial and Ethnic Diversity in the American Bar Association," American Bar Association's *Goal IX Report, 2003–2004*, 13–14.

18. Ron Ward, "Why Diversity? Rendering the Service of Reflecting the Persons We Serve, Leveling the Profession's Economic Playing Field, and Achieving True American Community," *Bar News* (April 2005), 2. www.wsba.org/media/publications/barnews/2005/apr-05-president.htm

19. This population comprised the base for the random sample of Washington attorneys used as a comparison group for the Latino attorney survey.

20. This information can be found at www.ofm.wa.gov/pop/race/projections/default.asp.

21. For the complete demographic breakdown of Washington State lawyers, see the Washington State Bar Association's website at www.wsba.org/lawyers/wlisessions.htm.

22. Jerold Auerbach, *Unequal Justice: Lawyers and Social Change in Modern America* (New York: Oxford University Press, 1976).

23. Auerbach, *Unequal Justice*.

24. Ibid.

25. The demographics of the sample for this study were comparable to the information provided by the Washington State Bar Association's Member Statistics and demonstrated how the respondents for this study were representative of lawyers in Washington State. For example, 23 percent of Washington attorneys were in solo practice, 12 percent practiced in "Large Firms" of twenty-six attorneys or more, and 5 percent were employed as state attorneys. Similar to the survey sample, but less closely matched, were the following: 4 percent were federal government attorneys, 5 percent worked for county government, 2 percent worked for city government, and 16 percent worked in "Medium Sized" firms of six to twenty-five attorneys.

26. Minority Bar Association's Joint Committee on Law Firm Diversity (2010), accessed on July 22, 2010, www.wsba.org/wsbadiversity.htm.

27. Kevin R. Johnson, associate dean for academic affairs, and Mabie-Apallas, public interest professor of law and Chicana/o studies at the University of California at Davis, School of Law, made this observation in an email exchange on July 12, 2006.

28. Maureen Milford, "Law Firms Short on Diversity," *The News Journal* (April 10, 2005), www.delawareonline.com/newsjournal/local/2005/04/10lawfirmsareshor.html.

29. American Bar Association, *Miles to Go: Progress of Minorities in the Legal Profession* (Washington, DC: Commission on Opportunities for Minorities in the Profession, 1998).

30. I am indebted to scholarly collaboration and discussions with eminent scholar, Luis Fraga. For a fuller discussion of this particular study, see Maria Chávez and Luis Ricardo Fraga, "Social Trust, Civic Engagement and Social Mobility." Paper presented at the annual conference of the Western Political Science Association, Denver, CO, 2003. The ideas in this section build on the material that we developed and presented at this conference.

31. Since this discussion, the most successful Latina attorney in the study had made it to the level of partner at a major Seattle law firm. After experiencing years of "patronizing treatment," as she put it, she has resigned and opened up her own practice.

CHAPTER 4

1. Jody Agius Vallejo, "Latina Spaces: Middle-Class Ethnic Capital and Professional Associations in the Latino Community," *City & Community* 8:2 (June 2009).

2. Lavariega Monforti, Jessica L. "La Lucha: Latinas Surviving Political Science." In *Presumed Incompetent: The Intersections of Race and Class for Women in Academia*, ed. Y. Flores-Niemann, A. Harris, C. González, and G. Gutiérrez y Muhs (Logan, UT: Utah State University Press, in press).

3. Kimberlé Crenshaw, "Demarginalizing the Intersection of Race and Sex: A Black Feminist Critique of Antidiscrimination Doctrine, Feminist Theory and Antiracist Politics," *Chicago Law Forum* (1989), 139–167.

4. bell hooks, *Feminist Theory: From Margin to Center*, 2nd ed. (Cambridge, MA: South End Press, 1984).

5. See Lisa García Bedolla, "Studying Inequality: Race, Class, Gender and Sexuality." Paper presented at the Woodrow Wilson International Center for Scholars, Washington, DC, May 2004, 18; Margaret Chon, "Race and Gender Plenary." Paper presented at the (Re)Examining Race and Gender Conference, Seattle, WA, March 4–5, 2005.

6. Chon, "Race and Gender Plenary."

7. García Bedolla, "Studying Inequality," 1.

8. This statement from one of the Latina respondents in this study was made in an email correspondence discussing the obstacles for women of color, with the author on January 6, 2011.

9. García Bedolla, "Studying Inequality," 9.

10. Luis Fraga, Valerie Martinez-Ebers, Ricardo Ramirez, Linda Lopez, and Christina Bejarano, "Gender and Ethnicity: The Political Incorporation of Latina State Legislators." Paper presented at the annual meeting of the American Political Science Association, San Francisco, CA, August 30–September 2, 2001.

11. For example, see Lisa García Bedolla, *Fluid Borders: Latino Identity, Community, and Politics in Los Angeles* (Berkeley: University of California Press, 2005); Carol

Hardy-Fanta, *Latina Politics, Latino Politics: Gender, Culture and Political Participation in Boston* (Philadelphia: Temple University Press, 1994); and Mary Pardo, "Mexican American Women Grassroots Community Activists: 'Mothers of East Los Angeles,'" in *Pursuing Power: Latinos and the Political System*, ed. F. Chris García (Notre Dame, IN: University of Notre Dame Press, 1997), 151–168.

12. Parts of this chapter were published by Maria Chávez, "Intersections of Race, Class, and Gender: The Experiences of Latina Lawyers," in *Black and Latino/a Politics: Issues in Political Development in the United States*, ed. William E. Nelson, Jr. and Jessica Lavariega Monforti (Miami: Barnhardt & Ashe, 2005), 80–89.

13. For example, see bell hooks, *Feminist Theory: From Margin to Center*, 2nd ed. (Cambridge, MA: South End Press, 2000); Gloria Anzaldúa, *Borderlands/La Frontera: The New Mestiza* (San Francisco: Spinsters/Aunt Lute, 1987); Aida Hurtado, *The Color of Privilege: Three Blasphemies on Race and Feminism* (Ann Arbor, MI: University of Michigan Press, 1996); and Ana Castillo, *Massacre of the Dreamers: Essays on Xicanisma* (New York: Plume, 1995).

14. Lavariega Monforti, "La Lucha."

15. For example, see the joint project of the ABA Commission on Women in the Profession and Commission on Opportunities for Minorities in the Profession, *The Burdens of Both, the Privileges of Neither: A Report of the Experiences of Native American Women Lawyers*, a report of the Multicultural Women Attorneys Network in cosponsorship with the Federal Bar Association and the Native American Bar Association, August 1998.

16. Maura Dolan, "Female Lawyers Suffer Bias, Study Finds," *The Los Angeles Times*, April 27, 2001.

17. Dolan, "Female Lawyers Suffer Bias."

18. Multicultural Women Attorneys Network, *The Burdens of Both*, 7.

19. American Bar Association, *Miles to Go: Progress of Minorities in the Legal Profession* (Washington, DC: Commission on Opportunities for Minorities in the Profession, 1998).

20. Ron Ward, "Why Diversity? Rendering the Service of Reflecting the Persons We Serve, Leveling the Profession's Economic Playing Field, and Achieving True American Community," *Bar News*, April 2005, 2, www.wsba.org/media/publications/barnews/2005/apr-05-president.htm.

21. Ward, "Why Diversity?" 2–3.

22. This statement was made by one of the Latina respondents in this study in an email correspondence discussing the obstacles for women of color, with the author on January 6, 2011.

23. Vallejo, "Latina Spaces," 146.

24. Though I understand that Latinos too encounter many obstacles and frustrations in the professions that stem from many of the same sources, the focus of this chapter is on Latinas. This is not to discount the struggles that our Latino brothers endure. In fact, it is recognized that in many circumstances, they encounter obstacles that are unique to their location. We would all benefit from research that brings out these issues.

25. Lavariega Monforti, Jessica L. "La Lucha: Latinas Surviving Political Science" Eds Gabriella Gutiérrez y Muhs, et al. *Presumed Incompetent: The Intersections of Race*

and Class for Women in Academia (in press): Utah State University (USU) Press and Lavariega Monforti, Jessica and Melissa Michelson. 2008. "Diagnosing the Leaky Pipeline: Continuing Barriers to the Retention of Latinas and Latinos in Political Science." *PS: Political Science and Politics* 41, 1 (Jan.): 161-166.

26. See the Washington State Bar Association's website at www.wsba.org/lawyers/wlisessions.htm.

27. For an analysis of Mexican-American gender roles and their effects on college see Y. F. Niemann, A. Romero, and Consuelo Arbona, "Effects of Cultural Orientation on the Perception of Conflict between Relationship and Education Goals for Mexican College Students," *Hispanic Journal of Behavioral Sciences*, 22 (2000): 46–63. Although not specifically looking at law school, one can infer that the findings are applicable to law school students.

28. This is not to say that there are not systemic obstacles as well, but this question focused on the family.

29. Raffaelli and Ontai, "Gender Socialization," 287–299.

30. Two interviews were conducted in Yakima, and three additional interviews were conducted via an email questionnaire sent out to Latina attorneys using the same questions, for a total of five additional interviews of Latina lawyers.

31. Rosalind S. Chou and Joe R. Feagin, *The Myth of the Model Minority: Asian Americans Facing Racism* (Boulder, CO: Paradigm, 2010).

32. Feagin, *The White Racial Frame*.

33. Multicultural Women Attorneys Network, *The Burdens of Both*.

34. José E. Cruz, "Latinos in Office," in *Latino Americans and Political Participation*, ed. Sharon Navarro and Armando Xavier Mejia (Santa Barbara, CA: ABC-CLIO, 2004), 209.

35. Cruz, "Latinos in Office," 210.

CHAPTER 5

1. I have changed the names of the Latino respondents in this study or have given them a participant number to protect their anonymity. However, this chapter is dedicated to Gabriel Ibarra for his dedication to the Latino community. So, in this case, I felt his real name should be used.

2. I learned most of this information from a memoriam written by Robert Perez, in the Washington State Bar Association, accessed August 10, 2010, www.wsba.org/media/publications/barnews/2005/feb-05-aroundthestate.htm

3. King County Bar Association, "In Memoriam of Two Neighborhood Legal Clinic Volunteers," accessed August 10, 2010, www.kcba.org/scriptcontent/KCBA/barbulletin/archive/2005/05-04/article8.cfm.

4. King County Bar Association, "In Memoriam of Two Neighborhood Legal Clinic Volunteers."

5. Robert Putnam, *Bowling Alone: The Collapse and Revival of American Community* (New York: Simon & Schuster, 2000), 19.

6. Joe R. Feagin, *Systemic Racism: A Theory of Oppression* (New York: Routledge, 2006), xiv.

7. Ibid.

8. Ibid., 2.

9. Ibid., 7.

10. Ibid., 38.

11. Robert Putnam, "*E Pluribus Unum*: Diversity and Community in the Twenty-first Century," *Scandinavian Political Studies*, 30:2 (2007), 137–174.

12. Maria L. Chávez, Brian Wampler, and Ross E. Burkhart, "Left Out: Trust and Social Capital Among Migrant Seasonal Farmworkers," *Social Science Quarterly*, 87:5 (December 2006), 1012–1029.

13. Chávez et al., "Left Out," 1026–1027.

14. Rodney Hero, *Racial Diversity and Social Capital: Equality and Community in America* (Cambridge, NY: Cambridge University Press, 2007).

15. Putnam, *Bowling Alone*, 411.

16. Rogers M. Smith, *Civic Ideals: Conflicting Visions of Citizenship in U.S. History* (New Haven, CT: Yale University Press, 1997).

17. Smith, *Civic Ideals*, 1.

18. Ibid., 22.

19. William G. Bowen and Derek Bok, *The Shape of the River: Long-Term Consequences of Considering Race in College and University Admissions* (Princeton, NJ: Princeton University Press, 1998), 23.

20. The C&B database includes data on over 80,000 undergraduate students who enrolled in twenty-eight elite (highly selective) colleges and universities during the fall semesters of 1951, 1976, and 1989.

21. Bowen and Bok, *The Shape of the River*, 160.

22. Ibid., 167.

23. The SCCBS was conducted in 2000. Latinos and blacks were oversampled in the national sample of 3,000 respondents, resulting in the participation of 502 Latino respondents (Executive Summary, p. 11).

24. While the SCCBS sample is not the same as the Latino attorneys surveyed here, I am making only descriptive comparisons of variables in the two databases.

25. These included "Low," "Medium," or "High" for two different categories based on associational membership. I created indices that matched the SCCBS. The first index of interest is the Associational Involvement Index. This index was divided into categories of "Very Low," for people who indicated no associational memberships; "Low," for people involved in one or two groups; "Medium," for people involved in three or four groups; and "High," for people involved in five or more associational and/or group memberships. To compare these findings with the data collected in this study, thirteen categories for civic activity were summarized and ranked in the same way they were in the SCCBS. The frequency of each occurrence per type of associational activity was computed as a count and then recoded into four categories, in which a score of "Very Low," for membership in no associational groups, was recorded; "Low," for involvement in one or two groups;

"Medium," for involvement in three or four associations; and "High," for involvement in five or more civic associations. Cronbach's alpha for this index is 0.57.

26. Bowen and Bok, *The Shape of the River*, xxi-xxii.

27. Bowen and Bok asked about civic participation activities for one specific year, 1995. This study is focused on the civic participation patterns of Latino professionals generally. Therefore, the question focused on civic activities of respondents since becoming attorneys rather than with respect to a single year.

28. The independent sample Mann-Whitney results confirm similar outlooks. There is no statistically significant difference between them on trust and honesty (Mann-Whitney Z-score = -1.59, df = 836, sig = .113 for trust; Mann-Whitney Z-score = $-.99$, df = 834, sig = .323 for honesty).

29. "Aside from attending your church or synagogue, in the past twelve months, did you spend any time on charitable or voluntary service activities?" "Aside from contributions to your church or synagogue, did you contribute any money to charitable or voluntary service activities and organizations?" "Aside from attending services, in the past twelve months have you been an active member of your church/synagogue in the capacity of serving on a committee, giving time for special projects, and/or helped organize meetings?"

30. This table summary was originally prepared for a conference presentation. See Maria Chávez and Luis Ricardo Fraga, "Social Trust, Civic Engagement and Social Mobility." Paper presented at the annual conference of the Western Political Science Association, Denver, 2003.

31. Ron Ward, "Why Diversity? Rendering the Service of Reflecting the Persons We Serve, Leveling the Profession's Economic Playing Field, and Achieving True American Community," *Bar News* (April 2005), www.wsba.org/media/publications/barnews/2005/apr-05-president.htm.

32. Ana Castillo, *Massacre of the Dreamers: Essays on Xicanisma* (New York: Penguin, 1995), 5.

33. Bowen and Bok, *The Shape of the River*, 169.

34. Lisa García Bedolla, *Fluid Borders: Latino Power, Identity, and Politics in Los Angeles* (Berkeley: University of California Press, 2005).

35. Gretchen Livingston and Joan R. Kahn, "An American Dream Unfulfilled: The Limited Mobility of Mexican Americans," *Social Science Quarterly* 83:4 (2002), 1003–1012.

36. This information comes from the U.S. Census Bureau report "The Hispanic Population in the United States: March 2002 Population Characteristics" (*Current Population Reports*, P20-545).

CHAPTER 6

1. Alejandro Portes and Rubén G. Rumbaut, *Legacies: The Story of the Immigrant Second Generation* (Berkeley: University of California Press, 2001).

2. For example, see the article "Choosing a Legal Career, Making a Difference," by Latina lawyer, Lisa Castilleja, describing a trip to Yakima for a student leadership conference: www.wsba.org/media/publications/denovo/archives/jun-02-student.htm.

3. Paul Attewell and David E. Lavin, *Passing the Torch: Does Higher Education Pay Off Across the Generations?* (New York: Russell Sage Foundation, 2007), 7.

4. I am referring to a lower status within the educational system among the students. For example, Latino students were segregated within the classrooms, overwhelmingly being tracked into vocational programs as opposed to having the opportunity to take the college preparatory courses. This is similar to Rodney Hero's idea of a two-tiered political system, in which he argued Latinos' political influence is diminished by being stuck in a lower tier within our political system. Being in such a position impacts their political influence regardless of their efforts to participate in politics. See Rodney E. Hero's book *Latinos and the U.S. Political System: Two-Tiered Pluralism* (Philadelphia: Temple University Press, 1992).

5. Rodolfo Acuña, "Mexicans Are Not Dumb; The Schools Fail," *La Prensa San Diego* vol. 34, no. 26 (San Diego, July 2, 2010), 6.

6. Earl Shorris, *Latinos: A Biography of the People* (New York: W. W. Norton, 1992).

7. David Montejano, *Anglos and Mexicans in the Making of Texas, 1836–1986* (Austin: University of Texas Press, 1987).

8. Montejano, *Anglos and Mexicans*, 168.

9. Shorris, *Latinos: A Biography of the People*.

10. Montejano, *Anglos and Mexicans*, 167–169.

11. For example, see Ronald T. Takaki, *A Different Mirror: The Making of Multicultural America* (Boston: Little, Brown & Company, 1994).

12. Montejano, *Anglos and Mexicans*, 196.

13. For example, see the documentary *Waiting for Superman*, by filmmaker Davis Guggenheim, 2010.

14. For example, see Philip H. Pollock, *The Essentials of Political Analysis* (Washington, DC: CQ Press, 2003), 1–5.

15. Lisa García Bedolla, *Fluid Borders: Latino Power, Identity, and Politics in Los Angeles* (Berkeley: University of California Press, 2005), 189–190.

16. García Bedolla, *Fluid Borders*, 190.

17. Professor Jensen details many aspects of white privilege in his article, "White Privilege Shapes the U.S.," *Baltimore Sun*, July 19, 1998, C-1.

18. Pollock, *The Essentials of Political Analysis*, 3.

19. Eugene J. Meehan, *Reasoned Argument in Social Science: Linking Research to Policy* (Westport, CT: Greenwood Press, 1981).

20. From the American Political Science Association's homepage at www.apsanet.org/studyingps.cfm.

21. Ibid.

22. Will Kymlicka, *Multicultural Citizenship* (New York: Oxford University Press, 1995).

23. Molly McDonough, "Demanding Diversity: Corporate Pressure Is Changing the Racial Mix at Some Law Firms," *ABA Journal* (March 2005), 54.

24. Richard Zweigenhaft and G. William Domhoff, *Diversity in the Power Elite: Have Women and Minorities Reached the Top?* (New Haven, CT: Yale University Press, 1998).

25. McDonough, "Demanding Diversity," 52.

26. Ibid.

27. Ibid., 54.

28. Ron Ward, "Why Diversity? Rendering the Service of Reflecting the Persons We Serve, Leveling the Profession's Economic Playing Field, and Achieving True American Community," *Bar News* (April 2005), www.wsba.org/media/publications/barnews/2005/apr-05-president.htm: 1 of 8.

29. Ward, "Why Diversity?"

30. This information can be found at www.aspiringdocs.org/site/c.luIUL9MUJtE/b.2108701/k.596E/Poll_Results_Incorrect_Answer. htm.

31. www.aspiringdocs.org

32. U.S. Census Bureau (2003) data indicated that only 57 percent of Latinos aged twenty-five or older have graduated from high school compared to 88.7 percent of the non-Hispanic white population.

33. Michelle Alexander, *The New Jim Crow: Mass Incarceration in the Age of Color-blindness* (New York: The New Press, 2010).

34. Garth Massey, "Thinking about Affirmative Action: Arguments Supporting Preferential Policies," *Review of Policy Research* 21:6 (2004), 783-797.

35. Massey, "Thinking about Affirmative Action," 792.

36. Ibid., 794.

37. William G. Bowen and Derek Bok, *The Shape of the River: Long-Term Consequences of Considering Race in College and University Admissions* (Princeton, NJ: Princeton University Press, 1998).

38. Wallace D. Loh, "Making a Case for an Equal Start," *Seattle Post Intelligencer*, July 11, 1999.

39. Excellent sources on affirmative action are Terry H. Anderson, *The Pursuit of Fairness: A History of Affirmative Action* (New York: Oxford University Press, 2004); and John David Skrentny, *The Ironies of Affirmative Action: Politics, Culture and Justice in America* (Chicago: University of Chicago Press, 1996).

40. Richard Zweigenhaft and G. William Domhoff, *The New CEOs: Women, African American, Latino, and Asian American Leaders of Fortune 500 Companies* (New York: Rowman & Littlefield, 2011).

41. For example, see Samuel R. Lucas, *Tracking Inequality: Stratification and Mobility in American High Schools* (New York: Teachers College Press, 1999).

42. Zweigenhaft and Domhoff, *The New CEOs*.

43. For example, see Luis Ricardo Fraga, Kenneth J. Meier, and Robert E. England, "Hispanic Americans and Educational Policy: Limits to Equal Access," in *Pursuing Power: Latinos and the Political System*, ed. F. Chris Garcia (Notre Dame, IN: University of Notre Dame Press, 1997).

44. Harriett D. Romo and Toni Falbo, *Latino High School Graduation: Defying the Odds* (Austin: University of Texas Press, 1995), xvi.

45. Ibid.

46. Denise A. Segura, "Slipping Through the Cracks: Dilemmas in Chicana Education," in *Building With Our Hands: New Directions in Chicana Studies*, ed. Adela de la Torre and Beatríz M. Pesquera (Berkeley: University of California Press, 1993), 212.

47. Ruth H. Gordon-Bradshaw, "A Social Essay on Special Issues Facing Poor Women of Color," *Women and Health* 12 (1987), 243–259.

48. Romo and Falbo, *Latino High School Graduation*, xvii.

49. Ron Glass, "Education and the Ethics of Democratic Citizenship," *Studies in Philosophy and Education* 19:3 (2000), 275–296.

50. Ronald Schmidt, *Language Policy and Identity Politics in the United States* (Philadelphia: Temple University Press, 2000).

51. Zweigenhaft and Domhoff, *The New CEOs*.

52. Ibid.

53. Sylvia R. Lazos Vargas, "Deconstructing Homo[geneous] Americanus: The White Ethnic Immigrant Narrative and Its Exclusionary Effect," *Tulane Law Review* 72 (1998), 1522–1523, Lexis-Nexis, accessed January 27, 2000.

54. For example, see Tomás Almaguer, *Racial Fault Lines: The Historical Origins of White Supremacy in California* (Berkeley: University of California Press, 1994). Also, see Kevin R. Johnson, *How Did You Get to Be a Mexican? A White/Brown Man's Search for Identity* (Philadelphia: Temple University Press, 1999).

55. Peggy Levitt, *The Transnational Villagers* (Berkeley: University of California Press, 2001).

56. See Maria L. Chávez, Brian Wampler, and Ross E. Burkhart, "Left Out: Trust and Social Capital Among Migrant Seasonal Farmworkers," *Social Science Quarterly* 87:5, Supplemental/Special Issue on Ethnicity (December 2006).

57. Calvin Goldscheider, *Studying the Jewish Future* (Seattle: University of Washington Press, 2004), 112.

58. This quote is taken from a conversation I had on October 14, 2004, with Russ Lidman, who is Jewish and the director of the Institute of Public Service at Seattle University.

59. Goldscheider, *Studying the Jewish Future*, 122.

60. Ibid..

CHAPTER 7

1. Race was not the only topic off limits. Discussions of patriarchy were not welcome either.

2. Joe Feagin, *The White Racial Frame: Centuries of Racial Framing and Counter-Framing* (New York: Routledge, 2010), vii.

3. Joe Feagin, *Systemic Racism: A Theory of Oppression* (New York: Routledge, 2006).

4. Ibid.

5. Feagin, *Systemic Racism*, 290.

6. For an example, see www.racismreview.com/blog/2010/07/23/children-march-against-anti-immigrant-federal-action/.

7. For a good analysis of America's immigration policy toward Mexicans, see Douglas S. Massey, Jorge Durand, and Nolan J. Malone, *Beyond Smoke and Mirrors: Mexican Immigration in an Era of Economic Integration* (New York: Russell Sage Foundation, 2002).

8. There are some exceptions. For example, see Jessica L. Lavariega Monforti, "La Lucha: Latinas Surviving Political Science," in *Presumed Incompetent: The Intersections of Race and Class for Women in Academia*, ed. Y. Flores-Niemann, A. Harris, C. González, and G. Gutiérrez y Muhs (Logan, UT: Utah State University Press, in press); Jody Agius Vallejo and J. Lee, "Brown Picket Fences: The Immigrant Narrative and 'Giving Back' among the Mexican-Origin Middle Class in Los Angeles," *Ethnicities*, 9:1, March 2009, 5–31; and Patricia Gándara, *Over the Ivy Walls: The Educational Mobility of Low-Income Chicanos* (Albany: State University of New York Press, 1995).

9. This information was obtained from www.racismreview.com, Joe Feagin, "Austerity and Poverty Are Not Shared in this Bush Depression: New UFE Report," January 2011. For more information on this blog report, go to www.racismreview.com/blog/2011/01/15/austerity-and-poverty-are-not-shared-in-this-bush-depression-new-ufe-report/.

10. For more information on this report, go to www.pewhispanic.org/page.jsp?page=reports.

11. U.S. Census Bureau, "The Hispanic Population in the United States: Population Characteristics," *Current Population Survey* (Washington, DC: U.S. P20-545, 2002).

12. This information was obtained from the U.S. Census Bureau, Ethnicity and Ancestry Statistics Branch, Population Division, "Annual Social and Economic Supplement," *Current Population Survey* (2004), www.census.gov/population/www/socdemo/hispanic/cps2004.html.

13. This information was obtained from "Excelencia in Education Inc.," June 29, 2006, www.edexcelencia.org/research/facts.asphttp://www.edexcelencia.org.

14. Joe Feagin, "White Supremacy and Mexican Americans: Rethinking the 'Black-White Paradigm,'" *Rutgers Law Review* 54 (Summer 2002), 959–987.

15. Rosalind Chou and Joe Feagin, *The Myth of the Model Minority: Asian Americans Facing Racism* (Boulder, CO: Paradigm, 2010).

16. Jennifer Hoschchild, *Facing Up to the American Dream: Race, Class, and the Soul of the Nation* (Princeton, NJ: Princeton University Press, 1995).

17. Feagin, "White Supremacy and Mexican Americans."

18. Robert Lieberman, *Shifting the Color Line: Race and the American Welfare State* (Cambridge, MA: Harvard University Press, 1998).

19. "Psychological warfare" is a term used by a colleague of mine in describing his tenure process, one in which he could not document the many obstacles put in his way,

but put there, nonetheless, in careful and malicious ways. The same may be occurring in the law firm environment for Latino lawyers.

20. Lieberman, *Shifting the Color Line*, 12.

21. For a discussion of systemic racism, see Jessie, "Rethinking Racism" (July 25, 2010), accessed July 26, 2010 at www.racismreview.com/blog/2010/07/25/rethinking-racism/.

22. For a complete discussion of systemic racism in America, see Feagin, *Systemic Racism*.

23. K. Anthony Appiah and Amy Gutmann, *Color Conscious: The Political Morality of Race* (Princeton, NJ: Princeton University Press, 1996), 106.

24. This is also true for Asian Americans. For a description of how Asian American professionals remain marginalized and vulnerable, see Mia Tuan, *Forever Foreigners or Honorary Whites?: The Asian Ethnic Experience Today* (New Brunswick, NJ: Rutgers University Press, 1998).

25. Appiah and Gutmann, *Color Conscious*,107.

26. Feagin, *The White Racial Frame*, 205.

27. Michelle Alexander, *The New Jim Crow: Mass Incarceration in the Age of Color-blindness* (New York: The New Press, 2010).

28. Feagin, *The White Racial Frame*, 213.

29. Ibid.

30. Roger Davidson, Walter Oleszek, and Frances Lee, *Congress and Its Members*, 12th ed. (Washington, DC: CQ Press, 2010).

31. Feagin, *The White Racial Frame*, 219.

32. I am indebted to Gary Segura for this idea based on his comments as the discussant for two of the chapters in this book, which I presented at the National Association of Chicana/Chicano Studies Conference on March 22, 2007 at the University of Washington.

33. Feagin, *Systemic Racism*; Feagin, *The White Racial Frame*; Eduardo Bonilla-Silva, *Racism Without Racists: Color-Blind Racism and Racial Inequality in Contemporary America* (New York: Rowman and Littlefield, 2010); José A. Cobas, Jorge Duany, and Joe R. Feagin, *How the United States Racializes Latinos: White Hegemony & Its Consequences* (Boulder, CO: Paradigm, 2009); and Michael Omi and Howard Winant, *Racial Formation in the United States: From the 1960s to the 1990s* (New York: Routledge, 1994).

34. Bonilla-Silva, *Racism Without* Racists, 1.

35. Bonilla-Silva, *Racism Without Racists*, 1–2.

36. W. E. B. DuBois, *The Souls of Black Folk* (New York: Penguin Putnam, 1985 [originally published in 1903], 245–263.

37. DuBois, *The Souls of Black Folk*, 260.

38. Bonilla-Silva, *Racism Without Racists*, 3–4.

39. Feagin, *The White Racial Frame*, 210.

40. Appiah and Gutmann, *Color Conscious*, 111.

41. Ibid., 170.

42. Ibid.

43. Charles N. Weaver, "The Effects of Contact on the Prejudice between Hispanics and Non-Hispanic Whites in the United States," *Hispanic Journal of Behavioral Sciences* 29:2 (2007), 254–274.

44. For example, see Lisa García Bedolla, *Fluid Borders: Latino Power, Identity, and Politics in Los Angeles* (Berkeley: University of California Press, 2005); Cornel West, *Race Matters* (New York: Vintage Books, 1994); Will Kymlicka, *Multicultural Citizenship: A Liberal Theory of Minority Rights* (New York: Oxford University Press, 1995); Michele Moses, *Embracing Race: Why We Need Race-Conscious Educational Policy* (New York: Teachers College Press, 2002); and Amy Gutmann, *Identity in Democracy* (Princeton, NJ: Princeton University Press, 2003).

45. Kymlicka, *Multicultural Citizenship*.

46. Steven Brint and Charles S. Levy, "Professions and Civic Engagement: Trends in Rhetoric and Practice, 1875–1995," in *Civic Engagement in American Democracy*, ed. Theda Skocpol and Morris P. Fiorina (Washington, DC: Brookings Institution Press, 1999), 163–210.

47. John P. Heinz et al., "Lawyers' Roles in Voluntary Associations: Declining Social Capital?" *Law & Social Inquiry* 26 (2001), 597–629.

48. American Bar Association, *Miles to Go: Progress of Minorities in the Legal Profession* (Commission on Opportunities for Minorities in the Profession, 1998).

49. It is important to note that there is research that demonstrated that many of these same experiences can be found in academia. For example, see Christine Marie Sierra, "The University Setting Reinforces Inequality," in *Chicana Voices: Intersections of Class, Race, and Gender*, ed. Teresa Cordova, Norma Elia Cantú, Gilberto Cardenas, Juan García, and Christine M. Sierra (Albuquerque: University of New Mexico Press, 1993); or María de la Luz Reyes and John J. Halcón, "Racism in Academia: The Old Wolf Revisited," in *Latinos and Education: A Critical Reader*, ed. Antonia Darder, Rodolfo D. Torres, and Henry Gutiérrez (New York: Routledge, 1997).

50. Jerold Auerbach, *Unequal Justice: Lawyers and Social Change in Modern America* (New York: Oxford University Press, 1976).

51. Luis R. Fraga, John A. Garcia, Rodney E. Hero, Michael Jones-Correa, Valerie Martinez-Ebers, and Gary M. Segura, *Latino Lives in America: Making It Home* (Philadelphia: Temple University Press, 2010).

52. Fraga et al., *Latino Lives in America*, 188.

53. Ibid.

54. Moses, *Embracing Race*, 9.

BIBLIOGRAPHY

Acuña, Rodolfo. "Mexicans Are Not Dumb; The Schools Fail." *La Prensa San Diego* 34:26 (July 2, 2010): 6.

Acuña, Rodolfo. *Occupied America: A History of Chicanos*. New York: HarperCollins, 1988.

Alexander, Michelle. *The New Jim Crow: Mass Incarceration in the Age of Colorblindness*. New York: The New Press, 2010.

Almaguer, Tomás. *Racial Fault Lines: The Historical Origins of White Supremacy in California*. Berkeley: University of California Press, 1994.

American Bar Association, Commission on Racial and Ethnic Diversity in the Legal Profession. *Miles to Go: Progress of Minorities in the Legal Profession* (Washington, DC: 1998).

American Bar Association, Commission on Women in the Profession and the Commission on Opportunities for Minorities in the Profession. *The Burdens of Both, the Privileges of Neither: A Report on the Experiences of Native American Women Lawyers*. A Report of the Multicultural Women Attorneys Network in co-sponsorship with the Federal Bar Association and the Native American Bar Association, August 1998.

Anderson, Terry H. *The Pursuit of Fairness: A History of Affirmative Action*. New York: Oxford University Press, 2004.

Anzaldúa, Gloria. *Borderlands/La Frontera: The New Mestiza*. San Francisco: Spinsters/Aunt Lute, 1987.

Appiah, K. Anthony, and Amy Gutmann. *Color Conscious: The Political Morality of Race*. Princeton, NJ: Princeton University Press, 1996.

Arizona State Legislature, Committee on Military Affairs and Public Safety. SB 1070 summary. Accessed June 14, 2010, www.azleg.gov/FormatDocument.asp?inDoc=/legtext/49leg/2r/summary/h.sb1070_04-15-10_houseengrossed.doc.htm

Attewell, Paul, and David E. Lavin. *Passing the Torch: Does Higher Education for the Disadvantaged Pay Off Across the Generations?* (American Sociological Association's Rose Series in Sociology). New York: Russell Sage Foundation, 2007.

Auerbach, Jerold S. *Unequal Justice: Lawyers and Social Change in Modern America.* New York: Oxford University Press, 1976.

Bauer, Janet. "Speaking of Culture: Immigrants in the American Legal System." In *Immigrants in Courts*, ed. Joanna I. Moore with Margaret Fisher. Seattle: University of Washington Press, 1999.

Bennett, Ryan Blaine. "Safeguards of the Republic: The Responsibility of the American Lawyer to Preserve the Republic Through Law-Related Education." *Notre Dame Journal of Law* 14 (2000). Lexis-Nexis, accessed February 4, 2001.

Bonilla-Silva, Eduardo. *Racism Without Racists: Color-Blind Racism and Racial Inequality in Contemporary America*, 3rd ed. New York: Rowman and Littlefield, 2010.

Bowen, William G., and Derek Bok. *The Shape of the River: Long-Term Consequences of Considering Race in College and University Admissions.* Princeton, NJ: Princeton University Press, 1998.

Brint, Steven, and Charles S. Levy. "Professions and Civic Engagement: Trends in Rhetoric and Practice, 1875–1995." In *Civic Engagment in American Democracy*, ed. Theda Skocpol and Morris P. Fiorina. Washington, DC: Brookings Institution Press, 1999.

"Broken Border." Television documentary, originally aired April 25, 2005, Canadian Broadcasting Corporation (CBC).

Calavita, Kitty. *Inside the State: The Bracero Program, Immigration, and the I.N.S.* New York: Routledge, 1992.

Castilleja, Lisa. "Choosing a Legal Career, Making a Difference." Pre-Law Student Leadership Conference, Washington State Bar Association, Washington Young Lawyers Division. *DeNovo* 16:2 (June 2002), www.wsba.org/media/publications/denovo/archives/jun-02-student.htm.

Castillo, Ana. *Massacre of the Dreamers: Essays on Xicanisma.* New York: Plume, 1995.

Chávez, Maria. "Intersections of Race, Class, and Gender: The Experiences of Latina Lawyers." In *Black and Latino/a Politics: Issues in Political Development in the United States*, ed. William E. Nelson, Jr., and Jessica Lavariega Monforti. Miami: Barnhardt & Ashe, 2005.

Chávez, María, and Luis Ricardo Fraga. "Social Trust, Civic Engagement, and Social Mobility." Paper presented at the annual conference of the Western Political Science Association, Denver, CO, 2003.

Chávez, Maria L., Brian Wampler, and Ross E. Burkhart. "Left Out: Trust and Social Capital Among Migrant Seasonal Farmworkers." *Social Science Quarterly* 87:5 (December 2006): 1012–1029.

Chon, Margaret. "Race and Gender Plenary." Paper presented at the (Re)Examining Race and Gender Conference, Seattle, WA, March 4–5, 2005.

Chou, Rosalind S., and Joe R. Feagin. *The Myth of the Model Minority: Asian Americans Facing Racism.* Boulder, CO: Paradigm, 2010.

Citrin, Jack, Amy Lerman, Michael Murakami, and Kathryn Pearson. "Testing Huntington: Is Hispanic Immigration a Threat to American Identity?" *Perspectives on Politics* 5:1 (March 2007): 47.

Cobas, José A., Jorge Duany, and Joe R. Feagin. *How the United States Racializes Latinos: White Hegemony & Its Consequences*. Boulder, CO: Paradigm, 2009.

Crenshaw, Kimberlé. "Demarginalizing the Intersection of Race and Sex: A Black Feminist Critique of Antidiscrimination Doctrine, Feminist Theory and Antiracist Politics." *University of Chicago Legal Forum*, vol. 1989:139–167.

Cruz, José E. "Latinos in Office." In *Latino Americans and Political Participation*, ed. Sharon A. Navarro and Armando Xavier Mejia. Santa Barbara, CA: ABC-CLIO, 2004.

Davidson, Roger H., Walter J. Oleszek, and Frances Lee. *Congress and Its Members*, 12th ed. Washington, DC: CQ Press, 2010.

de la Luz Reyes, María, and John J. Halcón. "Racism in Academia: The Old Wolf Revisited." In *Latinos and Education: A Critical Reader*, ed. Antonia Darder, Rodolfo D. Torres, and Henry Gutiérrez. New York: Routledge, 1997.

Dolan, Maura. "Female Lawyers Suffer Bias, Study Finds." *Los Angeles Times* (April 27, 2001).

DuBois, W. E. B. *The Souls of Black Folk*. New York: Penguin, 1986 [originally published in 1903].

Eberly, Don. E. *America's Promise: Civil Society and the Renewal of American Culture*. Lanham, MD: Rowman & Littlefield Publishers, Inc., 1998.

Excelencia in Education. "Facts" (June 29, 2006), www.edexcelencia.org/research/facts. asphttp://www.edexcelencia.org

Feagin, Joe R. *Systemic Racism: A Theory of Oppression* (New York: Routledge, 2006).

Feagin, Joe R. *The White Racial Frame: Centuries of Racial Framing and Counter-Framing*. New York: Routledge, 2010.

Feagin, Joe R. "White Supremacy and Mexican Americans: Rethinking the 'Black-White Paradigm.'" *Rutgers Law Review* 54 (Summer 2002): 959–987.

Feagin, Joe R., and José Cobas. "Latinos/as and White Racial Frame: The Procrustean Bed of Assimilation." *Sociological Inquiry* 78:1 (February 2008): 39–53.

Fraga, Luis, Valerie Martinez-Ebers, Ricardo Ramirez, Linda Lopez, and Christina Bejarano. "Gender and Ethnicity: The Political Incorporation of Latina State Legislators." Paper presented at the annual meeting of the American Political Science Association, San Francisco, CA, August 30–September 2, 2001.

Fraga, Luis R., and Gary M. Segura. "Culture Clash? Contesting Notions of American Identity and the Effects of Latin American Immigration." *Perspectives on Politics* 4:2 (June 2006): 283–284.

Fraga, Luis Ricardo, John A. Garcia, Rodney E. Hero, Michael Jones-Correa, Valerie Martinez-Ebers, and Gary M. Segura. *Latino Lives in America: Making It Home*. Philadelphia: Temple University Press, 2010.

Fraga, Luis Ricardo, Kenneth J. Meier, and Robert E. England. "Hispanic Americans and Educational Policy: Limits to Equal Access." In *Pursuing Power: Latinos and the Political System*, ed. F. Chris Garcia. Notre Dame, IN: University of Notre Dame Press, 1997.

Fu, Mingying. "Diverse Campus, Polarized View: The Controversy over Affirmative Action in a Multi-ethnic Environment." Paper presented at the annual meeting of the Western Political Science Association, Oakland, CA, March 17–19, 2005, 6–7.

Gándara, Patricia. *Over the Ivy Walls: The Educational Mobility of Low-Income Chicanos.* Albany: State University of New York Press, 1995.

García Bedolla, Lisa. *Fluid Borders: Latino Power, Identity, and Politics in Los Angeles.* Berkeley: University of California Press, 2005.

García Bedolla, Lisa. *Latino Politics.* Cambridge, MA: Polity Press, 2009.

Garcia Bedolla, Lisa. "Studying Inequality: Race, Class, Gender and Sexuality." Paper presented at the Woodrow Wilson International Center for Scholars, Washington, DC, May 11, 2004.

Garcia Bedolla, Lisa, and Becki Scola. "Race, Social Relations and the Study of Social Capital." Paper presented at the annual meeting of the American Political Science Association, Chicago, September 1–4, 2004.

Glass, Ronald David. "Education and the Ethics of Democratic Citizenship." *Studies in Philosophy and Education* 19:3 (May 2000): 275–296.

Goldscheider, Calvin. *Studying the Jewish Future.* Seattle: University of Washington Press, 2004.

Gonzalez, Juan. *Harvest of Empire: A History of Latinos in America.* New York: Viking, 2000.

Gordon-Bradshaw, Ruth H. "A Social Essay on Special Issues Facing Poor Women of Color." *Women and Health* 12:3-4 (1987): 243–259.

Griswold del Castillo, Richard. *The Treaty of Guadalupe Hidalgo: A Legacy of Conflict.* Norman, OK: University of Oklahoma Press, 1990.

Guinier, Lani, and Gerald Torres. *The Miner's Canary: Enlisting Race, Resisting Power, Transforming Democracy.* Cambridge, MA: Harvard University Press, 2002.

Gutiérrez, David. *Walls and Mirrors: Mexican Americans, Mexican Immigrants, and the Politics of Ethnicity.* Berkeley: University of California Press, 1995.

Gutmann, Amy. *Identity in Democracy.* Princeton, NJ: Princeton University Press, 2003.

Hardy-Fanta, Carol. *Latina Politics, Latino Politics: Gender, Culture, and Political Participation in Boston.* Philadelphia: Temple University Press, 1993.

Harris, Fredrick C. "Will the Circle Be Unbroken? The Erosion and Transformation of African-American Civic Life." In *Civil Society, Democracy, and Civic Renewal*, ed. Robert K. Fullinwider. Lanham, MD: Rowman & Littlefield, 1999.

Heinz, John P., and Paul S. Schnorr, with Edward O Laumann and Robert L. Nelson. "Lawyers' Roles in Voluntary Associations: Declining Social Capital?" *Law & Social Inquiry* 26 (2001).

Hero, Rodney E. *Latinos and the U.S. Political System: Two-Tiered Pluralism.* Philadelphia: Temple University Press, 1992.

Hero, Rodney E. *Racial Diversity and Social Capital: Equality and Community in America.* Cambridge, NY: Cambridge University Press, 2007.

Hero, Rodney E. "Social Capital and Racial Inequality in America." *Perspectives on Politics* 1:1 (2003): 113–122.

Hochschild, Jennifer L. *Facing Up to the American Dream: Race, Class, and the Soul of the Nation.* Princeton, NJ: Princeton University Press, 1996.

Hoffman, Abraham. *Unwanted Mexican Americans in the Great Depression: Repatriation Pressures, 1929–1939.* Tucson: University of Arizona Press, 1974.

hooks, bell. *Feminist Theory: From Margin to Center*, 2nd ed. Cambridge, MA: South End Press, 2000.

Huntington, Samuel. "Hispanic Immigrants Threaten the American Way of Life." *Foreign Policy* (March/April 2004). www.foreignpolicy.com/story/cms.php?story_id=2524

Huntington, Samuel P. *Who Are We? The Challenge to America's National Identity*. New York: Simon & Schuster, 2004.

Hurtado, Aida. *The Color of Privilege: Three Blasphemies on Race and Feminism*. Ann Arbor, MI: University of Michigan Press, 1996.

Jensen, Robert. *The Color of the Race Problem Is White*. YouTube video posted by freeedge369, July 1, 2009. Accessed July 26, 2010, www.youtube.com/watch?v=8aH-WSqanyQ&feature=related

Jensen, Robert. "White privilege shapes the U.S." *Baltimore Sun* (July 19, 1998): C-1. www.apsanet.org/studyingps.cfm

Jessie. "Rethinking Racism." *Racism Review*, July 25, 2010. Accessed July 26, 2010, www.racismreview.com/blog/2010/07/25/rethinking-racism/

Joe. "Land Mines to Stop Mexican Immigrants?: The Radical White Right." *Racism Review*, June 15, 2010. Accessed June 15, 2010, www.racismreview.com/blog/2010/06/15/land-mines-to-stop-mexican-immigrants-the-radical-white-right/

Johnson, Kevin R. *How Did You Get to Be a Mexican? A White/Brown Man's Search for Identity*. Philadelphia: Temple University Press, 1999.

Johnson, Kevin R., and Bill Ong Hing. "National Identity in a Multicultural Nation: The Challenge of Immigration Law and Immigrants." *Michigan Law Review* 103:6 (May 2005): 1380.

King County Bar Association. "In Memoriam of Two Neighborhood Legal Clinic Volunteers." Accessed August 10, 2010, www.kcba.org/scriptcontent/KCBA/barbulletin/archive/2005/05-04/article8.cfm

King, Gary, Robert O. Keohane, and Sidney Verba. *Designing Social Inquiry: Scientific Inference in Qualitative Research*. Princeton, NJ: Princeton University Press, 1994.

Kymlicka, Will. *Multicultural Citizenship: A Liberal Theory of Minority Rights*. New York: Oxford University Press, 1995.

Ladd, Everett Carll. *The Ladd Report*. New York: The Free Press, 1999.

Lavariega Monforti, Jessica L. "La Lucha: Latinas Surviving Political Science." In *Presumed Incompetent: The Intersections of Race and Class for Women in Academia*, ed. Y. Flores-Niemann, A. Harris, C. González, and G. Gutiérrez y Muhs. Logan, UT: Utah State University Press, in press.

Lavariega Monforti, Jessica, and Melissa Michelson. 2008. "Diagnosing the Leaky Pipeline: Continuing Barriers to the Retention of Latinas and Latinos in Political Science." *PS: Political Science and Politics* 41, 1 (Jan.): 161–166.

Lazos Vargas, Sylvia R. "Deconstructing Homo[geneous] Americanus: The White Ethnic Immigrant Narrative and Its Exclusionary Effect." *Tulane Law Review* 72 (1998). Online, Lexis-Nexis, accessed January 27, 2000.

Levitt, Peggy. *The Transnational Villagers*. Berkeley: University of California Press, 2001.

Lidman, Russ (Director of the Institute of Public Service at Seattle University). Discussion on October 14, 2004.

Lieberman, Robert C. *Shifting the Color Line: Race and the American Welfare State*. Cambridge, MA: Harvard University Press, 1998.

Lipsitz, George. *The Possessive Investment in Whiteness: How White People Profit from Identity Politics*. Philadelphia: Temple University Press, 1998.

Livingston, Gretchen, and Joan R. Kahn. "An American Dream Unfulfilled: The Limited Mobility of Mexican Americans." *Social Science Quarterly* 83:4 (2002): 1003–1012.

Loh, Wallace D. "Making a Case for an Equal Start." *Seattle Post Intelligencer* (July 11, 1999).

Lucas, Samuel R. *Tracking Inequality: Stratification and Mobility in American High Schools*. New York: Teachers College Press, 1999.

Ludden, Jennifer. "Customs Raids Cull Half of Ga. Town's Plant Workers." NPR, October 4, 2006, www.npr.org/templates/story/story.php?storyId=61967

Macedo, Stephen, et al. *Democracy at Risk: How Political Choices Undermine Citizen Participation, and What We Can Do About It*. Washington, DC: Brookings Institution Press, 2005.

Maria. "Children March against Anti-Immigrant Federal Action." *Racism Review*, July 23, 2010, www.racismreview.com/blog/2010/07/23/children-march-against-anti-immigrant-federal-action/

Marks, F. Raymond, Kirk Leswing, and Barbara A. Fortinsky. *The Lawyer, the Public, and Professional Responsibility*. Chicago: American Bar Foundation, 1972.

Massey, Douglas S., Jorge Durand, and Nolan J. Malone. *Beyond Smoke and Mirrors: Mexican Immigration in an Era of Economic Integration*. New York: Russell Sage Foundation, 2003.

Massey, Garth. "Thinking about Affirmative Action: Arguments Supporting Preferential Policies." *Review of Policy Research* 21:6 (November 2004): 783–797.

McClain, Paula D. "Social Capital and Diversity: An Introduction." *Perspectives on Politics*, 1:1 (2003): 101-102.

McDonough, Molly. "Demanding Diversity: Corporate Pressure Is Changing the Racial Mix at Some Law Firms." *ABA Journal* (March 2005).

Meehan, Eugene J. *Reasoned Argument in Social Science: Linking Research to Policy*. Westport, CT: Greenwood Press, 1981.

Michelson, Melissa R. "The Corrosive Effect of Acculturation: How Mexican Americans Lose Political Trust." *Social Science Quarterly* 84:4 (2003): 918–933.

Milford, Maureen. "Law Firms Short on Diversity." *The News Journal* (April 10, 2005). www.delawareonline.com/newsjournal/local/2005/04/10lawfirmsareshor.html

Minority Bar Association Joint Committee on Law Firm Diversity, 2010. Accessed July 22, 2010, www.wsba.org/wsbadiversity.htm

Montejano, David. *Anglos and Mexicans in the Making of Texas, 1836–1986*. Austin: University of Texas Press, 1987.

Moses, Michele S. *Embracing Race: Why We Need Race-Conscious Educational Policy*. New York: Teachers College Press, 2002.

National Center for Education Statistics. "Profile of Graduate and First-Professional Students: Trends from Selected Years, 1995–96 to 2007–08," Table 7, p. 22. U.S. Department of Education, NCES 2011-219, http://nces.ed.gov/pubs2011/2011219.pdf.

Niemann, Yolanda Flores, Andrea Romero, and Consuelo Arbona. "Effects of Cultural Orientation on the Perception of Conflict between Relationship and Education Goals for Mexican College Students." *Hispanic Journal of Behavioral Sciences* 22 (2000): 46–63.

O'Connell, Brian. *Civil Society: The Underpinnings of American Democracy*. Hanover, NH: University Press of New England, 1999.

O'Connell, Brian. "Civil Society: Definitions and Descriptions." *Nonprofit and Voluntary Sector Quarterly*. 29 (September 2000): 471–478. Online, Proquest, January 31, 2001.

Omi, Michael, and Howard Winant. *Racial Formation in the United States: From the 1960s to the 1990s*, 2nd ed. New York: Routledge, 1994.

Ong Hing, Bill. *Defining America Through Immigration Policy*. Philadelphia: Temple University Press, 2004.

Pardo, Mary. "Mexican American Women Grassroots Community Activists: 'Mothers of East Los Angeles.'" In *Pursuing Power: Latinos and the Political System*, ed. F. Chris Garcia. Notre Dame IN: University of Notre Dame Press, 1997.

Perez, Robert. "Around the State." Thurston County Report, In Memoriam, Gage Ibarra. Bar News. Accessed August 10, 2010, www.wsba.org/media/publications/barnews/2005/feb-05-aroundthestate.htm

Peterson, Daneen G. "Pro-Illegal Alien Shills True To Their Hispanic 'Roots.'" December 2, 2005, www.stopthenorthamericanunion.com/Roots.html

Pollock, Philip H., III. *The Essentials of Political Analysis*. Washington, DC: CQ Press, 2003.

Portes, Alejandro, and Alex Stepick. *City on the Edge: The Transformation of Miami*. Berkeley: University of California Press, 1993.

Portes, Alejandro, and Rubén G. Rumbaut. *Legacies: The Story of the Immigrant Second Generation*. Berkeley: University of California Press, 2001.

Portney, Kent E., and Jeffrey M. Berry. "Mobilizing Minority Communities: Social Capital and Participation in Urban Neighborhoods." *American Behavioral Scientist* 40:5 (March 1997): 632–644.

Price, Robert Arthur III. *Civic Engagement in Texas*. Ph.D. dissertation, The University of Texas at Austin, 1998.

Putnam, Robert. "*E Pluribus Unum*: Diversity and Community in the Twenty-first Century," *Scandinavian Political Studies* 30:2 (2007): 137–174.

Putnam, Robert D. *Bowling Alone: The Collapse and Revival of American Community*. New York: Simon & Schuster, 2000.

Putnam, Robert D., and Lewis M. Feldstein. *Better Together: Restoring the American Community*. New York: Simon & Schuster, 2003.

Raffaelli, Marcela, and Lenna L.Ontai. "Gender Socialization in Latino/a Families: Results from Two Retrospective Studies." *Sex Roles: A Journal of Research* 50:5/6 (March 2004): 287–299.

Rentería, Tamis Hoover. *Chicano Professionals: Culture, Conflict, and Identity*. New York: Garland Publishing, 1998.

Rhode, Deborah L. *Professional Responsibility: Ethics by the Pervasive Method*. Chicago: American Bar Foundation, 1972.

Romo, Harriett D., and Toni Falbo. *Latino High School Graduation: Defying the Odds*. Austin: University of Texas Press, 1995.

Schmidt, Ronald, Sr. *Language Policy and Identity Politics in the United States.* Philadelphia: Temple University Press, 2000.

Schmidt, Ronald, Sr., Yvette M. Alex-Assensoh, Andrew L. Aoki, and Rodney E. Hero. *Newcomers, Outsiders, and Insiders: Immigrants and American Racial Politics in the Early Twenty-first Century.* Ann Arbor, MI: University of Michigan Press, 2009.

Schudson, Michael. *The Good Citizen: A History of American Civic Life.* New York: The Free Press, 1998.

Segura, Denise A. "Slipping Through the Cracks: Dilemmas in Chicana Education." In *Building With Our Hands: New Directions in Chicana Studies*, ed. Adela de la Torre and Beatríz M. Pesquera. Berkeley: University of California Press, 1993.

Segura, Gary M., Harry Pachon, and Nathan D. Woods. "Hispanics, Social Capital, and Civic Engagement." *National Civic Review* 90:1 (Spring 2001): 85–96.

Shorris, Earl. *Latinos: A Biography of the People.* New York: W. W. Norton, 1992.

Sierra, Christine Marie. "The University Setting Reinforces Inequality." In *Chicana Voices: Intersections of Class, Race, and Gender*, ed. Teresa Cordova, Norma Elia Cantú, Gilberto Cardenas, Juan García, and Christine M. Sierra. Albuquerque: University of New Mexico Press, 1993.

Skocpol, Theda, and Morris P. Fiorina eds., *Civic Engagement in American Democracy.* Washington, DC: Brookings Institution Press, 1999.

Skrentny, John David. *The Ironies of Affirmative Action: Politics, Culture and Justice in America.* Chicago: University of Chicago Press, 1996.

Smith, Rogers M. *Civic Ideals: Conflicting Visions of Citizenship in U.S. History.* New Haven, CT: Yale University Press, 1997.

Sullivan, Teresa A. "A Demographic Portrait." In *Hispanics in the United States*, ed. Pastora San Juan Cafferty and David W. Engstrom. Piscataway, NJ: Transaction Publishers, 2000.

Suro, Roberto. *Strangers Among Us: How Latino Immigration Is Transforming America.* New York: Vintage Books, 1998.

Takaki, Ronald T. *A Different Mirror: The Making of Multicultural America.* Boston: Little, Brown and Company, 1994.

"The House We Live In." *Race: The Power of an Illusion, Episode III.* Produced by California Newsreel, in association with Independent Television Service (ITVS).

"The Status of Racial and Ethnic Diversity in the American Bar Association." American Bar Association's *Goal IX Report* (2003–2004).

Time Online. www.time.com/time/nation/article/0,8599,1135872,00.html

Trías Monge, José. *Puerto Rico: The Trials of the Oldest Colony in the World.* New Haven, CT: Yale University Press, 1997.

Tuan, Mia. *Forever Foreigners or Honorary Whites?: The Asian Ethnic Experience Today.* New Brunswick, NJ: Rutgers University Press, 1999.

Turnbull, Lornet. "Immigrants push state initiative targeting those here illegally." *The Seattle Times*, June 13, 2010. Accessed June 14, 2010, http//seattletimes.nwsource.com/html/localnews/2012110918_immigration14m.html

U.S. Census Bureau. "2010 Census Integrated Communications Campaign Plan: The Success of the Census Is in Our Hands." August 2008, http://2010.census.gov/partners/pdf/2010_ICC_Plan_Final_Edited.pdf

U.S. Census Bureau. "Educational Attainment in the United States: 2009—Detailed Tables," www.census.gov/hhes/socdemo/education/data/cps/2009/tables.html

U.S. Census Bureau. "The Hispanic Population in the United States: 2004—Detailed Tables." www.census.gov/population/www/socdemo/hispanic/cps2004.html

U.S. Census Bureau. "The Hispanic Population in the United States: Population Characteristics. Current Population Reports." Washington, DC: U.S. Census Bureau, 2001.

Uslaner, Eric M., and Richard S. Conley. "Civic Engagement and Particularized Trust: The Ties That Bind People to Their Ethnic Communities." *American Politics Research* 31:4 (July 2003): 331–360.

Valdez, Zulema. "Agency and Structure in Panethnic Identity Formation: The Case of Latino/a Entrepreneurs." In *How the United States Racializes Latinos: White Hegemony & Its Consequences*, ed. José A. Cobas, Jorge Duany, and Joe R. Feagin. Boulder, CO: Paradigm, 2009.

Vallejo, Jody Agius. "Latina Spaces: Middle-Class Ethnic Capital and Professional Associations in the Latino Community." *City & Community* 8:2 (June 2009):129–154.

Vallejo, Jody Agius. *The Mexican Origin Middle Class in Los Angeles*. Albany: State University of New York Press, 1995.

Vallejo, Jody Agius, and Jennifer Lee. "Brown Picket Fences: The Immigrant Narrative and 'Giving Back' among the Mexican-Origin Middle Class in Los Angeles," *Ethnicities*, 9:1, March 2009, 5–31.

Verba, Sidney, Kay Lehman Schlozman, and Henry E. Brady. *Voice and Equality: Civic Voluntarism in American Politics*. Cambridge, MA: Harvard University Press, 1995.

Ward, Ron. "Why Diversity? Rendering the Service of Reflecting the Persons We Serve, Leveling the Profession's Economic Playing Field, and Achieving True American Community." *Bar News* (April 2005), www.wsba.org/media/publications/barnews/2005/apr-05-president.htm

"Washington State Court Rules: Rules of Professional Conduct." www.courts.wa.gov/court_rules/?fa=court_rules.list&group=ga&set=RPC

Weaver, Charles N. "The Effects of Contact on the Prejudice between Hispanics and Non-Hispanic Whites in the United States." *Hispanic Journal of Behavioral Sciences* 29:2 (2007): 254–274.

West, Cornel. *Race Matters*. New York: Vintage Books, 1994.

Winthrop, John. "A Model of Christian Charity." In *Political Thought in America: An Anthology*, ed. Michael B. Levy. Chicago: Dorsey Press, 1988.

Wolfinger, Raymond E., and Steven J. Rosenstone. *Who Votes?* New Haven, CT: Yale University Press, 1980.

Wucker, Michele. *Lockout: Why America Keeps Getting Immigration Wrong When Our Prosperity Depends on Getting It Right*. New York: PublicAffairs, 2006.

Zweigenhaft, Richard L., and G. William Domhoff. *Diversity in the Power Elite: Have Women and Minorities Reached the Top?* New Haven, CT: Yale University Press, 1999.

Zweigenhaft, Richard L., and G. William Domhoff. *The New CEOs: Women, African American, Latino, and Asian American Leaders of Fortune 500 Companies*. New York: Rowman & Littlefield, 2011.

INDEX

Italic page numbers refer to figures and tables

ABOUT THE AUTHOR

Maria Chávez is associate professor in the Department of Political Science at Pacific Lutheran University. Chávez earned her B.A. in social science (cum laude) in 1992, her M.A. (with distinction) in political science in 1995, both from California State University, Chico, and her Ph.D. in political science from Washington State University in 2002. She teaches courses on American government, public policy, state and local government, and race and citizenship. She blogs for www.racismreview.com and lives with her husband and three youngest children in Lacey, Washington.